Canes & Walking Sticks

A Stroll Through Time and Place

Jeffrey B. Snyder

4880 Lower Valley Road, Atglen, PA 19310 USA

Courtesy of WITHERELLS.COM

Library of Congress Cataloging-in-Publication Data

Snyder, Jeffrey B.
    Canes & walking sticks : a stroll through time and place /
by Jeffrey B. Snyder.
       p. cm.
    ISBN 0-7643-2041-6 (hardcover)
1. Staffs (Sticks, canes, etc.)—Collectors and collecting—
Catalogs. 2. Staffs (Sticks, canes, etc.)—History. I. Title:
Canes and walking sticks. II. Title.
NK8645.S68 2004
745.51—dc22
                        2004000780

Designed by Ellen J. "Sue" Taltoan
Type set in Bernhard Modern BT/Souvenir Lt BT

ISBN: 0-7643-2041-6
Printed in China
1 2 3 4

Published by Schiffer Publishing Ltd.
4880 Lower Valley Road
Atglen, PA 19310
Phone: (610) 593-1777; Fax: (610) 593-2002
E-mail: Info@schifferbooks.com

For the largest selection of fine reference books on this and
related subjects, please visit our web site at
www.schifferbooks.com
We are always looking for people to write books on new
and related subjects. If you have an idea for a book please
contact us at the above address.

This book may be purchased from the publisher.
Include $3.95 for shipping.
Please try your bookstore first.
You may write for a free catalog.

In Europe, Schiffer books are distributed by
Bushwood Books
6 Marksbury Ave.
Kew Gardens
Surrey TW9 4JF England
Phone: 44 (0) 20 8392-8585; Fax: 44 (0) 20 8392-9876
E-mail: info@bushwoodbooks.co.uk
Free postage in the U.K., Europe; air mail at cost.

Dedication

To the memory of Mary Janis Cooksey.

I was one of the lucky sons-in-law. None of the standard
mother-in-law jokes applied. She and my father-in-law
both made me feel at home from day one. I was blessed.

Acknowledgments

Writing this book was a pleasure. It afforded me the opportunity and excuse to meet many interesting people—auctioneers, dealers, and collectors—who share my fascination for these objects, to discuss walking sticks in their many forms with them and swap stories, to handle exquisite examples of walking stick artistry spanning hundreds of years in time, and to capture these beautiful objects on film. Without the cooperation of these knowledgeable and generous individuals, this book would not have been possible.

I wish to thank the following contributors, who were generous with their time, their collections, and their information:

Ambassador Richard W. Carlson; Brant Mackley Gallery; Kimball M. Sterling Auctioneers; Henry A. Taron & Christopher H. Taron, Tradewinds Antiques, P.O. Box 249, Manchester-by-the-Sea, MA 01944-0249, Tel. (978) 526-4085; Ron Van Anda and Sandra Whitson; Dale Van Atta; Richard R. Wagner, Jr.; WITHERELLS.COM; and The World of the Walking Stick.

It was my great good fortune to work with you all.

I need to acknowledge my editor as well. Donna Baker has worked with me on a number of projects and always manages to set me straight when I stray too far afield.

Special thanks to my family, Sherry, Michael, and Madeline, who were always glad to see me when I drug my grubby self in at the end of a long shoot ... and who always listened when I discussed my research. Special thanks to my parents, Jim and Mary Alice, my brother, Marc, and sister-in-law, Marti ... they also heard an awful lot about this project.

Finally, I want to thank all the readers of this book and the others I have written. Without you, this book would truly never have been produced.

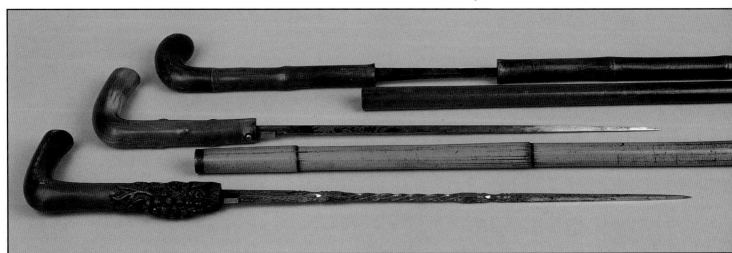

Courtesy of Richard R. Wagner, Jr.

Contents

Foreword

I hesitated when asked to write the foreword to this book; after all, I thought, what would people think when they discovered that the author is both editor of my own book and my son? Well, so what? Soldier on, say I. This is an exceptional piece of work, and I am a professional. So is Jeff.

Canes are a wonderful subject because they have marched in the human parade for so long. You can view them as apparel, a thing of beauty; as a symbol of authority or wealth; as a weapon or a crutch. Gentlemen of the nineteenth century were not properly dressed without a cane. Monarchs carried staffs, the ordinary man had his shillelagh. Only in recent times have canes lost favor to other personal exhibits such as briefcases or cell phones. Personally, I'll take the elegant and less obtrusive cane every time.

Jeffrey B. Snyder is one of the few people I know who could have written about Canes in this particular way. Trained as an archeologist and historian, Jeff takes investigative skills learned academically and in the field and applies them to storybooks about historic objects. In Jeff's books, the reader finds more than a simple description and price range of an object; he or she learns where it originated, how it was made, what purpose it served, and who used it. For the collector, his books are a wealth of information. Parenthetically, it's been a source of some satisfaction to his mother and me to see antique dealers using his books as reference on many of the popular TV shows.

This is Jeff's second book on Canes. That's not unusual; he did five books on Flow Blue China, thinking with each edition that he had said all he had to say, only to find more for a later book.

That's how it is with Canes. If you have the first book, you'll want this one, too, because Jeff found a lot more to say. Again.

I'm hoping he'll autograph my copy.

Jim Slade
McLean, VA
November 5, 2003

Jim Slade is both a highly-regarded journalist who has covered decades worth of history firsthand as it unfolded, most prominently the first forty years of the American space program, and the co-author with John Alexander of *Firestorm at Gettysburg*, Schiffer Books, 1998.

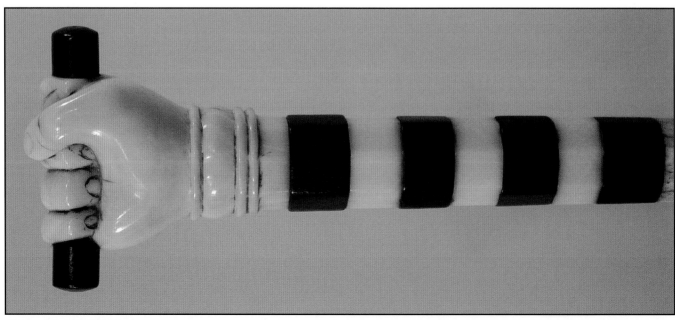

Courtesy of Kimball M. Sterling Auctioneers.

Introduction

Historically speaking, until recently the majority of the human race has gone from place to place on foot. Accompanying men, women, and children alike in their travels have been walking sticks in endless variety. Walking sticks, measuring roughly waist high, and staffs, their elongated cousins of shoulder height or greater, have always been more than mere travel aids or the firm third leg in old age, however. Walking sticks have also been symbols of authority and faith for pharaohs, kings, presidents, generals, field marshals, bishops, priests, and physicians.

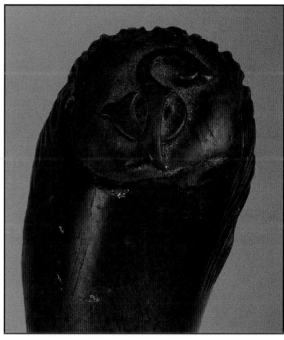

Historically, walking sticks have always accompanied people in their travels. Folk art beasts adorn these walking sticks and are not terribly common: the two-headed example in the center dates from the early eighteenth or possibly the seventeenth century and has a hole through the handle. The reddish-colored example has its tongue sticking out and is mounted on a hardwood branch. Dating from the mid-nineteenth century, this example features a 3-1/4" long metal ferrule. No ferrules were used on the other examples. *Courtesy of Richard R. Wagner, Jr.* $500-900 each.

Walking sticks have been made in tremendous variety. Many are the very embodiment of elegance. Far left: Solid 14k gold handle inscribed, "To Colonel H. A. Hayward from his friend." This is rose gold, which is pinker than the yellow, 14k gold as seen in the handle next to it. Rose gold handle, $900-1400. Second from left: Solid 14k gold handle with a white sapphire set into the top of the handle. The knob handle is inscribed, "1844, Presented To Field M. Citron from his friends." Both are mounted on ebonized shafts. $900-1400. Third: A fine cloisonné handle with a dragon on top and a bamboo shaft, $500-600. Fourth: A bloodstone handle in a silver mounting on a rosewood shaft, $600-800. Fifth: Square cane with beveled corners, green jadeite handle, $900-1200. Sixth: Blue stone and silver handle set with seed pearls and a monogram, mounted on a rosewood shaft, $1200-1400. Seventh: Rock crystal handle on a snakewood shaft, marked "Tiffany & Co.," $700-1100. Far right: Silver skull with bony fingers holding a crown in place. An amethyst adorns the top of the handle and garnets are set into the sides of the crown. $4000-5000. *Courtesy of Richard R. Wagner, Jr.*

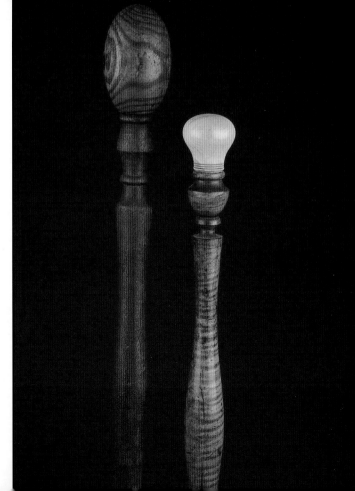

Right:
Two Hudson River Valley walking staffs (hiking) with pointed metal ferrules measuring 2-1/2" long for rough terrain. Gripped by the oak shaft. The left hand example is all wood; the right hand example is tiger wood with an ivory knob handle. *Courtesy of Richard R. Wagner, Jr.* Wood handle: $200-400; ivory knob handle: $400-600.

As most walking stick aficionados know, when Howard Carter opened the tomb of the boy king Tutankhamen, the archaeologist discovered over 130 walking sticks, some in an antechamber scattered between two disassembled chariots. However, less well known are the recent discoveries revealing that this pharaoh and at least one of his children were sufferers from diseases affecting the spine. Portrayals in the tomb show Tut leaning on a cane. While many of the sticks recovered were beautiful artifacts, real tributes to the skill of ancient Egyptian artists, the most intriguing of the walking sticks was a potent symbol of Egyptian power. The base of the shaft was rounded into a broad open crook. Rendered on either end of that crook were two elaborately carved figures representing an African Nubian and Asian Syrian, both enemies of Egypt. Carter assessed these figures as "unique in Egyptian art." (Carter & Mace 1977, 214) Egyptologist and professor of classical languages, Claude Rilly, explains that this walking stick was carried by the pharaoh with the crook down so that when he strode among his people, all could see that Egypt's enemies bit the dust with Pharaoh's every step. (Rilly 2001)

Exerting his authority, President Andrew Jackson is said to have altered the once straight and simple lines of Pennsylvania Avenue forever with a single rap of his walking stick. As the tale is told, the President's team picked an inopportune moment to ask the strong-willed Jackson where to construct the Treasury Building. Jackson, standing in the middle of Pennsylvania Avenue, rapped his cane on the street and snapped "Build it here!" And so they did.

Victorian Phrenologists carried Phrenology canes with them as symbols of their "scientific" authority. The handle of such a stick was fashioned in the shape of the human head. Upon that head was marked the complex landscape of the human brain, with good and evil traits shown housed in particular areas. The better developed the area of a particular trait, the more likely you were to fall under its sway. Well-developed regions of the brain were enlarged, rising above lesser regions, creating a cerebral topography of hills and valleys. The "professor of phrenology" proclaimed that he could judge the character of any person by carefully examining the rolling geography of the human skull, as enlarged areas of the brain thrust the skull outward while diminished areas left depressions.

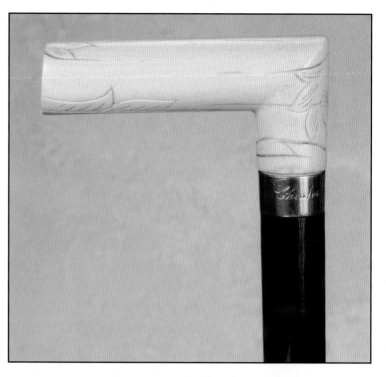

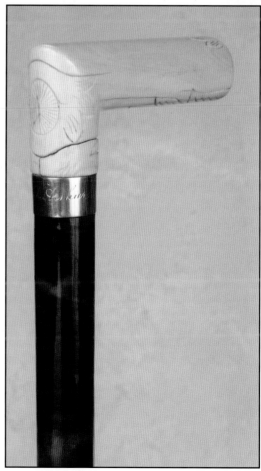

President Chester A. Arthur's cane, inscribed with his name on the 1/3" solid 18k gold collar. The L-shaped handle is elephant ivory decorated with flowers and leaves and the wooden shaft is covered with a tortoiseshell veneer. The base of the shaft ends in a 2" bone ferrule. Handle: 3-3/4" x 1-3/4". Overall length: 33-1/2". *Courtesy of Henry A. Taron, Tradewinds Antiques.* $4500-6500.

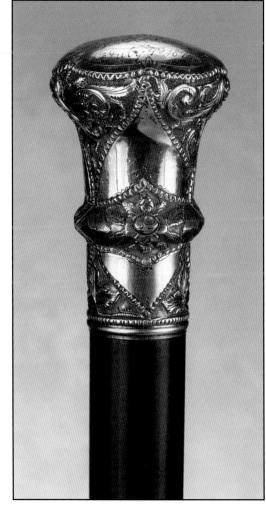

These three canes were owned by the Union General Americus Vespuccio Rice. The eight paneled elephant ivory knob handle measures 2" high x 1-1/3" in diameter. It has a 2/3" gold collar inscribed "Gen'l A.V. Rice from Court Ewing, 1882." The shaft is natural hickory with a 1" white metal ferrule. Overall length: 34-1/4". The gold-filled knob handle measures 1-1/4" high x 1-1/2" in diameter and is inscribed, "A.V. Rice, from sister Sallie, July 4th, 1877." The ebony shaft has a 3/4" white metal and iron ferrule. Overall length: 34-1/4". The L-shaped, eight-paneled, gold-filled handle is inscribed, "Gen'l A. V. Rice, The Soldier, The Statesman, The Democrat, The True Friend." The shaft is ebony and has a 1-1/8" long silver ferrule. This cane dates from c. 1890. Overall length: 35". *Courtesy of Henry A. Taron, Tradewinds Antiques.* Together these canes are valued at $4000-6000.

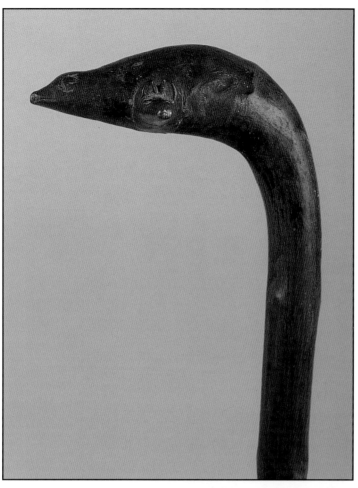

Woodland Indian Medicine Cane, mid-nineteenth century. Overall length: 30-1/2". *Courtesy of Brant Mackley Gallery.* $1200-1500.

Of course, historical records are filled with tales of cane wielding individuals using walking sticks as weapons, both in self-defense and in brutal assaults. For protection in town, citizens of the Roman Empire carried specially made birch canes to drive off the feral dogs that frequented their streets. While the image of toga clad citizens swinging cudgels at angry curs does not jibe with the modern cinematic vision of the Roman Empire, it should be noted that in the early 1840s Charles Dickens remarked on the many free roaming pigs in the streets of New York City, "Take care of the pigs. Two portly sows are trotting up behind this carriage, and a select party of half a dozen gentlemen hogs have just now turned the corner … They are the city scavengers, these pigs." (Snyder, 1995, 18) In the Roman Empire's military, Centurions encouraged stiff-necked raw recruits to obey orders with alacrity and precision by beating them with canes carried especially for that purpose.

Speaking of persuasion, it was once common practice for school teachers to strike recalcitrant young men misbehaving in class with stout walking sticks. Different sized sticks were recommended for boys of different ages and physiques. London's newspaper, *The Daily Mirror*, reported in 1953 that one ardent advocate of corporal punishment in schools had been lecturing on the virtues of a walking stick he described as a "dragon smoking malacca" in a Staffordshire private school in 1948 when outraged pupils swarmed the stage. Grabbing the lecturer, they gave him six strokes with his own stick.

Weapons of all sorts were also hidden beneath innocuous shafts and decorative handles. Many a wealthy gent had nerves steadied while walking down ill-lit streets late at night by the knowledge that a well-disguised sword, dagger, pistol or bludgeon was close at hand. However, in an unusual twist, a determined woman and a pair of walking sticks are said to have thwarted a pistol duel in the old South! As the story goes, Robert Henry Glass, the father of Virginia's Senator Carter Glass (the Senator was born in 1858 and would later be recognized as the nation's last Senator born in the antebellum South, a man Franklin Roosevelt would refer to as an "Unreconstructed Rebel"), became entangled in a deadly dispute in 1860. Robert Glass owned the leading Democratic newspaper in southwestern Virginia, the *Lynchburg Daily Republican*. He was also Lynchburg's postmaster. While Glass was away on business, George Hardwicke, the *Daily Republican's* associate editor, took it upon himself to defend Glass's honor. A rival newspaperman had claimed Glass was using his position as postmaster to prevent delivery of his competitor's newspapers. For this, Hardwicke killed the man but the issue remained unresolved. Upon his return, Robert Glass reached for his dueling pistols to settle the matter once and for all. His wife, however, had other ideas. She had warrants issued against both would-be duelists and replaced their pistols with walking sticks. If the duel was to continue, Mrs. Glass had seen to it that it would not be a quick affair ended with a single shot, but a slow, bruising, painful business for both parties involved as each attempted to bludgeon the other into submission with a walking stick. History does not relate whether the duel was held with its alternative weaponry or whether cooler heads prevailed.

Not all walking sticks have been put to such anti-social uses. Canes—it is understood that the terms "walking stick" and "cane" are interchangeable today—served as fashion accessories for centuries. Women in eleventh century France carried slender apple wood walking sticks. History records that during this period Constance, the second wife of King Robert, put out her confessor's eye with her apple wood stick. Rules of etiquette concerning proper stick handling would later be developed in an attempt to avoid such unfortunate incidents. Gentlemen would begin to adopt canes as fashion accessories to be "worn" rather than merely carried in the West in the sixteenth century, although this trend would take several hundred years to reach its climax. In the Western world, during the nineteenth century, gentlemen and ladies alike would "wear" canes in an astonishing variety of forms, produced from every exotic material available. Ladies and gentlemen of means were known to have many canes to choose from: canes to wear as accessories to a wide variety of clothing; canes for city and country outings; and even sticks for day and nighttime use.

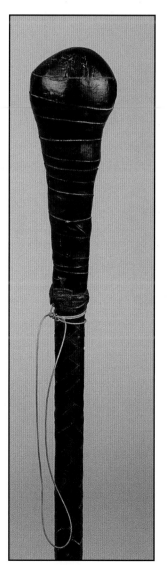

Phrenology handle cane (all the rage in the nineteenth century), silver handle with a "CS" monogram, black painted shaft, metal ferrule. Handle: 4" h. Overall length: 36". This is the genuine article. *Courtesy of Ambassador Richard W. Carlson.* $2600-2860.

For bludgeoning: A walking stick with a leather-wrapped metal head on a springy metal shaft. The entire piece is wrapped in leather and the base is protected with a metal ferrule. Handle: 2" d. Overall length: 36-1/2". *Courtesy of Ambassador Richard W. Carlson.* $425-470.

Introduction   13

When walking sticks were the height of fashionable attire, cane wearers were critiqued on their stick handling abilities. Author Thomas Holley Chivers, a contemporary of Edgar Allan Poe writing in Georgia, remarked on Poe's stick handling abilities, "When I first became acquainted with him, he used to carry a crooked-headed hickory walking-cane in his hand whenever we went out to walk ... This he flourished, as he walked, with considerable grace—particularly so when compared to a man who had never been in the habit of carrying a cane." (Davis 1952, 53)

Published in 1873, *The Bazar Book of Decorum* warned against poor cane handling, "[The awkward man] goes and places himself in the very place of the whole room where he should not. There he soon lets his hat fall down, and, in taking it up again, throws down his cane; in recovering his cane, his hat falls a second time, so that he is a quarter hour before he is in order again." (Tomes 1873, 76) Further, a Victorian man was dismissed as a "masher" who wore a little hat rigidly on his head, gave a stony stare, and carried a large cane.

Walking sticks were often presented to loved ones, esteemed friends, and colleagues as gifts. Frequently, a cartouche on the handle or the metal collar strengthening the joint between the handle and the shaft would be inscribed with the names of the gift giver and the recipient being honored, along with the date and, at times, the occasion at which the cane was presented. Writing as Special Correspondent to San Francisco's *Alta California* newspaper on February 5, 1868, Mark Twain remarked on the number of canes presented to President Andrew Johnson, "All of a sudden the President has grown mightily in favor, and everybody that can raise money enough buys a present for him and goes up to the White House and inflicts it on him. I believe he has received eleven different kinds of canes in the last three weeks. He got one from that same old inexhaustible Charter Oak, day before yesterday."

English pique cane dated 1691 on the top of the elephant ivory knob handle. The handle is finely decorated with intricate patterns of crosses and elaborate scrollwork. The wrist cord hole is surrounded with pique work. A 2/3" silver collar hides the joint between the ivory handle and the malacca shaft. The base of the shaft is covered with a 4" brass and iron ferrule. Handle: 3" x 1- 1/3". Overall length: 35-1/2". *Courtesy of Henry A. Taron, Tradewinds Antiques.* $5000-7000.

Right:
These are early sticks dating from 1750 through the American Revolution and are always tall. Knob of copper with gold wash, large eyelets of the same material, malacca shaft, and a worn brass ferrule measures 4-1/2" long. Handle: 2-1/4" l. Overall length: 48". Walrus ivory knob handle on a malacca shaft with silver eyelets, and a worn metal 2" l. ferrule. The name "Thomas Cushman" is carved on the knob handle. Handle: 1-3/4" h. Overall length: 46" l. Ceramic handle decorated with flowers, malacca shaft, long elephant ivory ferrule measuring 8-1/2". Handle: 2" l. x 2" w. Overall length: 45-1/2". *Courtesy of Richard R. Wagner, Jr.* $800-1100 each.

Men's Wear
for
Fall

Mark Twain mentions a type of cane closely associated with presentation canes, the relic cane. Relic canes were made from material taken from aging historical buildings, ships, forts, and, in this case, from Connecticut's Charter Oak, which once safely hid Connecticut's liberal charter. Twain went on to wonder, "Do you suppose that relic [the Charter Oak] will ever give out? They have already taken more wood out of it than would build a couple of steamboats, but it still holds out." Relic canes also bear inscriptions on handles, collars, or shafts stating from which famous object the wooden shaft, or at times the metal handle, originated. Among President James Madison's favorite walking sticks was a relic cane made from a timber taken from the USS *Constitution* during one of the periodic renovations of the United States Navy's most famous warship.

During the nineteenth and early twentieth centuries, the well-dressed gentleman never went out in public without his walking stick. This advertisement reads, "Men's Wear for Fall" and is signed "Edwin Tunis 1925 [with a dragonfly logo]." *Courtesy of Richard R. Wagner, Jr.*

Left:
Mineral handle (blue) with an unmarked gold collar, black shaft, and a 2-1/2" long ferrule. Handle: 2-1/2" h. Overall length: 36-1/2". *Courtesy of Richard R. Wagner, Jr.* $1000-1200.

Right:
Multi-year three-banded knob handled wood presentation cane. Inscribed in the silver of the top band it reads on the top line, "Presented to Daniel Fogg 1680." The next inscription below it reads "Also Presented to Joseph Kennard by Joseph Fogg 1866." The middle band reads " Presented to Samuel Kennard 1892." And "Perly L. Kennard 1903." The bottom band reads " Walter Kennard 1908" and leaves room below for a final presentation that never occurred. Overall length: 35", with a long ferrule with an iron tip.

Research suggests the Daniel Fogg first listed on the handle may have been an individual born on April 16, 1660, in Hampton, New Hampshire. This Daniel Fogg had a varied and interesting career, first as a blacksmith, then as a constable in Black Point. Having trouble with local Indians, he moved to Portsmouth, New Hampshire, in 1690. By 1714, Daniel Fogg was the constable of Kittery, Maine, where he continued to face hostilities from Indians, and helped organize the local church in 1721. Daniel Fogg died in 1747, leaving his estate to his children. *If* this is the correct individual, history does not record an event associated with the presentation of this impressive cane in 1680.

Joseph F. Kennard, listed second on the handle, lived in Manchester, New Hampshire, and was a member of the New Hampshire State Senate from the third district from 1868 to 1870. This impressive cane was purchased by its current owner in Maine. *Courtesy of Ambassador Richard W. Carlson.* $850-935.

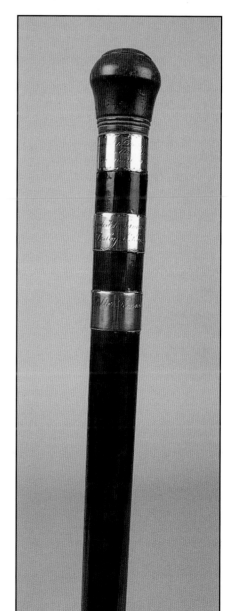

Canes have also been used in playful ways by cultures around the world. Performers have used walking sticks for dance, juggling, and magic. During the nineteenth century, as advances in technology allowed for the creation and mass-production of increasingly sophisticated objects, artisans "played" with new tools and techniques, creating—and patenting—over 1500 different types of "system sticks" before they were done. System sticks could be loosely described as "walking sticks with a hidden agenda." These sticks serve a dual purpose; hidden within their handles and shafts are a vast array of items to be used in quieter moments, ranging from billiard cues and fishing poles to musical instruments and writing sets. Professional men of all sorts also owned system sticks that held tools of their trade. Doctors carried vials of medicine and surgical instruments hidden in their system sticks … and when the doctor failed, the mortician carried a measuring stick in his to determine the length of his newest customer.

Every time the USS *Constitution* was refitted, new canes were made. The two shown here date from 1831 and 1908. Each is made from oak removed from the United States Navy's most famous frigate. On the 1831 example is inscribed, "A Rib of the Constitution, 1797. Thaddeus Page." This early example has an elephant ivory knob handle and a 3" long ferrule. Overall length: 34-1/2". The 1908 example has a copper handle and a copper ribbon that wraps around the oak shaft and identifies the ship by name and provides the date. Overall length: 33". *Courtesy of Richard R. Wagner, Jr.* Values: 1831: $1200; 1908: $500-600. USS *Constitution* relic canes are valued on a sliding scale by age.

While walking sticks are no longer necessary accessories for the well dressed gentleman and lady about town—although they are still offered with tuxedo rentals for formal weddings—nor generally seen as symbols of status and prestige, they remain ever fascinating to a growing collecting community. An ever-increasing number of collectors are struck by the artistry, history, and romance of these intriguing objects. Most of the antique canes readily available to collectors today date from the 1840s to World War I. Created during the period when mass production was in its ascendancy, walking sticks were produced in greater numbers and shorter times than ever before in human history. What you will find here is a cross section, a sampling if you will, of that immensely varied output. It is not encyclopedic in nature. There were simply too many canes produced to make such an enumeration practical.

The purpose of this book is to introduce you, the reader, to a wide variety of canes, to familiarize you with the broad categories canes fall into, and above all to explore why these artifacts of another age were once so important to the people who owned them. This will be accomplished with a blend of history and photos that I hope will help to bring these fascinating objects to life in your imagination.

While photographing my previous book on canes, it was my privilege to examine three violin canes up close while visiting with Frank Monek in Illinois. Here is another of these rare and beautiful instruments cleverly housed within a cane. This probably Austrian piece dating from around 1850 features a large tau-shaped mahogany handle, a 3/4" lined nickel collar at the joint where the handle unscrews, allowing the musician access to the horsehair fitted bow of exotic dark wood with ebony and ivory fittings hidden within a recess at the back of the shaft. The instrument is exposed when a 21-3/4" mahogany panel is removed from the side of the shaft. The violin features internal ebony seats, a maple sounding board, and bird's-eye maple bridge. There are four adjustable tuning pins turned by a small key to tune the strings. A lower 1/4" nickel ring helps secure the panel over the violin. A 3/4" white metal ferrule protects the lower end. Handle: 6-1/2" x 3". Overall length: 35". *Courtesy of Henry A. Taron, Tradewinds Antiques.* $10,000-15,000.

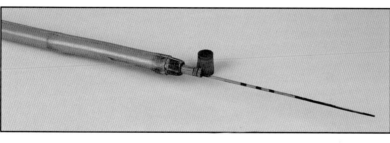

Japanese bamboo fishing cane with a pole that comes out of the base when the short metal ferrule is removed. Overall length: 35-3/4". *Courtesy of Dale Van Atta.* $450-495.

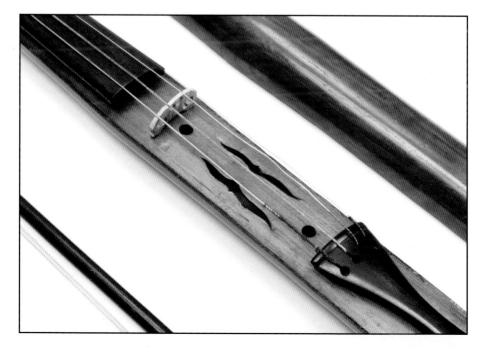

Sticks of Power & Prestige

Here we first open the door to the world of the walking stick in all its astounding variety. We begin with a review of basic information necessary to understand walking stick anatomy, stick types, their values, and care. Experienced collectors and readers of my previous work on canes, *Canes: From the Seventeenth to the Twentieth Century* (Schiffer Publishing, 1993), may wish to skip ahead to the subheading, **Notable Walking Stick Owners**. The vast majority of the walking sticks presented in this chapter are formal sticks, elegant examples of high cane artistry.

A Primer for the New Collector

Walking Stick vs. Cane

In *Accessories of Dress*, Katherine Lester and Bess Oerke state that prior to the sixteenth century, the term "cane" was not used in the Western world in reference to a fashionable walking stick. However, with the importation and use of a variety of reeds, canes, palms, rattans, and bamboo in shafts—the best known and most coveted of these being malacca—the name "cane" entered into use specifically to define sticks made from these new materials. (Lester & Oerke 1954, 392) How-

ever, today both terms, walking stick and cane, are used interchangeably. The author Francis Monek summed up the situation well in his book *Canes Through the Ages*, "People today try to make a distinction between canes and walking sticks. I personally think it is an unnecessary sophistication." (1995, 22)

The Formal Stick

Walking sticks may be divided into two broad categories, formal and folk art, by their method of manufacture and their purpose. Formal canes were produced by a variety of professionally trained artists for the commercial market: woodworkers, jewelers, metal workers, ceramists, and enamellers working for a variety of large manufacturing concerns and professional studios. Canes manufactured by these firms range from ordinary walking sticks and elegant dress canes to the vast array of

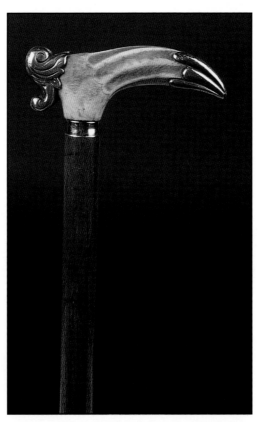

system sticks (also known as gadget canes), those sticks with a second purpose hidden within the confines of the handle or the shaft. Conversely, folk art sticks were made by independent artists working alone, creating walking sticks that reflected the prowess of the artist in the complexity of their designs. Folk art canes will be discussed in detail later.

Elaborately carved bone handle with silver fittings on silver collar, metal ferrule with iron tip. Handle: 4-1/2" w. Overall length: 34-1/2". *Courtesy of Ambassador Richard W. Carlson.* $725-800.

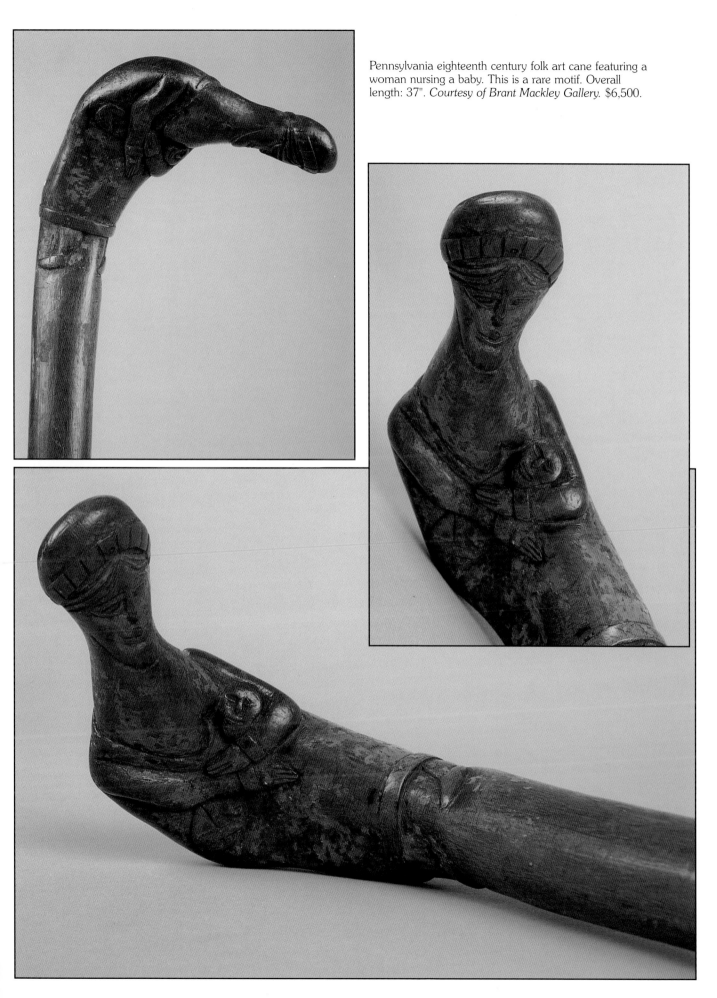

Pennsylvania eighteenth century folk art cane featuring a woman nursing a baby. This is a rare motif. Overall length: 37". *Courtesy of Brant Mackley Gallery.* $6,500.

Formal canes were produced by the cooperative efforts of several artists and were usually assembled from several separate parts and frequently have both collars and ferrules. The purpose of the formal cane is to draw attention to the wearer of the stick. Elegant, beautifully crafted, expensive formal canes also added to the wearer's prestige. The personalities of the artisans producing formal canes were unimportant to their work and the individual artists involved are rarely known. The handles bear most of the decoration and the shafts, while complementing these handles, were designed simply, drawing attention back to the handle. Formal cane handles are rarely made from the same material as the shaft. Formal handles were sometimes fashioned from wood; however, more often handles were crafted of ivory, silver, gold, or other precious materials. The fine craftsmanship and great stylistic variety are the significant features of formal canes.

Formal canes were made from local and imported woods, reeds, and canes. During the eighteenth and nineteenth centuries, demand for formal canes increased dramatically, bringing with it a desire for more exotic and innovative materials as we shall soon see.

Anatomy of the Walking Stick

Formal walking sticks may be divided into the following four parts: the handle, collar (or band), shaft (or shank), and the ferrule. Piercing shafts of certain ages are eyelets, located along the upper third of the shaft, used to thread a strap allowing the cane to dangle from the wearer's wrist while the hand is occupied with other business. Generally speaking, different handle and ferrule types, and the presence or absence of eyelets, are helpful in dating a cane to a particular period.

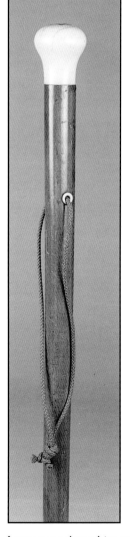
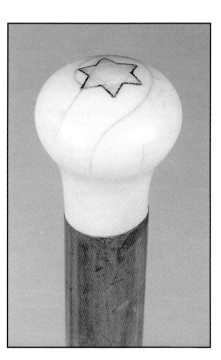

Carved ivory dog's head with glass eyes and a shoe in its mouth. Gold collar marked 18k and hallmarked, malacca shaft with 1- 1/2" horn ferrule, late nineteenth century. Handle: 2-1/2" l. x 2" d. x 1-11/16". Overall length: 34-1/8". *Courtesy of The World of the Walking Stick.* $2350-2585.

Large pear-shaped ivory handle with mother-of-pearl six pointed Star of David on top. Malacca shaft with ivory eyelets and wrist cord, 7/8" l. horn ferrule, c. 1870. Handle: 2" h. x 1-3/4" w. Overall length: 36". *Courtesy of The World of the Walking Stick.* $1975-2175.

Handles: The handle is the most important part of the cane in many respects. With formal canes especially, the handle draws the eye and is the center of attention. The handle is also the part in most constant contact with the user and it must be durable and comfortable, as well as stylish. Handles range in form from purely utilitarian to highly decorative and have been produced in many materials including gold, silver, enamel, and various metals, semi-precious stones, horn, tusk, bone, ivory (a favorite material of many cane artists who produced wildly innovative and elaborate ivory handles, many in the forms of animals and people), snake or shark skin, leather, glass, and ceramics. Well-known firms such as Meissen and Sèvres produced a wide variety of porcelain handles. While much sought for their beauty, porcelain-handled canes are rare due to their fragility. The Wedgwood ceramists produced some truly stunning handles in jasperware as well.

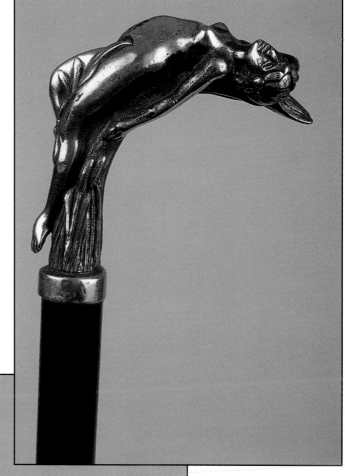

Silver-plated bronze nude woman in repose, draped across the handle above a dark rosewood shaft. Handle: 3" h. x 3" w. *Courtesy of Richard R. Wagner, Jr.* $700-1200 for such ladies.

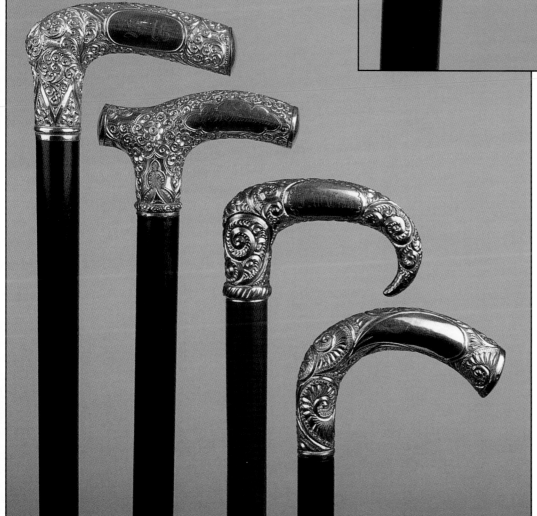

Four rolled gold handles in varying shapes. The quality of the gold is told by the color and by any black seam bleeds (very thin gold will show the seams, lowering the value). Three of these handles are on black shafts, with one on a brown shaft. *Courtesy of Richard R. Wagner, Jr.* Gold L-shaped and tau handles are more utilitarian to use, rather than knobs, and are of higher values: $400-800, depending on quality of gold and the patterns on the shafts. Solid gold handles are much more expensive, nearly doubling the value.

Four silver knob handles, including two examples of Anglo-Indian canes dating from the late nineteenth century. The Anglo-Indian example with the carved shaft ranges from $250-350 in value. The large malacca Anglo-Indian cane has a huge handle. Handle: 4-1/2" h. x 2" d. $550-650 due to the size of the handle. Silver handle, similar to a rolled gold knob handle in form, although much less common than gold examples, ebony shaft. $200-350. Plain silver knob with a carved ebony shaft with ivory in every nub. The carved ebony increases the value, $300-400. *Courtesy of Richard R. Wagner, Jr.*

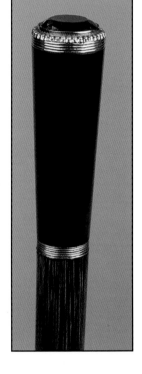

Left and above:
This is an elaborate jeweled handle featuring jade with gold mounts, seed pearls, and a large amethyst at the top. The shaft is partridge wood. Handle: 3" h. Overall length: 35-1/2". *Courtesy of Richard R. Wagner, Jr.* $1200-1800.

Rock crystal and enamel handle, possibly with gold, on a rosewood shaft. Handle: 3-1/2" l. Overall length: 39". *Courtesy of Richard R. Wagner, Jr.* $800-1000.

Unique rhino horn and ivory handle. The top portion of the handle is an ivory dog's head emerging from the horn and resting on its front paws. The dog has crystal eyes. The rhino horn is carved to match the contours of the malacca shaft with its 1-1/8" horn ferrule, late nineteenth century. Overall length: 34-7/8". *Courtesy of The World of the Walking Stick.* $1950-2145.

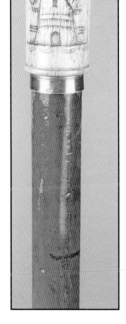

Tusk handled cane with brass collar fitted to a large horn shaft from South Africa. The tip of the antler is protected with a tiny metal ferrule. Handle: 4" h. Overall length: 35". *Courtesy of Ambassador Richard W. Carlson.* $275-300.

Bone straight support handle with relief carvings on either side with a windmill on one side and a Dutch woman on the other. Small silver collar, malacca shaft with 1-1/4" metal ferrule. Overall length: 33-1/2" *Courtesy of The World of the Walking Stick.* $775-855.

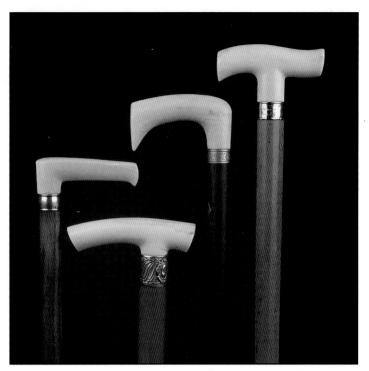

Four comfortable, plain ivory handles. Two are in walrus ivory, one in elephant, one in whale's tooth. Two malacca and two hardwood shafts. Ivory L-shaped handles started as early as the 1850s, and early examples have white metal eyelets, in this case with a sharply down turned point on the handle. The tau crutch handle is in whale ivory. The tau is a lopsided T-shaped handle. Walrus ivory is identified by the mottled center, which has been described as "looking like tapioca." This mottled area is the center of the tooth. Whale's tooth has a distinctive yellow discoloration banding. Elephant ivory has cross-grain, just like wood. Both elephant and whale's tooth also have a black dot at the center of the tooth. Bone has dark spots throughout. *Courtesy of Richard R. Wagner, Jr.* $300-500 each.

Walrus ivory. *Courtesy of Richard R. Wagner, Jr.*

Whale's tooth. *Courtesy of Richard R. Wagner, Jr.*

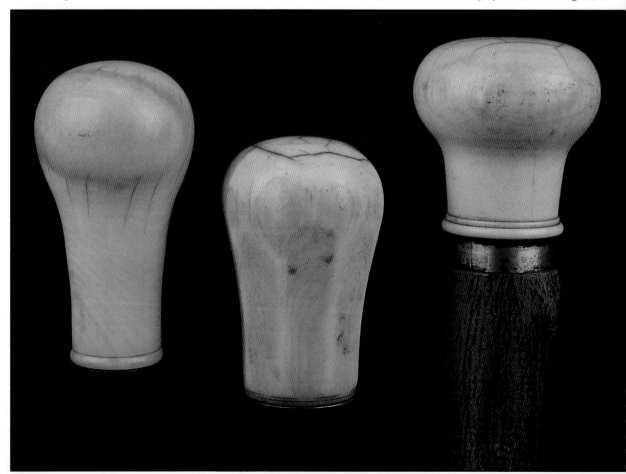

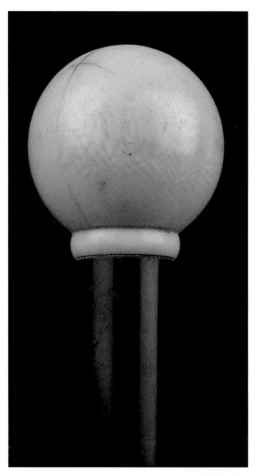

Elephant ivory. *Courtesy of Richard R. Wagner, Jr.*

Canes come in many materials. Rattlesnake skin crook handled cane. The rattle is attached near the base on the back of the cane. Overall length: 37". *Courtesy of Ambassador Richard W. Carlson.* $125-140.

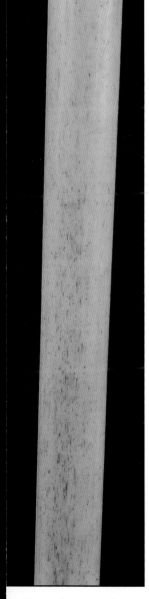

Bone. *Courtesy of Richard R. Wagner, Jr.*

Glass ball cane handle measuring 1-1/2" in diameter filled with multi-colored glass rods. Ringed silver collar, mahogany shaft, and black horn ferrule. Overall length: 36". *Courtesy of Kimball M. Sterling Auctioneers.* $400-600.

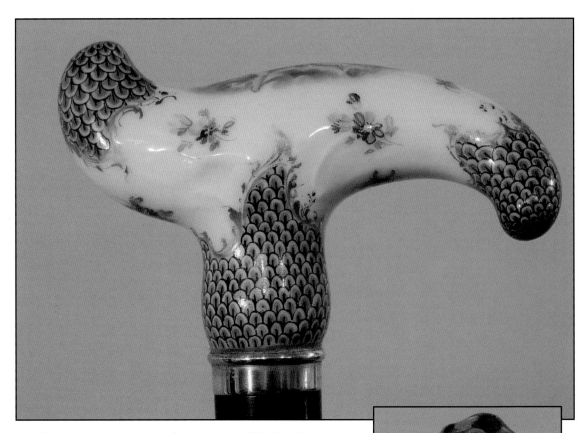

Continental porcelain handled dress cane. The handle features an idyllic scene of cherubs in the clouds on the top of the handle. Gold collar, black ebony shaft, and bimetal ferrule. Handle: 4" x 2-1/8". Overall length: 37-1/4". *Courtesy of Kimball M. Sterling Auctioneers.* $900-1100.

Glass paperweight handled cane with brass collar and rubber ferrule tip over brass ferrule. Handle: 2" h. Overall length: 36-1/2". *Courtesy of Ambassador Richard W. Carlson.* $425-470.

Porcelain handle by KPM (Koenigliche Porzellan-Manufaktur) of Berlin of unusual length, c. 1860-1880. Gold collar, snakewood shaft, horn ferrule. Handle: 4" x 1-1/8". Overall length: 38-1/4". *Courtesy of Kimball M. Sterling Auctioneers.* $800-1200.

From the second half of the nineteenth century on through the 1920s, silver-handled canes were manufactured in abundance and provide an excellent starting point when creating a collection of formal sticks. Both well crafted silver and gold handles were given as presentation canes, some featuring truly fascinating inscriptions. Ornate silver handles took figural form, representing a wide variety of animals and people.

Silver niello ("chern" in Russian) handles on black wood and snakewood shafts. Such items were produced in Russia and France predominately. These examples are French. One company in America also produced niello work handles. A great deal of craftsmanship was involved in successfully executed niello handles. *Courtesy of Richard R. Wagner, Jr.* These examples range from $350-500. Russian silver niello work brings more; add $200-300 more for Russian examples.

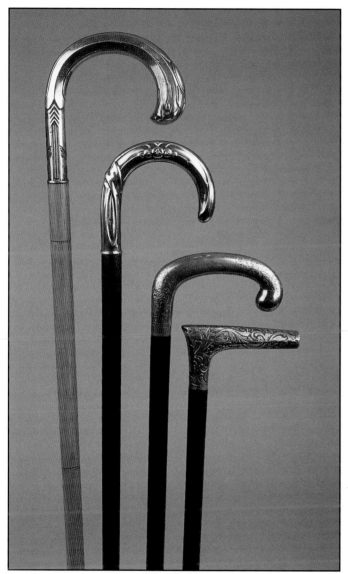

Silver handled canes. Crook handled, early twentieth century, designed to look elegant whether in use or hanging over the arm. Silver L handle, etched floral pattern on a snakewood shaft. Handle: 2" h. x 4" l. Overall length: 35". *Courtesy of Richard R. Wagner, Jr.* $250-400 each.

Right:
Figural silver wild boar and bird handles in 800 coin silver. Both handles are on black shafts. The bird has glass eyes. *Courtesy of Richard R. Wagner, Jr.* Canes with silver figural handles run $500-900, depending on the quality of the work. Whether sterling, plate, or coin silver, the prices are differentiated by figure quality alone.

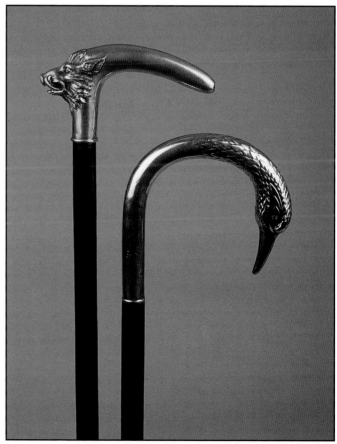

Gold handles tend to be among the highest priced canes available to collectors today. Look for the gold content marking on such handles. Most gold handles were placed on elegant shafts such as ebony and were intended as eveningwear.

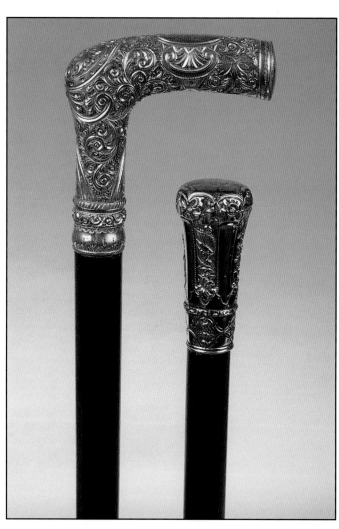

Gold knob handles: All on ebonized (black painted) or ebony shaft. Dated canes are more desirable. Historical canes are more valuable still. These canes date from the post-Civil War era to c. 1910. The largest cane handle reads, "Honorable George Gray, U.S. Judge, Wilmington, Delaware, from MJS." Largest handle: 3-3/4" h. x 2-1/8" w. Smallest handle: 3/4" h., 1" d. *Courtesy of Richard R. Wagner, Jr.* Rolled gold presentation canes vary in price by the size of the handle, anywhere from $200 for small handles to over $1000 for a very large handle.

Gold and silver presentation canes. Gold L handle reads on top "H H Judd" and on the end cap "From Nebraska Lumbermen's Excursion Feby 1902." Silver handled cane reads on top: "Gen. Millay from Soph. Class 55-6." The first s in class reads as an F. Left: overall length: 35-1/4"; right: overall length: 36". *Courtesy of Ambassador Richard W. Carlson.* Together these presentation canes are valued around $650+.

Rolled gold dog's head handle on a heavy ebonized shaft. Figural gold handles very uncommon. This is an Odd Fellow's cane (showing the three linked rings symbol). *Courtesy of Richard R. Wagner, Jr.* $300-1000, depending on the size and quality of the figure. Horse's hoof, $300-330; this piece, $700-800 range.

Figural handles are rarely found before the nineteenth century. Ivory was a favorite medium for artists producing figural handles. These handles take the forms of virtually every animal imaginable, along with the likenesses of men, women, and children produced as busts and full figures from head to toe. Remarkable porcelain figural handles were also made.

Carved ivory sad-eyed dog's head with 3" silver collar, hallmarked, hardwood shaft, c. 1900. Overall length: 33-1/4". *Courtesy of The World of the Walking Stick.* $1100-1210.

Porcelain figural handle signed by the German firm KPM, c. mid-nineteenth century, featuring a classic KPM cavalier in a purple cap with gilded and turned plinth. Honey-toned malacca shaft and horn ferrule. Handle: 3" x 1-1/2", Overall length: 35". The Koenigliche Porzellan-Manufaktur was established in 1763, receiving its name and symbol (a royal blue scepter) from Frederick the Great. The company is known for its elegant handmade, hand-painted porcelain work, including this handle. *Courtesy of Kimball M. Sterling Auctioneers.* $800-1000.

Left:
Bacchus bronze silver-plated figural handle, snakewood shaft. *Courtesy of Richard R. Wagner, Jr.* $500-700.

Left:
Bronze with silver plate figural handle formed in a very good representation of a snake and large cat facing each other. Handle: 3-1/2" h. x 1-3/4" w. *Courtesy of Richard R. Wagner, Jr.* $350-550.

Handles were made in many shapes. *Crook handle* shapes include the shepherd's neck-crook and shepherd's leg-crook; the crook (or umbrella) shape; and the carved crook. *Round handle* shapes include the ball knob (or pommel); flattened knob; and the carved knob (or turk's head). *Between round and straight support handles* are the molded knob (or cap); the pear-shaped; and the pistol grip handles. *Straight support handles* include the crowned straight support; flattened straight support; ornate straight support; rounded straight support; and short straight support. Among the *crutch handles* are the crooked crutch; derby crutch; fritz crutch (or opera style); and tau crutch. *Additional handle shapes* include the bec de corbin; crooked tau; epsilon (or thumb rest); figured or Imago; hunting hook; the L-shaped or crop; the L-shaped antler; and the T-shaped handle.

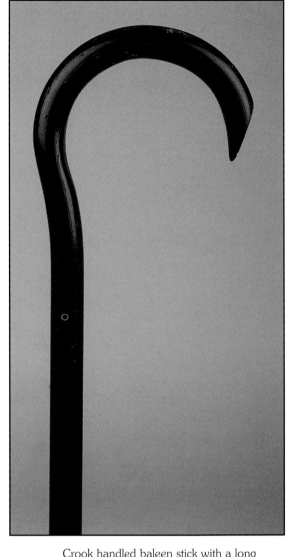

Crook handled baleen stick with a long white metal ferrule inscribed with the gentleman's name on the ferrule, "J. Chance Philadelphia." Eyelets in the shaft. Mid-nineteenth century. Handle: 2-3/8" l. Overall length: 35-1/2". *Courtesy of Richard R. Wagner, Jr.* $500 to $1000, depending on age and size.

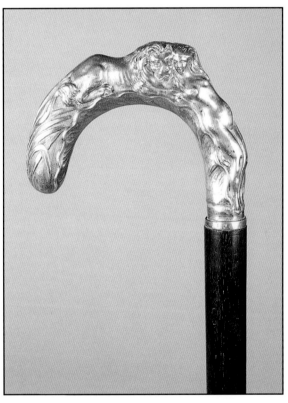

Silver Art Nouveau crook handle depicting a lion lying on the crook handle with his head being embraced by a nude woman with long flowing tresses. Ebony shaft with 1-1/4" metal ferrule, Continental, c. 1890. Handle: 4-1/4" w. x 3-1/2" h. Overall length: 35-1/2". *Courtesy of The World of the Walking Stick.* $1750-1925.

Ivory ball knob handle carved in the form of wrinkled fabric with the heads of three different dog breeds sticking through torn holes in the fabric; the dogs carved in relief include an English bulldog, Great Dane, and Spaniel, all with glass eyes. Silver collar with unknown hallmark of "FK." Walnut shaft, 1-1/2" metal ferrule. Handle: 2" d. Overall length: 35-1/2". *Courtesy of The World of the Walking Stick.* $1350-1485.

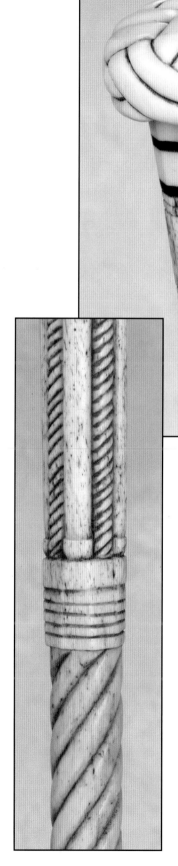

Chinese relief carved ivory ball knob handle depicting two dragons. Small horn collar, hardwood shaft with 1-1/4" brass and iron ferrule, late nineteenth century. Handle: 1-3/4" d. Overall length: 36-3/4". *Courtesy of The World of the Walking Stick.* $1425-1570.

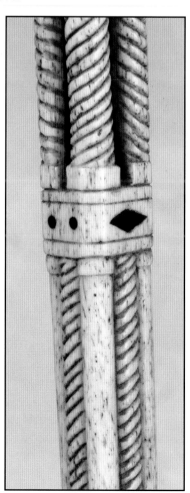

Fantastically carved, possibly American c. 1850, architectural nautical cane of whale ivory and whalebone produced by a sailor and requiring a great deal of time and skill. The ivory handle is fashioned in a carved knob or turk's head knot design. Two thin baleen separators separate the handle from the intricately carved whalebone shaft. The shaft is carved for the top 7-1/2" with open twisted columns with a twist-carved rope motif on the interior. Baleen diamonds and dots decorate around the columns. There is another 10" of twist carving, then the shaft is smooth. There was apparently no need for a ferrule. Handle: 1-1/4" x 1-1/2". Overall length: 34-1/2". *Courtesy of Henry A. Taron, Tradewinds Antiques.* $6000-8000.

Intricately carved ornate straight support ivory handle with a black shaft and ivory ferrule, no collar. Overall length: 39-1/4". *Courtesy of The World of the Walking Stick.* NP (**N**o **P**rice)

Above and right:
Ceramic handles. Left: Tau crutch handle on a stepped partridge wood shaft. Handle: 2" h. x 4" w. Overall length: 35". Center: two-piece ceramic handle with gold. Handle: 7" tall, flattened knob, 2" d. Black shaft. Overall length: 35". Right: short straight support handle, bamboo shaft. Handle: 2-1/4" h. Overall length: 35-3/4". *Courtesy of Richard R. Wagner, Jr.* $250-350 each. These go up to $900+ for elaborate examples.

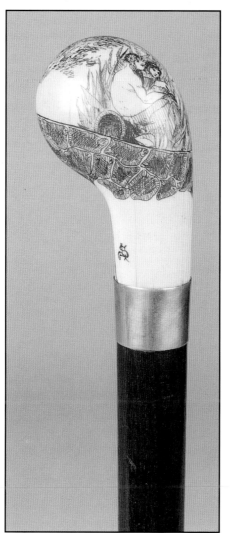

Unique ivory pistol grip handle depicting a scene done in black ink of a semi-clad man and woman along with two nude children frolicking in a garden surrounded with a bird and bear. Signed by the artist, silver collar hallmarked, hardwood shaft with 1-1/2" horn ferrule, late nineteenth century. Handle: 2-1/2" h. x 1-1/4" w. Overall length: 37-1/2". *Courtesy of The World of the Walking Stick.* $2500-2750.

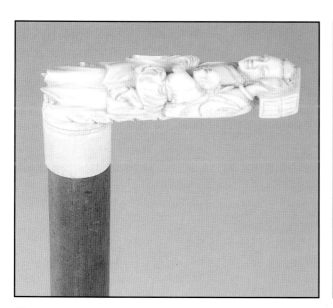
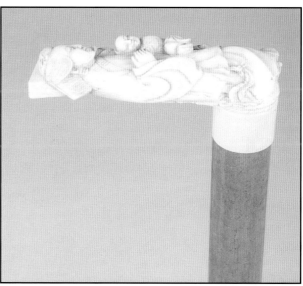

Chinese export carved ivory L-shaped handle featuring a mother with her child carved in relief. The mother is depicted in traditional Chinese dress holding her child while reclining on a pillow block. Malacca shaft with 1-1/4" l. light colored horn ferrule, late nineteenth century. Handle: 4" l. x 1-1/2" h. Overall length: 36-3/4". *Courtesy of The World of the Walking Stick.* $1500-1650.

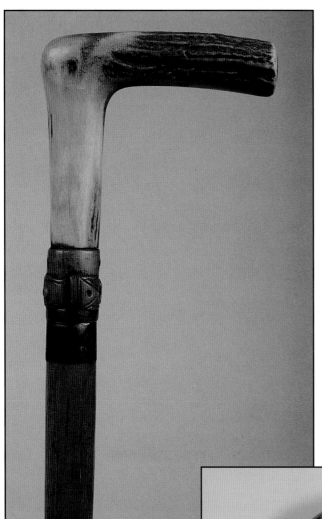

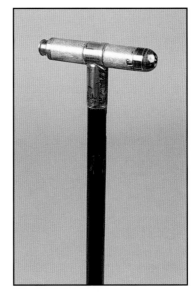

T-shaped handle English flashlight silver gadget cane, (i.e. English Silver Torch), bone ferrule. Handle: 3-1/4" wide. Overall length: 36-1/2". *Courtesy of Ambassador Richard W. Carlson.* $360-400.

L-shaped stag horn handle with a malacca shaft, this is a sword cane with a wonderful gilded and fire blued, heavy blade marked London. It is shown with a group of sword canes later under the weapons canes. *Courtesy of Richard R. Wagner, Jr.* Such sword canes range from $1000 to $1500 or $2000 in some cases.

Right:
This modified shepherd's crook handle features a soccer player's (er ... football player's) booted foot kicking the ball. English folk art cane carved from a single piece of wood and dating from the late nineteenth to early twentieth century. Gold and brown polychrome paint finish the piece and the base of the shaft is protected by a bimetal ferrule. Handle: 4-1/4" x 6". Overall length: 36". *Courtesy of Kimball M. Sterling Auctioneers.* $1600-2000.

Figured wooden handle carved as a bearded man wearing a hat. Under the bust is carved "Boggis '78." Overall length: 37-1/2". *Courtesy of Dale Van Atta.* $400-440.

There are some general rules of thumb that will aid in determining the age of a cane. However, it should be noted that a single feature alone might not provide an accurate date. It is best to consider the walking stick and all its features as a whole before estimating the age of that cane. From the late seventeenth century in the Western world, formal canes had vertically mounted handles, usually of ivory or bone and occasionally of precious metal or porcelain. Until 1800, these vertically mounted handles were shaped as elongated, cylindrical, flaring, sometimes bulbous or scrolled knobs.

From 1800-1840, handle materials remained unchanged but shapes evolved away from cylindrical knob to more rounded, bulbous forms. Antler handles also became popular during this period. These handles were made from the portion of the antler nearest the skull, allowing the natural rosette to be used as a decorative feature. Antler handled canes were particular popular with gentlemen who enjoyed spending time in the country. The antler shank was polished and was often fitted with a small silver, gold, or brass panel. Such panels were frequently engraved with the owner's initials or name.

Around 1840, bulbous knob handle forms were replaced with the first L-shaped handles. These handles were set at right angles to the shaft and were most com-

monly produced of either ivory or bone. L-shaped handles remained popular until around 1865.

By the early 1850s, improvement in equipment brought about by the Industrial Revolution allowed modern crook handle forms to be readily manufactured. Early crook handles curved gently but gradually tightened into the modern form. An exception to the crook handle was the vertically mounted grip that was in fashion on formal canes from roughly 1870 to 1915. Many of these handles were flaring, ornate knobs of gold, gold plate, or silver mounted on rosewood, ebony, or other exotic wood shafts.

The Sears, Roebuck and Company catalog for 1902 (reproduced in 1993) features several crook handle canes described as made from "genuine hickory," "natural Congo," and "genuine Congo." The most expensive of the lot was priced at $1.25 and featured a sterling silver ornament on the crook handle.

Not all handle shapes follow the rules of thumb for handle dating listed above. In the 1902 Sears catalog, the least expensive cane listed featured a plain knob handle. While Sears described this innocuous looking cane simply as a "very nice cane;" in actuality this was a weapon—a dangerous weapon that could be purchased for a dime. It was a "loaded" cane, meaning that heavy metal was hidden beneath the spun cloth outer sheath to disguise its true nature, in other words the cane was loaded with a heavy metal interior that increased the force of a blow when the cane was swung at an opponent. This loaded cane was designed to disable an unsuspecting villain with a single blow.

Four ornate gold handles were also displayed in the 1902 Sears catalog among the fine jewelry and watches. Ranging in value from $4.45 to $14.00, three were knob handles of the forms popular from 1870 to 1915 with raised floral decoration that left an open surface on top for an inscription. The fourth handle was an opera or fritz crutch style, described by Sears as a "Polo crook," which also featured raised surface decoration.

By the 1930s, canes all but disappear from the scene unless required for support while walking or hiking.

Collars: The collar or band is a metal strip located below the cane's handle which conceals the joint between the handle and the shaft when the two pieces are made from different materials. Not only an aesthetic feature, the collar also strengthens the joint and helps prevent the shaft from splitting at the joint when pressure is applied to the handle during use. When a cane was presented as a gift, the collar frequently was inscribed with a message from the gift giver and the name of the honored individual.

Prior to roughly 1750, most canes were produced without collars; even metal handled canes rarely had collars to disguise the joint between metal and wood. From 1750 through 1800, the collars supplied were nar row metal bands decorated with either simple incised lines or small stamped dots in straight or wavy line patterns. These collars were most often made from silver, although they were also produced at times from gold or brass.

From approximately 1800 to 1850, collars widened and were decorated with high relief bead work reminiscent of twisted rope. Toward the end of this period, both undecorated collars and collars with raised beads along the edges made their appearance. These collars were produced primarily in silver.

From around 1840 to 1865, many collars were made smooth and wider still. During the 1850s, the most popular bands were decorated with lines of raised beads along the edges.

From roughly 1865 to 1920, collars were mainly produced from brass plated with silver, and toward the end of the nineteenth century, with nickel and chrome. Mass production brought uniform sizes and shapes to collars. Many such collars were heavily decorated with the exception of an enclosed panel or cartouche of smooth metal intended for an inscription or initials, as presentation canes became very popular during this period. American silver collars were marked Sterling during this period and the karat marking appeared on gold collars. Hallmarks vouching for the purity of gold, silver, and platinum appear on British collars and are useful for dating. The British have used hallmarks to indicate the purity of such metals since the 1300s.

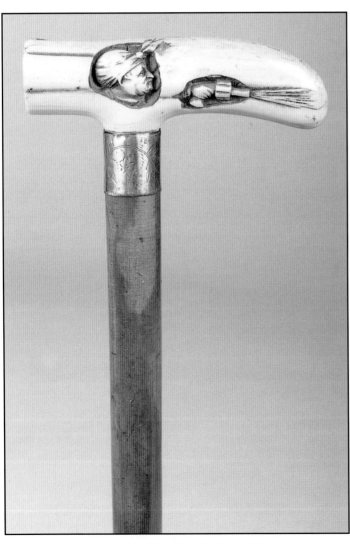

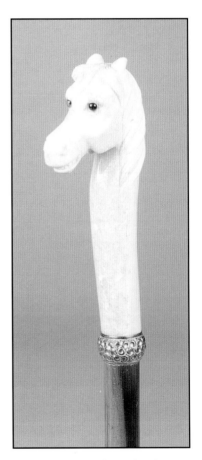

Victorian gold collar. Carved walrus ivory horse head handle with red glass eyes. Cherry wood shaft with 1-1/2" metal ferrule, American, late nineteenth century. Handle: 5" h. x 2-1/4" at its widest, 3/4" d. Overall length: 35-1/4". *Courtesy of The World of the Walking Stick.* $1195-1315.

Engraved silver collar. Ivory handle with the head of a man firing a pistol carved into one side of the handle. The man's hand and the discharge from the pistol are also carved into the handle. Malacca shaft with 3/8" metal ferrule, late nineteenth century. Handle: 4" l. x 1-1/4" h. Overall length: 33". *Courtesy of The World of the Walking Stick.* $1350-1485.

Here is an example of silver eyelets. Elephant ivory knob handle, c. 1850s, child's or ladies cane, silver collar and eyelets, malacca stick with a long 2-3/4" brass ferrule. Handle: 2-1/4" h. Overall length: 29-1/2". *Courtesy of Richard R. Wagner, Jr.* $200-250.

Shafts (or Shanks): While the majority of cane shafts were made from branches, stems, or side-shoots of almost every sturdy tree or shrub imaginable, virtually every material has been used to make a cane shaft at one time or another. Among the materials used are ivory, bone, horns and tusks, tortoiseshell, canes (malacca, bamboo, partridge, sugar cane…), kelp, vegetable ivory, Jersey cabbage stalks, amber, metal, glass, plastic and gutta-percha, snakeskin, and even unfortunate bulls' penises. At the Columbian Exposition in Chicago in 1893, canes made from cactus were on display in one of the pavilions. For a very detailed listing of cane materials used in shafts, see Canes.org, a website maintained by the Israeli Society for Cane Collectors.

Among the woods used for shafts, favorites were mahogany, ebony, maple, holly, ash, beech, and hickory. Among the canes used, malacca and partridge were coveted. Making a wooden cane shaft required time and patience. No green sticks could be used and it took several years before wood gathered was dry enough to de-bark and use.

Eyelets: Eyelets are often found on canes dating from roughly the mid-eighteenth through the mid-nineteenth centuries. The eyelet was a hole drilled through the shaft near the handle. This hole was often trimmed with the same material as the collar and ferrule, which was frequently metal ranging from silver and brass to gold. A tasseled cord could be passed through the eyelet, allowing the cane wearer to pass his or her wrist through the cord and let the cane dangle, freeing busy hands for other activities.

Ferrules: Ferrules are found at the base of the cane. Frequently, ferrules were designed with a solid piece of iron or steel at the base that was very durable, while the cone-shaped sides of the ferrule were made of another, softer metal. However, in some instances ferrules were made of bone, horn, or ivory. The ferrule protected the base of the cane shaft both from wear caused by direct contact with the ground and from rot caused by repeatedly plunging the wooden shaft into puddles and other muck. The ferrule took the beating and the wear of long use and could be replaced when necessary while ensuring the lower end of the shaft remained sound.

In 1890, the British manufacturer Henry Howell & Company advertised their selection of walking stick ferrules. The company described their ferrules as being made of copper with a riveted round iron end. They also produced a copper ferrule with a pointed end, "for Alpenstocks." Finally, the firm also offered "Ashdown's Patented India-rubber" ferrules which were both noise-less and non-slipping. (Monek 1995, 88)

As a general rule: the longer the ferrule, the earlier the stick. During the eighteenth and early nineteenth centuries, ferrules were made of plain brass, could measure as much as seven or eight inches long, and had that iron tip protruding at the base to protect the brass. Rough traveling conditions on difficult roads made these long ferrules necessary. In cities, for example, population densities were high, the roads were poorly drained, and they were rarely cleaned. Streets were generally covered with a thick layer of horse manure. In some areas, townsfolk swore that no one in living memory had ever seen the actual road surface!

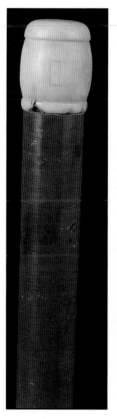

This is a 1770s era stick with a long metal ferrule measuring 6-1/4". Weighted ivory handled malacca cane with "B E" carved on either side of the handle. Overall length: 33-1/2". *Courtesy of Dale Van Atta.* $500+.

By the mid-nineteenth century, road conditions were improving and ferrules were shortening down to less than two inches. These shorter ferrules were made of nickel, silver-plated brass, or plain iron. Generally speaking, the closer to the twentieth century the cane dates, the shorter the ferrule becomes until it measures no more than an inch in length.

Ferrules are generally found on formal walking sticks. Folk art sticks were most often produced without ferrules. The folk artist expected to the wood he worked with to be sufficiently sturdy to withstand regular use. Occasionally folk artists will paint mock ferrules on the base of their canes. Folk art sticks with actual ferrules tend to date from later periods and do not necessarily correspond in size with their formal counterparts.

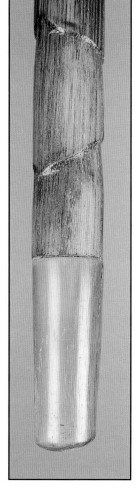

A 1-1/2" blond horn ferrule, German, dating from the late 19th century. *Courtesy of The World of the Walking Stick.*

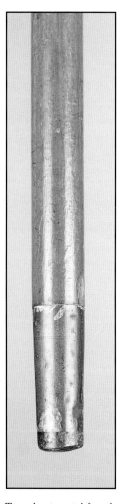 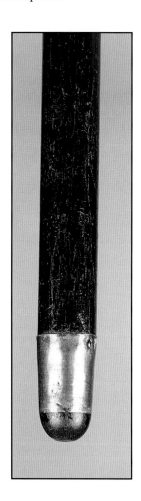

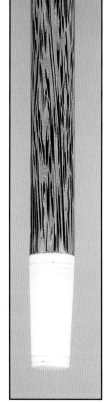

A 1-3/4" ivory ferrule dating from c. 1900, found on a Japanese cane. *Courtesy of The World of the Walking Stick.*

Two short metal ferrules with iron tips. *Courtesy of The World of the Walking Stick.*

A serious mountaineer's ferrule that has a spike on the end to facilitate climbing in rough terrain. *Courtesy of Ambassador Richard W. Carlson.*

Cane Values

The age of a walking stick alone will not determine its value on the market today. Values depend upon a variety of factors including the quality of the materials used, the workmanship involved, the amount of decoration, the rarity of the theme displayed, and the condition of the walking stick itself. Walking sticks that combine several materials such as ivory and sterling will also draw higher prices, as will well fashioned canes with an erotic theme carved from ivory or cast in sterling silver. Complete weapon canes and system sticks draw high values, as do walking sticks with interesting, proven historical provenances.

Walking sticks produced by world renowned manufacturers such as Tiffany and Fabergé frequently sell for over $15,000. Fabergé produced stunning enamel and diamond cane handles, while Tiffany was known for their handsome gold handles on ebony or tortoiseshell shafts. Some of the gun canes produced by Remington, rarities to be sure, also command prices in excess of $15,000.

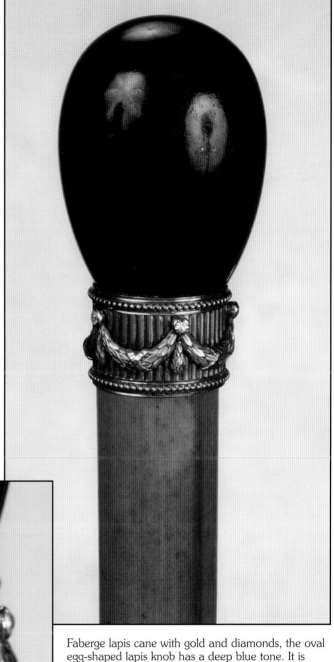

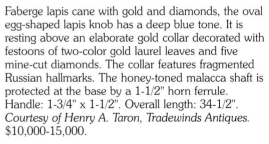

Faberge lapis cane with gold and diamonds, the oval egg-shaped lapis knob has a deep blue tone. It is resting above an elaborate gold collar decorated with festoons of two-color gold laurel leaves and five mine-cut diamonds. The collar features fragmented Russian hallmarks. The honey-toned malacca shaft is protected at the base by a 1-1/2" horn ferrule. Handle: 1-3/4" x 1-1/2". Overall length: 34-1/2". *Courtesy of Henry A. Taron, Tradewinds Antiques.* $10,000-15,000.

It was not all that long ago that folk art sticks were generally overlooked by the collecting community. This is no longer the case and the values of well-made, interesting folk art canes have risen accordingly. For example, a beautifully carved Amelia Earhart folk art cane measuring thirty-six inches long sold at auction in 1995 for over $3,500 (*to view this cane see Snyder 1993, p. 38*).

Walking sticks of lesser value include those that lack workmanship, are devoid of interesting features or artistic motifs, have no historical connection, and cannot be readily dated. Damaged walking sticks and examples that have been repaired are also of lower value.

The values found in the captions for the walking sticks displayed are in United States dollars. Prices vary immensely based on the location of the market, the venue of the sale, the rarity of the stick, and the enthusiasms of the collecting community. Values in the Midwest differ from those in the West or East, and those at specialty shows or auctions will differ from those in dealers' shops or through dealers' web pages.

All of these factors make it impossible to create absolutely accurate price listings, but *a guide* to realistic pricing may be offered. Please note: these values are not provided to set prices in the antiques marketplace, but rather to give the reader a reasonable idea of what one might expect to pay for walking sticks in mint condition.

Caring for Walking Sticks

Walking sticks are organic artifacts and must be handled with care. They are quite sensitive to changes in humidity and temperature. Rises in humidity and temperature may lead to swelling and cracking of walking stick shafts and handles. Direct sunlight may also be damaging. In ivory, sunlight will raise the temperature, lower the humidity level, and eventually change the color of the ivory.

Take care when cleaning antique walking sticks. If you have any doubts at all about what you are about to do, seek out a professional before you proceed. A quick consultation could save you from considerable grief. It pays to remember that the accumulated "dirt of the ages" actually protects the sensitive organic material underneath. Once the surface grime has been removed, the exposed walking stick is all the more susceptible to the effects of changing temperature and humidity.

That said, to carefully clean wooden sticks, first wipe the wooden surface gently with a clean cloth. Apply a small amount of linseed oil. Allow the oil to dry and then polish the surface with a clean, soft cloth. Bees' wax also works well with wooden canes. In either case, use oil or wax sparingly. Apply too much of either and you will create a sticky surface that attracts dirt all over again. Once the oil or wax is dry, polish with a soft, clean cloth.

There are methods for removing and polishing silver handles, however, I suggest readers take this up with a specialist rather than forging ahead on their own. However, reasonably clean silver handles may be kept clean with conventional silver care products. Always protect the wooden shaft while cleaning as silver cleaners can damage the wood. Once cleaned, silver and other metal handles should be polished with a soft, clean cloth.

Great care must be taken when dealing with ivory canes as well. If the ivory appears to be dyed, pigmented, or inlaid with other materials, seek out a professional for cleaning. For ivory free of these restrictions, initially clean away surface grime by gently wiping the ivory with a soft, clean cloth. If the ivory is not cracked and dirt remains, you can create a solution that is fifty percent ethyl alcohol and fifty percent water. Dip a cotton swab into the solution, blot it on a paper towel to reduce the moisture content, and apply the cotton swab to a small and well-hidden portion of the ivory. Dry the area immediately and check the results. If no harm has been done, continue cleaning small areas, drying immediately, until the ivory is clean. (Drayman-Weisser 1993; Kadri 1993)

Walking Sticks & the Twenty-first Century

Collectors find antique walking sticks endlessly fascinating. The Smithsonian Institution alone owns over two thousand sticks, which they display about a dozen at a time distributed among their various museums. I have been privileged enough to meet passionate collectors who own even more. Additionally, while modern canes will never catch the eye of technophiles the way a multi-function cell phone or quality PDA will, there are a few firms producing quality sticks for those who require or desire them. Modern formal sticks of sterling silver and ebony may be purchased from the remaining American and English firms creating them for prices ranging from roughly $150 to $500+.

There is, however, at least one venue where an inexpensive, modern "tippler's" cane is currently in use. Every winter since 1894, for the three weekends prior to Lent, Quebec City hosts a winter carnival. Held on the Plains of Abraham, 310 wooden steps below the *Promenades des Gouveneurs* down the fortified city's cliff face, daily activities include toboggan runs, snow sculpting, and ice wall climbing. Once the day's soapbox derbies and dogsled races are done and the sun goes down, revelers keep away the chill with a variety of alcoholic beverages. Many carry their liquor in hollow plastic walking sticks.

Some suggest that as the baby boom generation ages, the walking stick will return to fashion. Only time will tell.

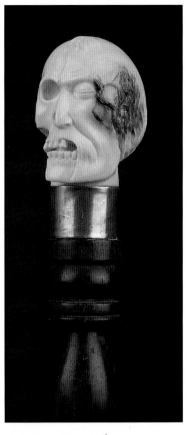

Modern ivory canes carved in Indonesia. Mostly these are found on palm wood shafts, sometimes rosewood. Today, makers use mastodon, moose, and walrus ivory to produce their handles. *Courtesy of Richard R. Wagner, Jr.* Values range from $200-500 depending on the quality of the carving and the material used.

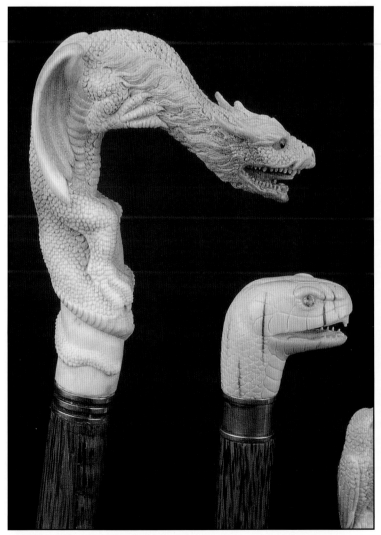

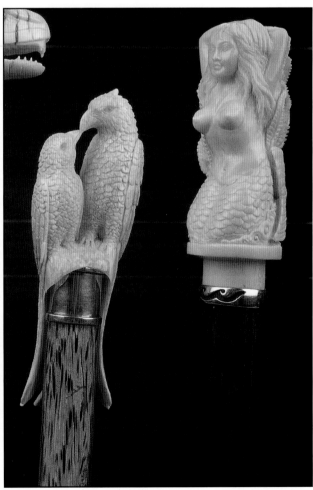

Black skull made from water buffalo horn, modern, carved in Indonesia. *Courtesy of Richard R. Wagner, Jr.* $250-400.

Modern silver cane handles with London hallmarks and marked "Sterling." Rosewood shafts. The handles are a ram's head and a British Beefeater. These are English examples from the 1970s-1990s. Similar silver handled canes are now made everywhere. *Courtesy of Richard R. Wagner, Jr.* $200-300 each.

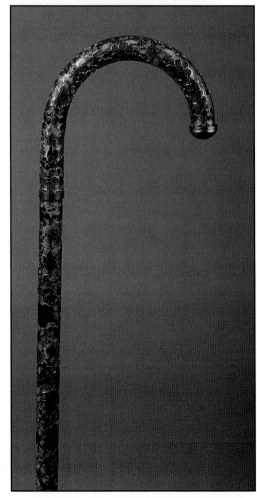

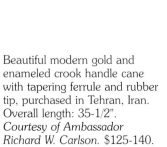

Beautiful modern gold and enameled crook handle cane with tapering ferrule and rubber tip, purchased in Tehran, Iran. Overall length: 35-1/2". *Courtesy of Ambassador Richard W. Carlson.* $125-140.

Modern crook handle traveler's cane with souvenir medal-
lions from various cities and points of interest, including
Obernai; Haut Koenigsbourg; Riquewihr; and Weinot
Markelsheim. One medallion is dated 1980. *Courtesy of
Ambassador Richard W. Carlson.* $275-300.

Notable Walking Stick Owners

If you are an owner of walking sticks, you are in august company. Many of the most powerful ladies and gentlemen of the past have been proud owners of walking sticks. Some were so loathe to part with a favorite stick that they were buried with it. In the introduction, mention was made of King Tutankhamen, Presidents James Madison, Andrew Jackson, and Andrew Johnson, and Edgar Allan Poe as cane owners of note. Famous stick owners in France included the Marquis de Lafayette (ally of General George Washington and a hero of the American Revolution) and Napoleon Bonaparte. In England, Queen Victoria was reputed to have had an impressive collection of walking sticks and Winston Churchill triumphantly saluted the Allied forces with his.

President James Buchanan, 15th President of the United States serving from 1856 to 1860, owned this impressive solid 18k gold handle cane. On the handle are the Presidential Seal on the top with Buchanan's name and the inscription on the side panels, "From George S. Fogleman, Holly Grove, Crittenden Co., Ark." One wonders what event(s) led to the dents in the gold handle. The shaft is natural hardwood, possibly hickory, that has been finished in dark brown. The tip of the shaft is protected by a 2" white metal and iron ferrule. Handle: 2-1/3" x 1-1/3". Overall length: 37-1/2". *Courtesy of Henry A. Taron, Tradewinds Antiques.* While the value of this cane presented to President Buchanan was estimated at $10,000-15,000, the historical cane brought $6000 at auction. Auctions are a great source of quality sticks for those who know their business.

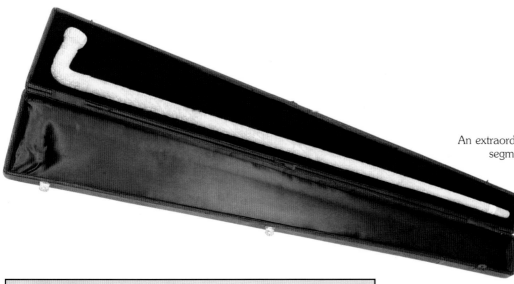

An extraordinary, rare Anglo/Indian Royal segmented elephant ivory cane elaborately decorated from handle to tip. The L-shaped handle features a circle of Prince of Wales feathers at the end with a 1/3" collar decorated with chains and crosses. On the handle's top, Queen Victoria's "St. Edwards Crown," the official crown of England, is carved in relief. On the lower side of the handle "E.V." is carved in script, probably representing "Empress Victoria." Queen Victoria became India's Empress in 1876. The rest of the cane is carved with doves, fruit, and vines. Overall length: 35". *Courtesy of Henry A. Taron, Tradewinds Antiques.* $20,000-30,000.

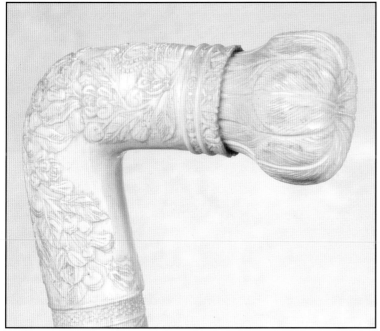

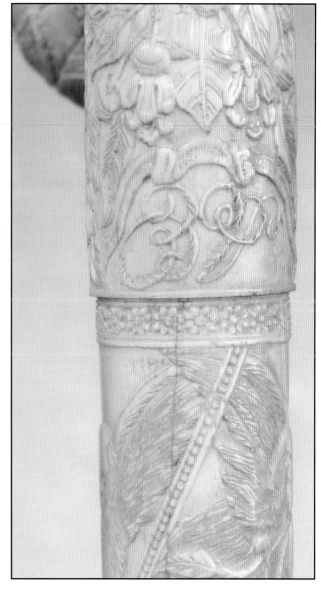

Gold and gold quartz walking stick: faceted octagonal gold quartz top, above eight cabochon side mounts alternating in light and dark gold quartz, scrolled and checked engraving overall with presentation flutes inscribed "A Token of Esteem to / John F. Taylor / from his San Francisco Friends / May 6th 1869." Solid gold handle measuring 2-5/8", mounted on a rosewood shaft with a steel ferrule. This stick was enclosed and protected in a ribbon mahogany velvet lined case.

The Witherells hypothesize that the San Francisco Friends in the inscription suggests it was presented to strengthen relations with an out of state diplomat. The date is just several days prior to the completion of the Transcontinental Railroad, the last spike driven home at Promontory Point, Utah, on May 10, 1869. With this information, the John Taylor in the inscription may well be Utah's territorial legislator, a prominent member of the Church of Latter Day Saints. $10,000+. *Courtesy of WITHERELLS.COM*

George Washington owned four canes at the time of his death. One, featuring a gold handle fashioned in the shape of a French liberty cap, had been bequeathed to Washington by Benjamin Franklin. Washington in turn passed Franklin's cane on to his brother, Charles Washington, in his will. Today, the Smithsonian Institution owns the Franklin/Washington walking stick. The first president also passed on two "gold-headed" canes to friends of his youth, Lawrence and Robert Washington. Each cane was engraved with George Washington's coat of arms. The former general and president also left Lawrence and Robert each a spyglass that he had used in the "late War."

It is difficult for us living in an era when canes play no major role to understand how much they were valued by their owners. A review of some of the other articles in George Washington's study, inventoried at the time of his death, will give the reader a sense of the regard Washington felt for these canes. He kept them in fine company among his most personal possessions, including seven swords, numerous guns and pistols, eleven spyglasses (at least two of which, from his will, we know were used during the Revolutionary War), one military silk sash, numerous military medals, a Battalion flag, presents from Native Americans, a case of surveyor's instruments, a life-cast plaster bust of General Washington himself, and a Japan box containing his Mason's apron.

Aside from his relic cane from the USS *Constitution*, President James Madison was especially fond of an animal horn walking stick given to him by Thomas Jefferson as a token of Jefferson's lasting friendship. Andrew Jackson owned a sword cane, although it is doubtful that was the stick he used to detour Pennsylvania Avenue. Concluding the tour of American presidents with canes, Warren G. Harding owned around twenty-five walking sticks. A fine black stick accompanied him on his last journey, a political tour that took him north to Alaska and west to San Francisco—and his death—in August of 1923.

Mark Twain kept his stick close at hand for walks. Brigham Young, leader of the Church of Jesus Christ of Latter-day Saints, owned two relic canes made from the oak coffin that carried the body of the faith's founder, Joseph Smith, from Carthage to Nauvoo, Illinois, in June of 1844.

Finally, Alexandre Mouton (b. November 19, 1804, d. November 12, 1885), was a United States Senator (1837-1842) with a colorful career. This Jacksonian Democrat was both the first native French-speaking governor of the state of Louisiana (1843-1846) and the first Democrat to hold that office. Mouton went on to preside over the Secession Convention held in Baton Rouge in 1861. He owned two canes inscribed with poetry, one poem in French, the other in English. The English poem read: "My son, by this thy simple plan forget not in temptation's hour that sin leads sorrow double power. Count life a stage upon thy way and follow conscience come what may. Alike with heaven and earth sincere, with hand and brow and bosom clear fear God and know no other Fear." Together, the Mouton canes were purchased for over $1400 at auction in 2000. (St. Germain 2000)

Walking Sticks Through Time

Both ancient Greek amphorae and Egyptian hieroglyphics show many individuals using walking sticks and staffs. Egyptian walking stick artistry was on display among those 130 sticks recovered from Tutankhamen's tomb. Among them were sticks decorated with ornamental bark work, elytra inlay, and the delicate decoration of iridescent beetle wings. One stick, with a broad crook curling back toward itself like an exaggerated shepherd's crook, was decorated with gold gilt and elaborate displays of colored bark. Biblical accounts tell of Moses and Egyptian priests dueling with their staffs.

Constantine the Great, the first Christian emperor of the Christianized eastern portion of the Roman Empire known as Byzantium, transferred his capital from Rome to Constantinople, located on the straights of the Bosporus at the entrance to the Black Sea between Europe and Asia, in 330 B.C. The capital city of Constantinople, on the site of the Greek city of Byzantium, was the center of the Byzantine Empire until the city fell to the Ottomans in 1453 A.D.

In 552 A.D., a pair of Byzantine priests added to the power of the empire by smuggling silkworms out of China in hollowed walking sticks in an age when textile production was a very important industry. Had the Chinese caught them in this act of industrial espionage, the two priests would have been put to death. Upon their return, a silk factory was established in the Marmara Eregli region, producing silk cloth to clothe the royal family—much to the consternation of the Chinese no doubt. This is a very early record of a dual-purpose system stick.

In Europe, during the tenth century, scepters came to symbolize the powers of the king. The king's power over the people was represented by the scepter in his right hand while the scepter in his left represented justice. In France, these symbols of authority were adopted around 987 A.D., while in England scepters were presented to Richard Coeur de Lion in the twelfth century.

During the age of the Crusades (1095-1291) and pilgrimages to the Holy Land, travelers found five foot high walking staffs just as useful as the Byzantine priests had. Called bourdons, these staffs had spiked ferrules and high handgrips to help negotiate the rough terrain and adversities of the journey. Bourdons also had a hollow space at the top of the shaft to carry religious relics and valuables. The top of the staff could be removed to gain access to this concealed carrying space.

During these Middle Ages, other holders of power were also presented with staffs of office to symbolize their authority. Bishops, priests, judges, and military commanders all carried staffs representing the power and authority of their offices. This practice would continue on into the seventeenth century. In this context, it is interesting to note that it is customary for the president of the United States to receive a presentation cane upon entering office.

Sixteenth century English aristocracy under the reign of Henry VIII (b. 1491, d. 1547) wore walking sticks when venturing out into the world. These elegant sticks of polished mahogany or ebony were decorated with gold or silver. They were also spiked with six inch long silver ferrules to deal with less than ideal roads, whether in town or in the country. In an age when bathing could bring on colds that could turn fatal, when beasts of burden hauled goods to and from markets daily, and slaughterhouses and tanneries dotted the towns and countryside, it was a truly fragrant world. In an attempt to counter the aromatic assault, many walking sticks were fitted with pouncet (or pomander) boxes containing pieces of sponge or cloth soaked in fragrant vinegar. The box lid was pierced to allow the scent to be inhaled. Along with masking odors, vinegar was also felt to have medicinal value. It was hoped that the regular use of the pouncet box would help ward off disease. One century later, little had changed concerning the unhealthful nature of the human condition, and *seventeenth* century pique canes fitted with pouncet boxes may be found by determined collectors today.

Rare ebony pique pomander (or pouncet) gadget cane dating from 1696. The top of the ebony handle is decorated with silver pique in the English style and the lid is pierced with holes so that aromatic vapors may be inhaled by the owner, with the hope of reducing the odors of the surrounding countryside and providing some health benefit to counter the generally unhealthful conditions. While on the topic of odor, it is interesting to note that in 1696 the English naturalist John Ray (1627-1705) describes the aromatic herb peppermint for the first time.

The top of the handle unscrews to reveal the shallow receptacle designed to hold a piece of cotton or wool soaked in aromatic, healthful liquids such as vinegar. The sides of the handle are decorated with rings of pique and a 3/4" inlaid silver bee. The owner's initials "I.W." and the date "1696" decorate the lower shaft of the handle above the wrist cord hole. Both a 2/3" scalloped edge silver collar and a thin ring of ivory finish the handle. The shaft is full bark malacca, the tip of which is protected by a 2-1/4" brass ferrule that has been dented from repeated use. Handle: 3-1/2" x 1-2/3". Overall length: 35-3/4". *Courtesy of Henry A. Taron, Tradewinds Antiques.* $4000-6000.

The king himself owned an extraordinary gold decorated stick. It housed a number of items, including a perfume dispenser (no nostrils, no matter how mighty, were free of the olfactory assault of the age), two golden compasses, a golden foot rule, tweezers, and a file and knife. While kings and aristocrats carried elegant sticks, the less affluent subjects of British and European kings continued to carry traveling staffs. These no-nonsense rods helped travelers navigate rutted roads, cross streams, and fend off attacks from animals and humans alike.

During the reign of King Louis XIV (b. 1638, d. 1715) walking sticks were a must of French fashionable dress for the aristocracy. The king himself was never out in public without a walking stick. Louis' court jeweler produced a walking stick for his majesty containing twenty-four diamonds. In an effort to keep up appearances, the aristocracy kept jewelers busy, calling for ever more elegant sticks of gold and silver, encrusted with jewels of all sorts. As a result, the sticks of this period were elaborately, flamboyantly decorated, frequently adorned with images of the natural world. By the middle of the eighteenth century, a more sober approach to cane decoration would follow.

By the 1740s, the habit of carrying dress swords had fallen by the wayside for civilian men. Bereft of the swords that had proclaimed their status as gentlemen, these men turned to carrying walking sticks as a substitute. Meanwhile, eighteenth century Americans were carrying more conservative sticks than their European counterparts. In times of conflict, American sticks were frequently decorated with eagles.

During the American Revolution, Eli Whitney, future inventor of the cotton gin, built a forge in his father's Westborough, Massachusetts, workshop with the intention of producing nails to fill the void left when British shipments ceased. Whitney also produced tools, hatpins, and a number of metal walking sticks.

In the eighteenth and early nineteenth centuries in America, the average citizen had a need for a stout walking stick. Most common folk traveled on foot. Americans without means regularly walked three to six miles to church, stores, or taverns. Children walked everywhere. In New England towns, school districts were established based on the distance a four or five year old could be expected to walk to attend school. Students of that tender age were expected to cover two miles in one direction. At fourteen, P.T. Barnum took his higher schooling at an Academy three miles from home.

Young New England men often worked away from home during the week as schoolteachers and farm laborers. They would walk eight to ten miles to return home for Sunday visits.

With the advent of the Industrial Revolution, larger numbers of people gained access to better jobs and increased opportunities to gather wealth. The middle class consumer became a powerful force. Likewise, technological developments allowed for better and faster transportation, better and more sophisticated tools and machinery, and vastly increased production capacities with significantly lowered production costs. As Victorians toured the globe in ever increasing numbers, a passion for natural history developed, as well as a passion for walking sticks made from exotic materials from romantic far off lands. With the newly acquired wealth of the rising middle class, demand for walking sticks of all sorts increased astronomically. With radically increased production capacities brought on by technological innovations, walking stick manufactories were up to the challenge.

James W.C. Pennington began life as James Pembroke, an African-American blacksmith living in slavery in Washington County, Maryland. During his captivity, Pembroke produced a wide variety of objects and took great pride in his skills at the forge. Among the finer items he produced were firearms, hatchets, hammers, penknife blades, and sword canes. Of course, at that time, it would have been illegal for Pembroke to actually carry most of the items he produced.

In 1827, Pembroke escaped and became a clergyman and antislavery orator in the second quarter of the nineteenth century known in New York and London. He also produced the first published African-American history studying African origins and civilization.

From the 1850s onward, European walking stick production centers in Berlin, Hamburg, and Vienna employed thousands to meet demands. By the 1870s, British stick makers were competing strongly with their European counterparts. By the 1890s, over four thousand workers would be producing walking sticks. Sheffield, England, produced pressed horn handled walking sticks during the nineteenth century and on into the late 1920s. Sheffield horn handles were known for fine decoration and the addition of ivory and pearl inlay. Birmingham, England, had been known for its production of cane handles, swords, snuffboxes, and other steel objects since the seventeenth century. To meet both production and consumer demands, plantations around the globe were dedicated to growing the raw materials for walking sticks. Approximately three million unfinished chestnut shafts were imported from Austria to the United States to meet the demand for "Congo" sticks.

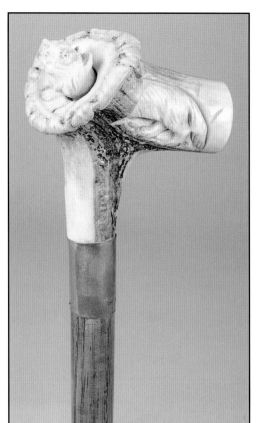

By the 1850s, one author would note that elderly gentlemen in the United States had all carried gold handled walking sticks. It was considered their mark of distinction.

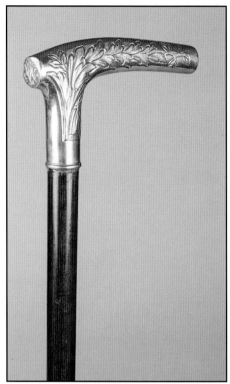

Stag horn handle carved in the shape of a hollow log with a dog inside. The dog's head and paws may be seen emerging from the end of the log and its body can be seen on one side where the log is cut away, 1-1/2" silver collar marked "Made in England" and having hallmarks for Birmingham, England – 1925, light brown hardwood shaft with 3/4" metal ferrule. Handle: 3-1/4" w. x 3-1/4" h. Overall length: 34-3/4". *Courtesy of The World of the Walking Stick.* $1275-1400.

Fritz crutch or opera shape gold handle engraved with leaves on both sides and monogrammed on the end, hallmarked with a lion and marked K18. Snakewood shaft, late nineteenth century. Handle: 4-1/2" w x 2-1/2" h. x 1/2" d. Overall length: 35-3/4". *Courtesy of The World of the Walking Stick.* $1500-1650.

Below and right:
Ivory handled ink well and pen gadget cane. The handle comes apart in two places. *Courtesy of Ambassador Richard W. Carlson.* $625-690.

History shows that dual purpose system sticks have been around for ages. However, the technological innovation of the nineteenth century led to a golden age for system sticks and weapon canes. Over 1500 patents were taken out for system sticks ranging from fishing poles to writing sticks.

In the 1860s, when the United States was torn in two by civil war, cane wielding citizens of cities and towns would flock to rumored entry points for opposing armies, ready to beat them back with their walking sticks, much to the amusement of their own troops. However, soldiers during the war kept family, friends, and curiosity seekers away from prisoners with walking sticks rather than firearms whenever possible.

By the 1870s, with the Civil War behind them, gentlemen enjoyed roaming the countryside with antler handled, thorny briar shafted rustic walking sticks. Hunters found these antler handled sticks appealing as well. Many such handles were decorated with carved figures of hunting dogs and game animals.

Formal cane manufacturers rarely signed their work and remain largely anonymous today. However, combing American business directories turned up a few. In 1868 in San Francisco, Albert Jellinek and Charles Doerger were listed as turners of ivory and hardwood, selling billiard materials and canes under the name Jellinek and Doerger. Located at 24 California Street, they produced rosewood, ebony, manzanita, and mountain mahogany sticks. The partnership dissolved the following year; however, both men continued to turn wood and ivory independently. The Brooklyn City Business Directory of 1873 lists Charles E. Smith of 170 Fulton Street as a manufacturer of Umbrellas, Parasols, and Walking Sticks. In Providence, Rhode Island, the firm Hearn & Braitsch (Nos. 2 to 12 Melrose Street) manufactured gold-headed canes, umbrella mountings, and novelties in gold and silver. Established in 1887, the firm claimed to be one of the leading makers of gold-handled canes in the United States.

However, as the nineteenth century passed into the twentieth, cane wearing began to decline. While the fashion conscious still tucked canes jauntily under their arms in the 1920s and anyone with a mind to drink in violation of Prohibition laws carried alcohol hidden in tippler's canes, by mid-century canes were relegated to orthopedic aids, hiking and climbing sticks, and the occasional formal wear accessory which would be handled with such lack of finesse by the inexperienced as to make wearers of previous centuries turn over in their graves.

Walking Stick Restrictions & Status

Throughout much of recorded history, beautifully made walking sticks were possessions of royalty and ar-istocracy. They were such coveted and expensive ornaments that they enhanced the prestige of the wearer. As such, those who owned sticks did their best to limit access to them, keeping walking sticks from the "lesser sort" whenever possible. The wealthy walking stick owner feared that free access to beautiful sticks would diminish their impact as status symbols and suspected that if the lower classes had access to such elegant sticks, they would use them to make fun of the wealthy and their ways. Conversely, those without formal walking sticks were often desperate to possess them.

King Louis XIV limited walking stick access to himself and his aristocracy during his reign. In the king's mind, his bejeweled walking sticks were indeed symbols of his authority and he had no desire to see such potent symbols in the hands of average citizens.

In eighteenth century England, carrying a walking stick was considered such a privilege that a license was required to carry one. A London license declared that the bearer was entitled to pass freely through London's streets and suburbs within ten miles with his stick "without theft or molestation." However, should the bearer of the license misuse his stick by carrying it under his arm, flailing it about in the air, or hanging it from a button, then his license was forfeit. Anyone seeing these violations *who felt it was safe to do so* was free to take the offender's cane away. (Lester 1940, 389-90)

English eighteenth century ivory pique handled pomander cane. The handle is of elephant ivory with a perforated lid that unscrews to gain access to the shallow inner chamber which receives a cloth soaked in aromatic liquids. The perforations in the lid are star shaped. The collar is 1/2" and has a decorative scalloped edge. The shaft is dark full-bark malacca protected at the tip with a 3" brass and iron ferrule. Handle: 2-3/4" x 1-1/4". Overall length: 34-3/4". *Courtesy of Henry A. Taron, Tradewinds Antiques.* $6000-8000.

In the nineteenth century, men of means continued to purchase very expensive walking sticks for themselves and their wives as a way to proclaim the level of their success. Throughout all of history, conspicuous consumption has been the time-honored means of declaring to the world that you have arrived. Archaeological investigations in the 1990s outside of Augusta, Georgia, shed light on some fascinating restrictions placed upon the African-American community in the antebellum South. In the early to middle nineteenth century in Georgia, the labor of free African-Americans was highly sought. Recognized as skilled craftspeople, free African-American laborers constituted fifteen percent of Charleston's work force. A Registry of Free Persons of Color from Augusta, dated 1819, records that over eighty percent of free African-Americans were occupied as tradesmen or watermen. They worked as barbers, blacksmiths, boat hands and boat pilots, carpenters, hostlers, and saddlers. Free African-American women worked as cooks, house servants, seamstresses, washers, and weavers.

Valued as they were for their skills, the free African-American population in Georgia was prevented from participating in much of Southern life by state and local laws. Legal prohibitions were tightened as tensions rose prior to the Civil War. Some of the restrictions prevented certain social behaviors. Among them was a prohibition against African-Americans using walking sticks or pipes in public. Both items were considered status symbols by the upper class white community and were declared to be white "privileges" that did not extend to the free African-American community. Only blind or infirm African-Americans could walk about in public with canes.

However in excavations in the free African-American community of Springfield, located outside of Augusta along the Savannah River from 1820 to 1850, an elegant ball clay pipe bowl was recovered. In West Africa, smoking was considered a symbol of social rank as well and free African-Americans were apparently loath to give up the practice, prohibition or no prohibition. The elaborate pipe bowl may have represented an act of defiance against Augusta city ordinances. One wonders if some of the wonderful walking sticks produced during this period by African-American artists were not also quiet acts of rebellion against Southern laws.

In London in the 1850s, over two hundred individuals would be busy selling walking sticks on the streets every Sunday. In 1853, Charles Smith describes, in *Curiosities of London Life*, how a middle class bargain hunter could be conned by a peddler. Umbrella peddlers would circulate among the homes of the wealthy in London, repairing broken umbrellas. These peddlers developed a keen eye for high quality wooden shafts. At times, these umbrella repairmen would purchase a secondhand umbrella from a gentleman's serving maid if that umbrella had a quality partridge wood shaft and handle. Once purchased, the peddler removes the partridge wood shaft and handle, replacing it with a common wood such as beech. He sells the umbrella and begins altering the removed partridge wood shaft, giving it the appearance of a nice walking stick. This is done by filling in the cavity that held the umbrella spring and varnishing the entire shaft and handle to remove all traces of the new cane's old life as an umbrella rod.

The peddler offers the "cane" at a bargain price to a middle class customer seeking a fine stick that just might be beyond his means under ordinary circumstances. Later, the customer discovers he has been fooled when he applies weight to the shaft. The shaft breaks at the fragile filled void and the customer realizes his mistake.

Walking Stick Etiquette

In a letter to the editor of the *New England Courant* in 1722, Benjamin Franklin, under the pseudonym Silence Dogood, mentioned some of the "diversions" he observed on a "night's ramble." Young men in love were the subjects of his observations and he found love-struck youth clapping their cheeks and swinging their canes.

Such behavior would be frowned upon by those who fastidiously observed the rules of walking stick etiquette. It was considered generally rude to swing a stick in the air as Franklin had observed young men in love doing, to carry a walking stick under your arm, or drag it along the ground. It seems much of walking stick etiquette revolves around how to behave with a stick in crowded conditions. The cane swung or tightly held under the arm while walking is bound to strike someone nearby. The inconsiderately drug stick is sure to trip the unwary pedestrian in a hurry.

In 1833, *The Carrolltonian*, a Maryland newspaper, reported on fashions in Boston. It also provided sound advice for gentlemen walking along those dirty city streets. The article, appearing in the "Ladies' Department," stated, "...fashion is a whimsical jade, but who ever dreamed that she would put canes in the ladies' hands! But so it is as the fashionable ladies of Boston exhibit themselves on Washington Street with these little sticks, which they flaunt with becoming grace. Gentlemen are warned to look out in the future and always give ladies with canes the inside of the walks or they may smart for it." (Graybeal 1998)

When visiting someone's home, polite gentlemen and ladies alike were to leave their walking sticks in the front hallway in a stand or rack designed for the purpose. In 1857, the National Gallery in Washington, D.C., had a staff member on hand to take visitors' walking sticks and umbrellas before entering the gallery. He was located inside the entrance door to the right near the Register of Visitors. This individual must have been very busy as the gallery estimated that around 100,000 visitors passed through their doors annually.

A witty book entitled *The Laws of Etiquette; or Short Rules and Reflections for Conduct in Society*, provided the following walking stick etiquette advice in 1836. When attending funerals, dress in black, lean solemnly on the top of your walking stick, and think about the previous night's party to ensure that you add to the sadness of the ceremony. At a concert or private musical party, never keep time with your feet or your walking stick as nothing is more unpleasant.

In nineteenth century America, public entertainment would change in scale and organization before and after the Civil War. Expected public behavior changed along with it. In the early nineteenth century, American entertainment was a loose and raucous affair. Theatergoers had a wide variety of entertainment to choose from including Shakespearean plays, dancers, comedy acts, singers, and acrobats. As the years passed, circuses began to tour the country, dime-museums cropped up, and amusement parks, riverboats, saloons, and music halls all provided lively diversions. In the 1840s, minstrel shows provided a variety performance that quickly grew in popularity. Traveling medicine shows also served up entertainment along with their tonics. Most of these entertainments were loosely organized and run on small budgets, catering to audiences of limited means and sophistication.

Audiences prior to the Civil War played an active role in their entertainment. They screamed and stomped to show how much they enjoyed or disliked a show, threw a distressingly wide variety of objects at the actors, and rushed the stage to either help remove bad acts or plead with their favorite stars for encore performances.

After the Civil War, urban middle class audiences had more disposable income and more urbane tastes. Vaudeville was post-war entertainment produced as big business by well-organized showmen to cater to those tastes and tap that extra income. Using the improving transportation systems, theater circuits were established and acts polished. The theaters themselves were luxurious fantasies of architecture based on Southern European palaces. The purpose behind the ostentatious design was to draw a crowd and keep them coming back. The newly established department stores were taking the same approach.

With a well organized show in luxurious surroundings, the old audience behavior would not do. The public needed to be educated in a different approach to the night out. Uniformed ushers and attendants provided printed cards with polite requests to refrain from wearing hats in the theater, carrying lit cigars in mouths in the building, or stamping feet or pounding canes on the floor as applause. Entertainment had become quite civilized and audiences were expected to watch, not to participate. There is a temptation to look back on such histories, smile, and think "how quaint." Yet, how different

are those little vaudevillian cards from the instructional messages preceding movies in theaters today? "Don't bang your cane;" "turn off your cell phone"—how different is it really?

The last word on walking stick etiquette here comes from *The Bazar Book of Decorum*, written in 1873: "There is nothing more annoying to other people who may be present than the noise which a person will sometimes make by snapping a toothpick, jiggling a watch-chain, creaking a chair, opening and shutting a pencil or knife, tapping the boot with a cane, or making any kind of noise or movement which irresistibly and disagreeably attracts the general attention." (Tomes 1873, 144)

So, behave!

Sticks of Faith, Sticks of Mortality

Church Uses

By the sixth century A.D., Christianity had adopted the pastoral staff as a symbol of authority. Pastoral staffs were presented to the Church's ranking leaders. This staff was clearly seen to represent the Bishop's authority over his flock and its form held symbolic meaning. The crook represented the Bishop drawing congregants to himself and to God; the point was the prod by which those less than enthusiastic about the cause were motivated.

Creek Indian Baptist deacons of the Thlewarle Indian Baptist Church near Dustin, Oklahoma, also made use of walking sticks they termed "deacon's staffs" as symbols of church authority during the nineteenth and twentieth centuries. These deacon staffs also served many practical uses during church ceremonies. In 1870, the Baptist congregants who had held church meetings since 1858 built their first Thlewarle Mekko Sapkv Coko (House of Prayer). Following the tradition of all Creek churches, this structure and its replacement (built in 1914) were constructed facing east. Creek tradition holds that Christ will come from the east with the sunrise when He returns.

Thlewarle Baptists appoint seven deacons to office. Their duties are to assist with Communion and baptisms, usher, and receive the tithes and offerings. Deacons are selected on the basis of their understanding of the church. At his ordination, a new deacon is presented with a staff and this staff will remain with him until he steps down from his position. Deacon's staffs are never replaced. They are handed down across the generations. These staffs are symbols of strength and support. Three of the deacon's staffs were hand-carved folk art sticks. The other four were commercially produced walking sticks. Of the hand-carved trio, one artist walked fifteen miles to donate the stick he carved to the church for services. This cane had raised designs on the handle. The second staff was decorated with carved monkeys. The third was carved by Joe Watson (1850-1914) and decorated with a reptile design.

Among the many practical uses for these staffs during services were pointing out open seats while ushering and assisting the pastor in baptisms. Baptisms occurred in creeks or rivers with waist deep free flowing water, which was required to wash away the sins of the believer being baptized. During baptism, once the believer had been tipped slowly, carefully back into the water, a deacon would gently place the crook of his stick behind the believer's neck and help the pastor raise the baptized individual from the water into new life. This was seen as more than a practical aid; it represented a shepherd helping one of his flock, drawing the sheep out of danger and into safety with his crook.

Rules of etiquette applied to the proper use of a deacon's staff. The deacon was not allowed to touch a person with the cane's tip as this might cause injury or knock the wind out of the individual. It would also be a source of embarrassment. If it was necessary for a deacon to touch someone with his staff, it was done by gently laying the side of the shaft against a congregant's arm. A deacon's staff was never to lay flat on the ground. It was to remain tilted with one end clear of the ground at all times, even if that meant leaning the staff against a deacon's foot under certain circumstances. If something was wrong, the deacon was allowed to lean on his staff.

Memento Mori

Once, while traveling through an old seaside community, I spotted the tombstone of an early nineteenth century sea captain. The epitaph on the stone was addressed to the wife and children he left behind. It read: "Do not cry for me, you will be here soon enough." At first glance, this appears to be cruel parting words from the captain. This sentiment however is an example of Memento Mori, a none-too-subtle reminder that we are

mortal and must have our souls prepared for death and reckoning at all times. Such reminders were used from the Middle Ages through the nineteenth century, when death visited families all too frequently. Memento Mori appeared in many different forms. An aged covered bridge in Lucerne, Switzerland, the *Spreuerbrüke* or Mill Bridge built in 1408, is "decorated" with a series of seventeenth century paintings, done in medieval style, depicting the plague in action. This series by Kaspar Melinger is entitled *Dance of Death*. The scenes feature people from all walks of life painted on the interior roof supports. In every scene, Death stands among the people. When you have walked from one end of the bridge to the other, you have seen clearly that no one, no matter what his or her station in life, escapes Death. Memento Mori take the forms of statues, photographs, and walking stick handles as well.

Most Memento Mori cane handles take the form of the human skull. Many times, the grinning skull takes up the entire handle. At other times the skull may be combined with a snake. Interpretations of this combination vary. The snake may represent humanity's fall from grace and certain knowledge of mortality. However, seen from a different perspective, the snake may be seen as a symbol of rebirth. In certain cultures the shedding of the snake's skin is seen as symbolic rebirth.

Far more rare and chilling is the Memento Mori handle featuring the skeletal specter of Death holding life in his arms, life represented in the form of a young, nude woman in repose. The message is clear, life and death remain entwined and death will be inevitable.

The message of the Memento Mori cane is not that different from the message a Roman Emperor would send to his general returning victorious from war. During the triumphal parade along the Sacred Way, while the general received a hero's welcome from the grateful citizenry, a messenger from the Emperor rode in the chariot behind the general and whispered into his ear "Remember, you are only a man."

Opposite page, photo:
Memento Mori! Skulls are a very popular motif in canes. Two of these have ivory skulls, one shrouded, one bare. Handles: shrouded: 3" h. x 2" w.; bare: 2" h. The other cane has a silver skull with bony fingers bracketing the grinning jaws, a crown perched on top. Remember the admonition here: no one escapes death! An amethyst adorns the top of the handle and garnets are set into the sides of the crown. Handle: 2" h. x 2" w. *Courtesy of Richard R. Wagner, Jr.* These ivory skulls range in value from $1600-2100 (ivory skulls, and ivory in general, is valued in part on the size of the piece). Silver skull: $4000-5000.

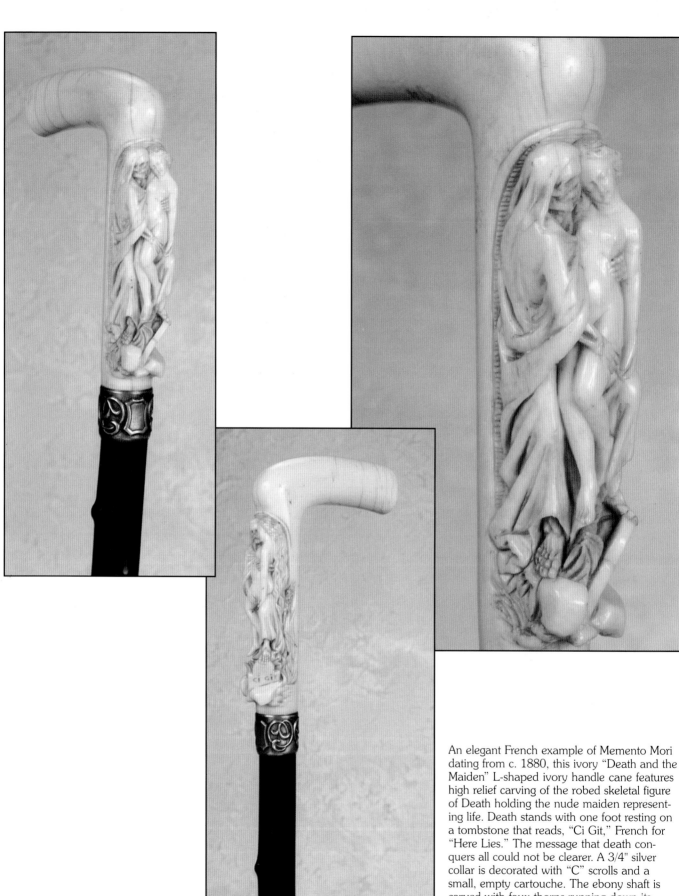

An elegant French example of Memento Mori dating from c. 1880, this ivory "Death and the Maiden" L-shaped ivory handle cane features high relief carving of the robed skeletal figure of Death holding the nude maiden representing life. Death stands with one foot resting on a tombstone that reads, "Ci Git," French for "Here Lies." The message that death conquers all could not be clearer. A 3/4" silver collar is decorated with "C" scrolls and a small, empty cartouche. The ebony shaft is carved with faux thorns running down its length and the base is protected with a 1-1/4" white metal and iron ferrule. Handle: 3-1/4" x 4-1/2". Overall length: 38". *Courtesy of Henry A. Taron, Tradewinds Antiques.* $3500-4500.

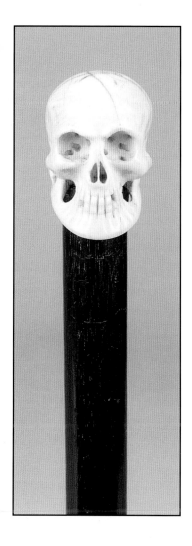

Very detailed carved ivory human skull. Silver collar, ebony shaft with 1" bullet-type metal ferrule, late nineteenth century. Handle: 1-3/4" l. x 1-1/2" d. Overall length: 35". *Courtesy of The World of the Walking Stick.* $995-1095.

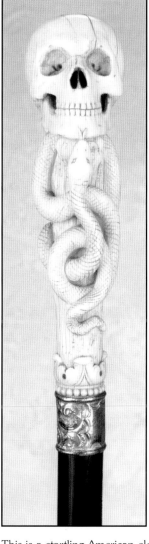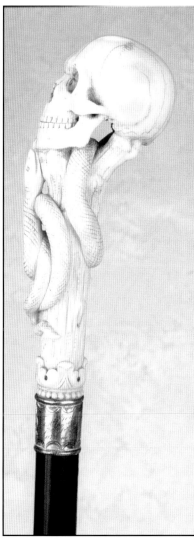

This is a startling American elephant ivory cane handle carved with a skull and snake motif dating from c. 1870. The decorated gold-filled collar is inscribed "Dr. Alfred Springer, Norwood, O." I wonder if the good doctor carried this cane on his rounds in Norwood, Ohio? The cane has an ebony shaft and a brass and iron ferrule. Handle: 4-2/3" x 2". Overall length: 34-1/8". *Courtesy of Henry A. Taron, Tradewinds Antiques.* The estimated value of $2000-3000 was exceeded in 2003 at auction, the final bid being $4500.

Elaborately carved skull handle over silver collar and bone ferrule. Handle: 2-3/4" l. Overall length: 34-3/4". *Courtesy of Ambassador Richard W. Carlson.* $525-580.

Phrenology Canes

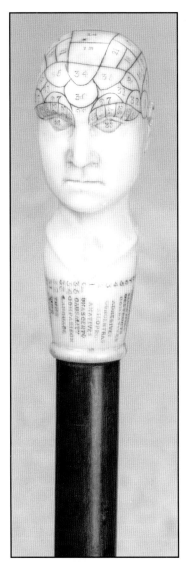
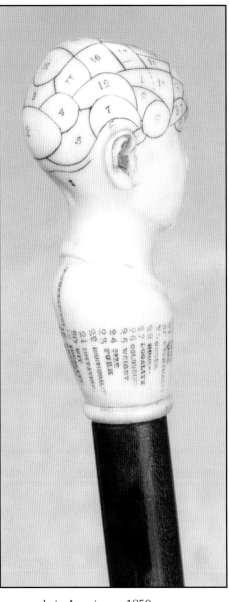

Elephant ivory handle phrenology cane made in America, c. 1850. The shaft is brown hardwood, the bottom of which is protected with a 1-1/3" white metal and iron ferrule. Handle: 2-1/2" x 1-1/2". Overall length: 34". *Courtesy of Henry A. Taron, Tradewinds Antiques.* $4000-6000.

Viennese physician Franz Joseph Gall (1758-1828) established the tenants of phrenology, "the only true science of the mind." (Van Wyhe n.d., 1) Gall stated his methods would allow the practitioner to divine the char-acter of anyone based on the shape of their skull. Gall hypothesized that the different faculties of the mind were housed in discrete portions and the power of each portion was directly proportional to its size in relation to other faculties. The shape of the brain there-fore would reflect the development of the various faculties and would be reflected in the shape of the skull, which took on the shape of the underlying brain. Put simply, skulls with protruding portions over areas housing positive traits will suggest a person with positive abilities or vice versa.

From the mid-1790s to the 1810s, only Germans were aware of Gall's science of Phrenology. However, in 1815, when the *Edinburgh Review* wrote a scathing review of Phrenology, the idea rapidly disseminated among many nations. Ironically, the first phrenological society was established in Edinburgh in 1820. Such societies would dot the landscape in Britain and America throughout the nineteenth century.

Middle class men eager to enter the weighty world of the growing scientific societies of the age promptly threw themselves into the "scientific study" of phrenology and established the Phrenological Association in 1838. Like the physician's gold handled walking stick, the phrenology stick became an outward symbol of a practitioner's authority.

Phrenology would grow in popularity in the United States and France in the 1830s and 1840s. While the original movement in Britain died away in the 1850s, it was rein-troduced in a vigorous, modified form from the United States in the 1860s. In the 1830s in New York City, L.N. Fowler established a more entrepreneurial phrenology. Not terri-bly interested in scientific status or preten-sions, phrenological Fowlers were much more focused on conducting lecture tours and reading heads for fees. Many of the an-tique phrenology canes and busts found today are marked "L.N. Fowler" and are traced back to this Ameri-can movement. In fact, head reading would become quite the craze in the latter half of the nineteenth century.

America's fertile soil for phrenological growth

Phrenology was only one of many pseudo-sciences to flourish in the United States in the nineteenth century. Their development was a response to unsettling discoveries in the Victorian age. Darwin's *Origin of Species* and the discovery of geological time shook the eighteenth century belief that all science and theology was in harmony. Western thought in the eighteenth century espoused that a careful search of the natural world would lead one directly to God. Nineteenth century discoveries appeared to contradict both this belief and a literal interpretation of the book of Genesis. Such discoveries were leaving individuals of all levels of education uncertain and unsettled. The pseudo-sciences proclaimed that the eighteenth century system was intact and their "science" provided the proof.

Along with phrenology, Americans seeking assurance passionately pursued creationism, electric medicine, Mesmerism, water cures, and spiritualism, with its séances featuring ghostly materializations, messages from beyond, ectoplasmic ooze, and mysterious table rapping. People across the educational spectrum were caught up in these movements.

In the early nineteenth century there was also a certain void in the American scientific community. Trained scientists were few and far between. Much useful work was to be accomplished by enthusiastic amateurs.

Into this mix steps the phrenologist, certainly an enthusiastic amateur, who proclaims the mysteries of the mind are knowable and orderly. When challenged, and skeptics challenged them often, phrenologists proclaimed the book of nature was open to all. Their accusers were dismissed as both closed-minded and undemocratic elitists who would try to decide everything for themselves rather than letting everyone judge the truth for themselves! Such arguments continue to be used by charlatans and snake oil salesmen of all stripes today. (MacDougall n.d., 1-2)

Presentation Canes

Below and on following page:

This cane was presented as a gift to President Grover Cleveland. It features a polished stag horn handle carved in the form of a stylized jumping fish. The silver collar measures 7/8" and is inscribed "From James McGowan, Troy, to Grover Cleveland." The shaft is rosewood and is carved with block letters, reading: "Cleveland and Stevenson / Troy N.Y. / The Record." After that is a spiraling ribbon carved with the names of the twenty-four states Grover Cleveland carried in the election of 1892, beginning with "Alabama" and ending with "Wisconsin." The base of the shaft is protected with a 1" white metal ferrule. Handle: 6-1/2". Overall length: 37". *Courtesy of Henry A. Taron, Tradewinds Antiques.* $12,000-15,000.

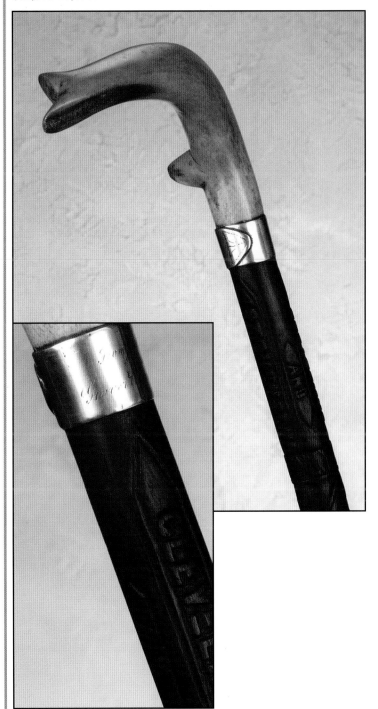

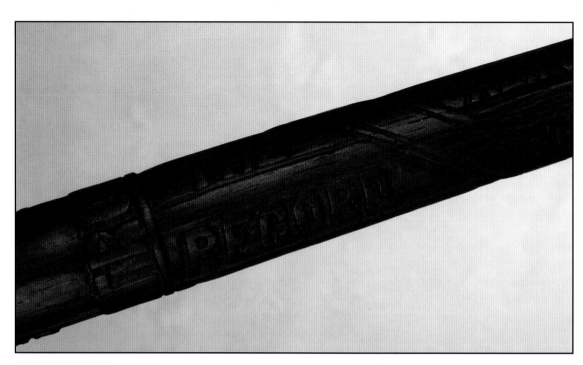

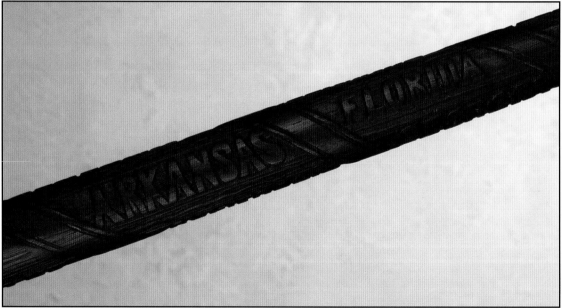

Cane from previous page.

Presentation canes and relic sticks are true walking sticks of story. Presentation canes bear inscriptions from the giver to the individual honored. Such canes were presented to mark major life events and accomplishments. Veterans of the American Civil War were presented with sticks at anniversaries of major battles when the elderly combatants returned to the field in ever diminishing numbers to remember and to reminisce. Both formal and folk art sticks have served as presentation canes.

As previously mentioned, ceremonial canes have long been presented to Presidents upon their election. Some to these Presidential canes are on display at the Smithsonian Institution's "Ceremonial Court."

In New Mexico, some very old presentation canes may be found. They belong to the governors of the nineteen Pueblos of New Mexico. The Pueblo Indians had been living in New Mexico roughly five hundred years before they encountered Spanish explorers in the 1590s. They lived in terraced, apartment-style homes and each Pueblo was a self-governing mini-nation unto itself. It is said of the Pueblo Indians that they have been in contact with Europeans longest but have changed the least. In 1620, the King of Spain issued a Royal Decree requiring each Pueblo to choose a governor by popular vote, along with a lieutenant governor, and other officials, independently of the Spanish Crown or the Catholic Church. As a symbol of authority, each pueblo governor received a silver-handled cane that was to be passed down to succeeding governors. A cross was inscribed in the silver as evidence of support for the church.

In 1864, Abraham Lincoln presented the Pueblo Governors with another set of silver-handled ceremonial canes with ebony shafts. This set of ceremonial sticks had been purchased from John Dodd in Philadelphia, Pennsylvania. They bore the inscription "1863, A. Lincoln, Pres. U.S.A." and were presented in recognition of the Pueblo tribes' loyalty to the North when Southern armies advanced on New Mexico during the Civil War.

Today, in a commingling of their native culture and Catholicism, Pueblo Governors are inaugurated during the feast of Epiphany. They bring the canes presented to them by Spain and the United States, placing them upon the altar to be blessed by a priest.

The first governor of united British Columbia, Frederick Seymour, presented walking sticks to each friendly tribe among the Northwest Coast First Nations. These presentation sticks were made with British India malacca shafts topped with cast silver handles. In the British Columbia Provincial Archives, historical photographs depict an Interior Salish man wearing a fringed leather coat and carrying a Seymour presentation cane.

Presentation Canes & the California Gold Rush, 1848-1864

On January 24, 1848, James Marshall, heading a work crew constructing a saw mill for John Sutter along the American River in Coloma, California, discovered tiny gold nuggets. Shortly thereafter, General John Bidwell found gold in the Feather River while Major Pearson B. Reading recovered gold from the Trinity River. The discovery was first printed in the March 15, 1848, issue of San Francisco's newspaper, *The Californian*. With these events, hopeful adventurers, entrepreneurs, merchants, and scoundrels from around the globe flocked to California in pursuit of untold fortunes. Before it was over in 1864, roughly a half-million people would have been drawn by gold's allure in one of history's largest voluntary mass migrations.

Of the inrush of fortune seekers, the *California Star* reported on June 10, 1848, "Every seaport as far south as San Diego, and every interior town, and nearly every rancho from the base of the mountains in which the gold has been found, to the Mission of San Luis, south, has become suddenly drained of human beings. Americans, Californians, Indians, and Sandwich Islanders, men, women, and children, indiscriminately. ... The probable amount taken from these mountains since the first of May last, we are informed is $100,000, and which is at this time principally in the hands of the mechanical, agricultural, and laboring classes." The *California Star* fell silent on June 14, 1848, as the staff deserted the paper in favor of the gold fields.

In 1849, the Mariposa mine opened in Mariposa County, California, extracting quartz veins filled with gold deposits. A year later, as California became a state, gold-bearing quartz was discovered in Grass Valley at Gold Hill. Subsurface mining began in earnest. In 1852, California's annual gold production reached record heights of $81 million.

Hope was spurred and imaginations fired in 1854 when a 195-pound gold mass was recovered at Carson Hill in Calaveras County. Further inspiration came in 1859 in the form of the 54-pound "Willard nugget" found in Butte County at Magalia. However, by 1864 the gold rush in California drew to a close. Subsurface mines would continue to extract gold for another twenty years, but the excitement was over.

Produced during this exciting period and beyond were elegant walking sticks with gold handles inlaid with gold-bearing quartz. With such a stick, an individual of means could give the appearance of one who had struck it rich in the rush without ever getting one's hands dirty. Of course, those who recovered gold could also have such impressive sticks made as testament to their fortune-seeking prowess.

Opposite page, bottom:
Gold crook handles with inlaid gold quartz from the California gold rush days. Left inscribed: "From Geo. N. Ewells August 1863." Right inscribed: "L.G.S. from J.C.", c. 1850-1870. *Courtesy of Ron Van Anda and Sandra Whitson.* Left: $6500; right: $5500.

Right and below:
Three gold handled gold quartz walking sticks. Overall lengths: 36" each. *Courtesy of Ron Van Anda and Sandra Whitson.* Right: inscribed: "From E.B. to G.B. June 12, 1869." $8,500. Center: inscribed "F.H. Allen to Capt. W. Baker. Ship Swallow." c. 1860. $12,500. Left: inscribed "John Limms / 1856 / J.F. McCauley." $15,500.

From previous page.

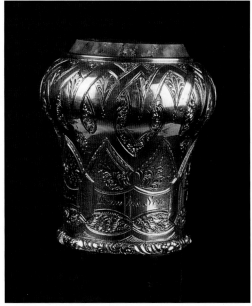

Gold handled walking stick inlaid with black gold quartz, inscribed "To my father from his son Phillip," c. 1850-1870. *Courtesy of Ron Van Anda and Sandra Whitson.* $12,500.

Gold and gold quartz
walking stick, inscribed
"San Francisco June 24th
A.D. 1856; A.L. 5856;
Olive Branch Lodge to J.
Wethington." *Courtesy of
Ron Van Anda and Sandra
Whitson.* $6500.

Gold and gold quartz walking stick,
inscribed "Presented by my oldest son,
Alphonso Sterling." Subsequently this
cane was presented again and
inscribed, "The gold and quartz in this
stick were mined at Sutter's Mill in
1853 by Byram D. Sterling. Made in
San Francisco in that year and sent to
my grandfather. Presented to John L.
Johnston in 1940 by Albert M.
Sterling." *Courtesy of Ron Van Anda
and Sandra Whitson.* NP (**N**o **P**rice).

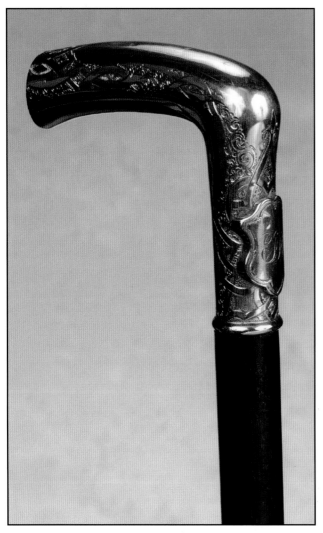

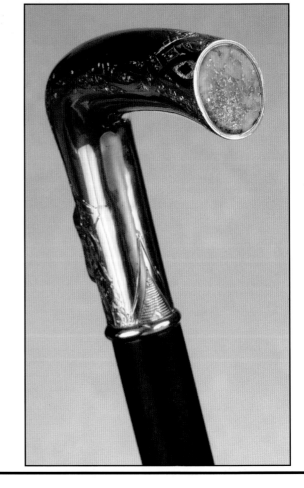

Gold and gold quartz L-shaped handle cane made in California, dating to c. 1875. Such canes were produced in California during the latter half of the nineteenth century. An oval of gold quartz inlay is found on the handle's tip, measuring 3/4". The handle itself is 18k gold and is decorated with intricate engravings. A 1" raised shield cartouche is engraved with the original owner's initials. The shaft is maccassar ebony that is protected at the tip by a 1-1/3" white metal and iron ferrule. Handle: 3" x 2-2/3". Overall length: 36". *Courtesy of Henry A. Taron, Tradewinds Antiques.* $3500-4500.

Rare California gold quartz disc mounted in a very large silver knob handle. The polished and beveled smoky gold quartz disc measures 1" in diameter and is well veined with many bright gold flecks. The silver handle is engraved with three small chains. Of the eight side panels, four are decorated with "C" scrolls and four are inscribed, "Presented to / Henry Lawrence / by his son / J. H. Lawrence." The shaft is a thick honey-toned malacca, the base of which is protected with a 1-1/3" brass ferrule. This American cane dates to c. 1860. Handle: 2-1/2" x 2". Overall length: 34-1/2". *Courtesy of Henry A. Taron, Tradewinds Antiques.* $8000-12,000.

Right:
Gold, gold quartz and enamel Wells Fargo presentation walking stick, c. 1866. It is engraved, "Presented to / Chas. Woodward / by the /Employe's of / Wells Fargo / & Co / Oregon / Department." Around the cane handle are six small gold doors engraved with the names of the employees presenting the cane: "J.L. Smith, W.A. Altee, T.M. Loop, G.W. French, W.C. Child and Tho. H Cann." These doors are encircled with black enamel and open to display a tintype image of each of the identified presenters. On top of the handle is a round piece of gold quartz from Grimus Creek where gold was first discovered in the Idaho Territory, near Pioneer City. The balance of the gold head is engraved with fancy scrolls and enamel. The shaft is made of Mountain Mahogany. The silver bullion ferrule is from Owyhee County, Idaho Territory. The cane handle was designed and manufactured in Idaho City from gold of that city.

The Witherells provided the following research: "In 1862, Charles Woodward was the Assistant Superintendent of the Oregon Department of Wells Fargo stationed in Portland. Between August and October 1863, Woodward worked for Wells Fargo as a stage-man on the line between what is now Lewiston, Idaho, and Walla Walla, Washington. On October 1, 1863, he was appointed Wells Fargo & Co. Superintendent for the Northern Idaho Territory, Oregon Department, living in Bannock City (February 1864, the city name changed to Idaho City). His command included Boise, Centerville, Lewiston, Idaho City, Pioneer, Placerville, Rocky Bar, Ruby City, Silver City, and Walla Walla. It is interesting to note that Pioneer was also called Hogem, on account of the first miners in the area who "hogged" up all the good placer gold." $10,000. *Courtesy of WITHERELLS.COM*

Presentation gold and gold quartz walking stick, c. 1861, the richly veined and faceted octagonal gold quartz top above eight cabochon side mounts of various colored gold quartz, the base inscribed, "TO GOVERNOR J. W. NYE NEVADA TERRITORY". Handle: 2-1/4" x 1".

The Witherells research reports, "Appointed by President Lincoln, James W. Nye was the first and only Governor of Nevada Territory, 1861-1864. James Nye, formerly Police Commissioner of New York City, was a close friend and confidant of President Abraham Lincoln who appointed him Brigadier General; thereafter, Lincoln called him 'The General' and gave him a private key to a side door in the White House, where he went nights to 'swap stories' with Lincoln. James Nye later served as U.S. Senator for Nevada from 1864-1872."

The Witherspoons assess the cane as follows: "This Nye cane is an excellent example of a California manufactured cane using native gold. It is well designed, executed, and in excellent condition. Taking into account its age, artistic merits, authenticity, and presentation to an important figure of the American West, its considered one of the finest examples known." $10,000+.
Courtesy of WITHERELLS.COM

Opposite page:
Gold and gold quartz walking stick, with rosewood shaft and steel ferrule. Richly veined and faceted, octagonal gold quartz top (1-3/16"), above eight oval and beveled side mounts alternating in gold quartz and California moss agate (7/16"). The engraving on the handle features scroll, foliate, and geometric designs, with presentation flutes inscribed, "PRESENTED TO / C. H. Randall P. G. R. / By the members of Sonora Lodge No 10 I. O. O. F. / as a token of their / high esteem of him as a / Brother and an Odd Fellow. / January 1876."

Of this cane, the Witherells report, "The emergence of the 'Randall' cane represents one of the most aesthetically significant and historically important gold quartz canes ever discovered. Its design, which incorporates California moss agate, is one of the most unique and its recipient, Charles H. Randall, is one of the most notable. Perhaps more than any other example, it best portrays one of America's defining moments, the California gold rush.

"Few forty-niners had a more romantic odyssey than Charles H. Randall. He arrived in California on board the ship, *Samoset*, September 9, 1849. His quests for gold led him to Webber Creek and Hangtown, an area near Coloma, where gold was first discovered. It was a region rich with gold in addition to 'murders and robbers'. It was dubbed 'Hangtown' just prior to his arrival for carrying out the first known hanging in the motherload. Today, it is considered, 'One of the most historically significant areas along the golden chain.'

"In 1850, Charles H. Randall left California with the intention of prospecting in Central America. He returned to California in 1851 and took up residence in the gold rich county of Tuolumne. It is presumed he continued prospecting in and around the area until 1853 when he returned to a professional life.

"He first gained employment in the Sheriffs office of Tuolumne County working with Major P. L. Solomon. In 1857, upon his appointment as Deputy United States Marshall, Mr. Randall relocated to San Francisco. It was reported, '...in 1857 he (Charles Randall) held the position of United States Marshal, during the absence of the United States Marshal (Major Solomon), for one year.'

"In 1858, he returned to Sonora (Tuolumne County), and entered into the mercantile business with James Lane, doing business as Lane & Randall. Mr. Randall was elected Supervisor in 1861 and served six years. In 1867 he was elected County Judge, serving from 1868 to 1872, and in 1869 he bought the Union-Democrat, a Sonora newspaper. He acted as editor for the paper until 1875 when he sold it and returned to San Francisco. In 1877, Mr. Randall re-acquired the Union-Democrat and returned to Sonora working again as editor. Charles H. Randall passed away in 1891 at the age of 67.

"His obituary states, 'the services were conducted by the order of chosen friends ... at the Odd Fellows Cemetery.' He was quite prominent in the Order of Odd Fellows having served as Grand Master of the State of California and Grand Representative.

"The town of Sonora was named after the Mexican state from which many forty-niners came. 'In its heyday it was one of the richest and wildest towns in the gold country.' The land in and around it was drenched in gold. The San Francisco *Alta California*, March 1 1852, recorded that in one week local banks received 3,412 ounces of gold.

"It was also wrought with lawlessness. As L. M. wrote in a letter home: 'Here there are no parents' eyes to guide, no wife to warn, no sister to entreat... in short, all the animal and vicious passions are let loose and free to indulge without any legal or social restraint.' In just one week in 1850 in Sonora, two Massachusetts men had their throats slit, a Chilean was shot to death in a gunfight, and a Frenchman stabbed a Mexican to death.

"The presentation of the C. H. Randall walking stick was likely consummated at the Odd Fellows', January 5, 1876, Installation Ball. As reported in the *Tuolumne Independent*, January 8, 1876, '...officers of the lodges... have been installed' and as a result Mr. Randall was likely presented with this token of high esteem as Past Grand Representative.

"In closing the gold, gold quartz, and moss agate walking stick presented to Charles H. Randall stands today as one of the preeminent examples, having been presented to an Argonaut of the first order in the venerable gold rush town of Sonora." $10,000+. *Courtesy of WITHERELLS.COM*

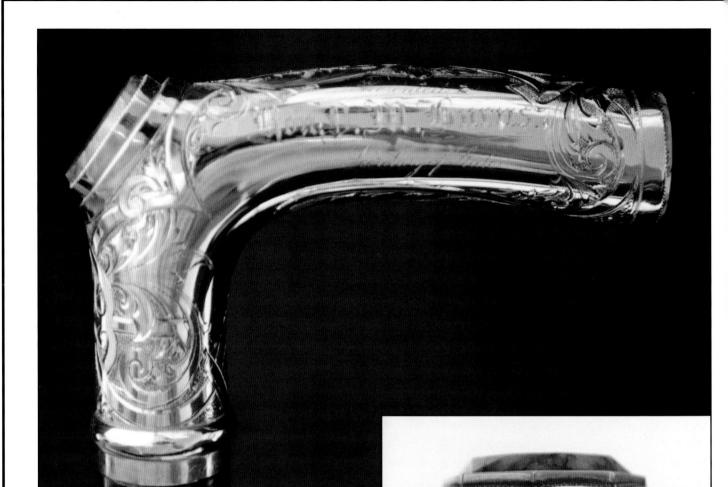

Gold presentation cane with L form handle with opposing black and white gold quartz caps, inscribed "Presented to / Hon. D. M. Burns / Secretary of State / by the employees of his department / January 8th 1883." The handle measures 3-1/2" x 2-1/2".

Daniel Monroe Burns (1845-1927) had moved west with his family from Tennessee. In his life he was a soldier, police commissioner, and politician. $10,000+. *Courtesy of WITHERELLS.COM*

Right:
Gold and gold quartz cane handle on a rosewood shaft with a steel ferrule. The flutes of the handle are engraved, "R. McElroy / San Francisco / -1869-." The large handle measures 2-3/8" h. x 1-7/8" w. The quartz top measures 1-1/4" across.

Robert McElroy, born in Albany, New York, on June 27, 1827, moved to California in 1853 for his health. In California more than his health flourished as he ran a successful real estate enterprise and helped organize the Mutual Savings Bank. He, along with his wife, was active in charity and church work until his death in 1909. $10,000+. *Courtesy of WITHERELLS.COM*

Gold quartz mounted in a silver handle is rare. This presentation cane has a large silver handle inset on the top with a 7/8" faceted and polished piece of gold quartz. Four of the eight panels on the sides of the handle read, "Presented by H. S. Allen to his mother, 1863." The thick shaft is heavy lignum vitae, wood so dense it will not float. Nevertheless, the shaft has a 2" silver and iron ferrule. Handle: 2-1/4" x 1-1/2". Overall length: 35-3/4". *Courtesy of Henry A. Taron, Tradewinds Antiques.* $9000-13,000.

In 1909, the publisher of the *Boston Post*, Edwin A. Grozier, embarked on a publicity stunt that became a New England tradition. Grozier announced he was having seven hundred gold-handled walking sticks manufactured in New York. These sticks were to be distributed to New England towns and presented to the oldest citizen in each town. Upon the death of the original recipient, the cane would be passed on to whomever qualified for the honor. While many of these presentation canes were lost and others remain in the hands of heirs reluctant to return them, some New England towns continue the tradition begun by Grozier.

The presentation cane is described as having a fist-sized gold handle with a black finished shaft and metal rounded ferrule. Upon the death of a recipient, the cane is intended to return to the Town Hall to await the next presentation. Elderly citizens of New England towns where the tradition continues like to joke about who will be next to receive a *Boston Post* golden cane.

As another sign that presentation canes are not strictly a thing of the past, in 1996 Britain's Prince Charles presented a gold-handled walking stick to the Sultan of Brunei. It was Sultan Hassanal Bolkiah's fiftieth birthday.

Above and right:
Gold presentation cane inscribed on the top, "Ziethen Co. No. 3 March 4, 1880 Presented to Capt. J. Dewald". Ebony shaft with 1-1/2" bullet type metal ferrule, American. Handle: 1-3/4" h. x 1-1/4" at widest point. Overall length: 35-5/8". *Courtesy of The World of the Walking Stick.* $695-765.

Silver and gold handled presentation cane reading on one side "Wm. M. Dunlevy" and on the other "From Anna Held Oct. 23 04" Overall length: 35".

Anna Held was a vivacious French actress who met Florenz Ziegfeld, Jr. in London in 1896 and married him in 1897. She was credited as the inspiration for the *Ziegfeld Follies* musical revues, first opening in 1907 at the New York Theater, featuring chorus girls in racy outfits, comedy, and unbridled pageantry. Anna Held was among the fifty chorus girls featured in that opening revue. Held worked with her husband to produce a number of shows, including *Miss Innocence* and *The French Maid*, and starred in both productions. Combining her husband's talent for promotion with her skill and beauty, Anna Held's popularity and fame grew rapidly in America. She was prominently featured in advertising and became one of the early stars among twentieth-century entertainers in the United States. *Courtesy of Ambassador Richard W. Carlson.* $825-900.

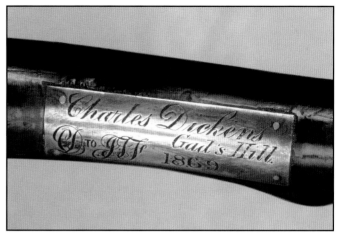

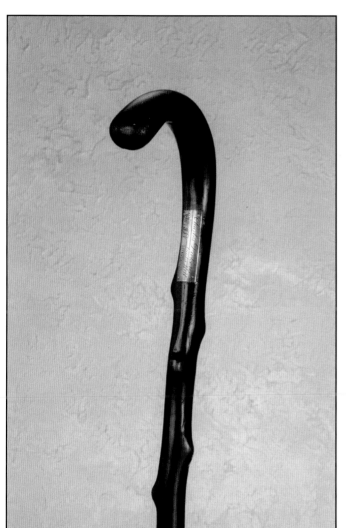

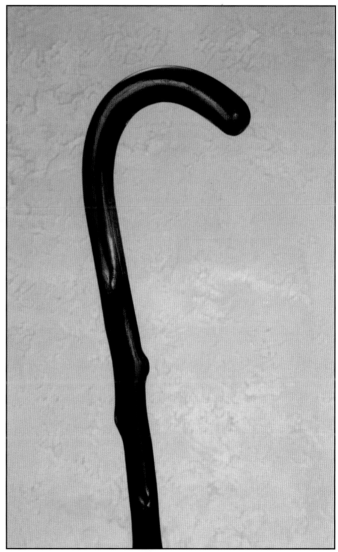

A presentation cane given by Charles Dickens in 1869 featuring a crook handle and shaft of English hardwood with a silver panel on the shaft's underside beneath the handle that reads, "Charles Dickens, Gad's Hill. / C.D. to J.T.F., 1869." Natural branch stubs are retained on the shaft, the base of which is protected by a 7/8" brass ferrule showing wear from repeated use. Overall length: 35-1/2". *Courtesy of Henry A. Taron, Tradewinds Antiques.* While the estimated values was established as $4000-6000, this cane sold at auction for $8000 in 2002.

Presentation cane from President Andrew Jackson (president from 1829 to 1837) to Silas E. Burrows, dated June 12, 1832 on the top of the handle. The inscribed gold handle is 18k and the sides of the handle are finished with two rope ring decorations. The shaft is made of barked hickory (as one might expect from "Old Hickory") and features decorated eyelets. The base of the shaft is protected with a 5-1/4" long brass and iron ferrule. Handle: 1-1/3" x 1". Overall length: 38". *Courtesy of Henry A. Taron, Tradewinds Antiques.* $4000-6000.

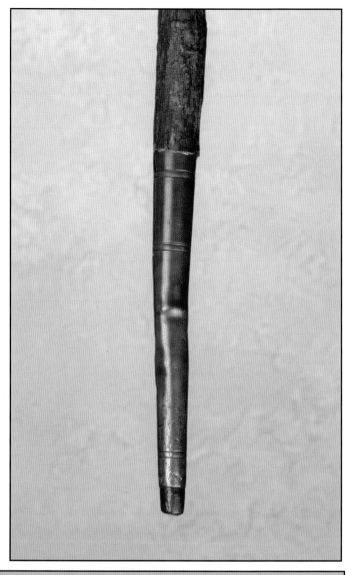

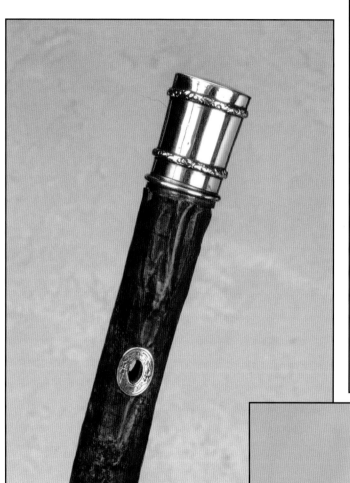

Relic Sticks & Souvenir Canes

Relic sticks are created from wood or metal removed from a site of historical significance, a vessel, or some other significant location one wished to remember. Wood from historical structures ranging from homes to forts has been used in relic sticks. Shipwrecks provide bountiful sources of raw material for relic canes. Civil War veterans were known to create grisly relic canes using the ends of bones from limbs removed in combat. Prisoners also created canes to commemorate their time of incarceration. Once again, these may be formal or folk art sticks.

Abraham Lincoln's birthplace in Larue County, Kentucky, was known to attract visitors. Locals had no interest in the site and were amused by the attention it received. Although the house fell into disrepair and by 1865 all that remained was the chimney stack and two pear trees at the edge of a barley field, travelers would stop to cut a branch from one of the trees as both a relic and a souvenir of their visit.

Relic sticks were, at times, sold as souvenirs. In 1906 in Citronelle, Alabama, the giant white oak beneath which General Richard Taylor (the son of Zachary Taylor, the twelfth President of the United States) surrendered to General E.R.S. Canby on May 4, 1865 at the close of the Civil War was downed by a hurricane. With permission of the property owner, Colonel W.D. Mann, the tree was used to make relic canes, souvenir gavels, and crutches. Canes and crutches were presented to Civil War veterans as gifts and those that remained were sold as souvenirs to cover the costs. Several of these relics are in the Smithsonian Institution's collection in Washington, D.C.

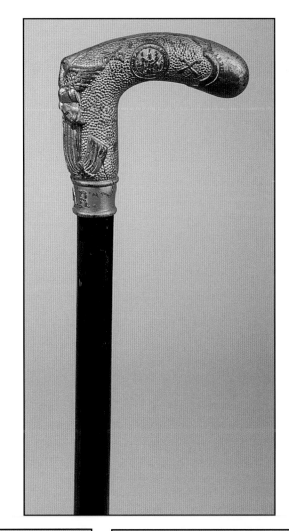

Right and above right:
GAR (Grand Army of the Republic) metal handled walking stick for Union soldiers' veteran's reunions. Metal ferrule. Handle 2-1/2" h. x 3" l. Overall length: 34-3/4". *Courtesy of Ambassador Richard W. Carlson.* $400-440.

Fort Wayne, Indiana, was home to five active forts between 1722 and 1819. Two of the forts were built by the French and three by Americans. The final fort was abandoned in 1819. In 1852, the decaying remnants of the fort were transformed into relic canes and sold as souvenirs.

Relic of the *Royal George*

Relic cane passed through several generations. The silver plate on top above the eyelets reads: "Relic of *Royal George* Sunk At Spithead 1782." The silver collar below tells whose hands the cane passed through: "Presented by Col. Palsey to Capt. Allez and by his Granddaughter to Richard W. Bricstock Esq. MD 1913. Ray – With Love Gerry & Peggy 1970." Metal ferrule. Overall length: 36". *Courtesy of Ambassador Richard W. Carlson.* $800-1400.

In 1756, when the *Royal George* was completed, she was the British Royal Navy's largest warship. With a hull measuring over two hundred feet long and fifty feet wide, the *Royal George* weighed 3,745 tons and carried one hundred cannons on three gun decks. Her masts towered over one hundred feet high and the quarterdeck rode thirty-two feet above the waves. *Royal George* was made the flagship of the Channel Fleet in 1756 as the Seven Years War began.

The *Royal George* played a significant role in thwarting the French invasion of Britain at the Battle of Quiberon Bay. The *Royal George* would see her last military victory in January of 1781, capturing two Spanish warships off Portugal. In 1782, the *Royal George* joined the fleet at the Isle of Wight along the north coast at Spithead in preparation for relieving the crews blockading Spanish forces off Gibraltar. While Spithead was the traditional anchorage of the Royal Navy and considered to be the safest part of the island coast to sail, Spithead would be the *Royal George's* grave.

On August 29, 1782, the fleet was assembled, including fifty men of war and three hundred merchant vessels. As the flagship, the *Royal George* had Rear Admiral Kempenfeldt on board. The ship was under the command of Captain Waghorn. This was the day for crewmembers to say goodbye to their loved ones before the fleet sailed for Gibraltar. However, due to desertion problems, shore-leaves were canceled. Sailors' wives and families were allowed on board the *Royal George* for their farewells. Along with them came moneylenders, merchants, and prostitutes. All told, an extra four hundred individuals were aboard ship.

Against the recommendations of the Master Attendant of the dockyard, Captain Waghorn ordered the replacement of a water-cock below the waterline. This valve provided water for deck cleaning. Despite warnings, the ship's heavy load of 548 tons of stores and 83 tons of ammunition, *and* the extra four hundred individuals on board, the Captain gave the order to heel the ship and replace the water-cock. To heel the ship, the crew had to move the cannons from one side of the ship to the other, creating an eight-degree list to starboard and raising the faulty water-cock above sea-level.

In spite of the revocation of shore-leave, the *Royal George's* Gunner, Boatswain, and Master were all ashore. These are the officers whose job it was to oversee this particular maneuver.

The captain further ordered the lower gun decks to keep their gun ports open to receive additional supplies while the ship was listing. Normally these ports would remain closed to ensure water would not enter through the ports, which were now much closer to the sea with the ship listing. By nine in the morning, when the merchant ship *Lark* arrived to supply the *Royal George* with rum, water was splashing in through the gun ports, which were a mere foot above sea-level. The weight of the rum tipped the gun sills below the waterline. At this point, it was noted that rats and mice were leaving the *Royal George* in favor of the *Lark*.

As the story goes, twice a carpenter reported this situation to the officer of the watch and twice he was rebuffed. The carpenter went directly to the captain, who sent the First Lieutenant to investigate. At 9:18 AM the Captain gave the order to Right Ship. However, the ship began to capsize immediately. With the increasingly steep slope of the deck the crew could not move a single cannon back into position.

The Captain ran to the Admiral's Cabin to warn the Rear Admiral of the situation but could not enter the cabin. The door was jammed. The masts began to fall and the Captain abandoned his ship. The *Royal George* capsized and sank so rapidly that only 255 of the 1,200 souls aboard survived.

At the court martial, the five Admirals decided to clear the Rear Admiral and Captain, blaming the dockyard authority for the disaster. The decision was made that the bottom of the ship was rotten and had fallen away due to neglect. It was well known that the Navy Board in charge of dockyard repair embezzled money meant for ship repairs. During the American Revolution, eighty-three British naval vessels sank due to rot resulting from the neglect of the Navy Board.

The Navy Board had no desire to find out if the decision was correct and was not happy when salvage expert William Tracey proposed raising the *Royal George* in 1783. They supplied Tracey with ships that sank under him and refused to pay his expenses. Tracey was forced to quit after moving the ship's hull no more than thirty yards. In 1832, the Navy Board was abolished and work resumed on the *Royal George*. Between 1836 and 1839, John and Charles Deane, inventors of the deep-sea diving suit, raised twenty-nine cannons and determined that the hull was now beyond salvage. In 1839, Colonel Palsey, a pioneer in marine demolition, raised the remaining cannon using gunpowder. Finally, in 1844, Alexander Siebe would prove the reliability of his "Improved Diving Dress" by diving to the *Royal George* and recovering the ship's bell.

Ironically, the cannons from the *Royal George* were melted down and used in Nelson's Column in Trafalgar Square, commemorating the wartime accomplishments of the *Royal George's* sister ship, the HMS *Victory*. The HMS *Victory* had been present the day the *Royal George* had gone down.

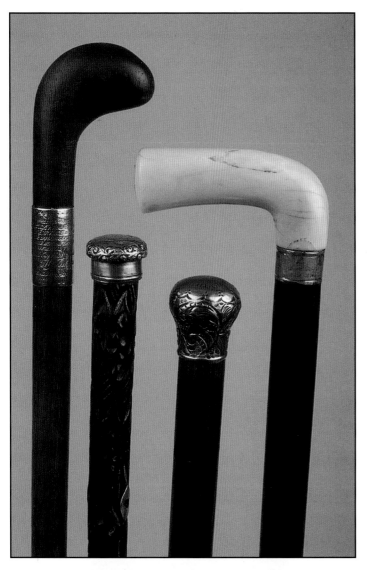

Four relic canes from British ships. They are identified on the canes as relics of the HMS *Eurydice*, HMS *Royal George*, *Great Eastern*, and HMS *Augusta*. All are silver mounted. The ivory handle is walrus ivory. All of the shafts are oak. The inscription on the HMS *Augusta* stick reads, "Irish oak from British frigate. Sunk off Fort Mifflin on the Delaware River, Oct. 23, 1777." *Courtesy of Richard R. Wagner, Jr.* $800-1400 each.

The warship HMS *Eurydice* met a tragic end. The 26-gun, 921 ton wooden-hulled frigate was launched in 1843. She was designed for speed with a broad sail expanse and sleek hull design. By the last quarter of the nineteenth century, ironclads and other iron-hulled vessels were gaining prominence. The HMS *Eurydice* was refitted in 1876, converted to a training ship under the command of Captain Hare. In November of 1877, she sailed on a three-month training mission through the West Indies and Bermuda. After a successful voyage, the ship met with disaster off the Isle of Wight while returning to Portsmouth.

The HMS *Eurydice* fell victim to a fast moving storm blowing snow and ice in high winds. Apparently caught unawares, the ship entered the storm under full sail with her gun ports wide open. Unable to reef the sails under the storm's assault, the *Eurydice* was soon capsized and sunk, water pouring though the open gun ports. Much of the crew was sucked down with the rapidly sinking ship. Others froze to death in the frigid waters before rescue was possible. In all, only two crewmembers survived the ill-fated journey.

The *Great Eastern*, a.k.a. the *Leviathan*, was a very large iron-hulled steamship designed to carry four thousand passengers. Launched in 1858 to compete against the swift wooden-hulled, sail driven clipper ships, the *Great Eastern* caused its parent company, the Eastern Steam Navigation Company, much trouble and expense. The ship proved to be too costly to operate in an era when coaling stations on route to the Indian Ocean and Pacific had yet to be fully established. In time, the ship would pass through several owners and would prove most useful from 1865 to 1874 while laying transatlantic telegraph cables. In 1867, the ship was refitted to transport four thousand American visitors from New York to the Paris Exposition. Jules Verne made this crossing and wrote of the imposing vessel in his novel, *Une Ville Flottante*. In 1886, the *Great Eastern*'s final mission was to act as a floating amusement park, complete with restaurants, music, and a fair. Her last voyage, in 1889, was to the scrap yard.

The HMS *Augusta* was the largest British warship lost in action during the Revolutionary War. On October 23, 1777, the 64-gun British warship was attempting to force its way up the Delaware River with other warships of the Royal Navy to reach and re-supply the British ground forces occupying Philadelphia. However, Pennsylvania had formidable defenses in place, including their own gunboat navy, shoreline fortifications, and underwater obstacles. The HMS *Augusta* ran aground near Fort Mifflin in the morning and caught fire. As the fire spread, the battered warship was abandoned, the crew escaping aboard the 44-gun HMS *Roebuck*, which was heavily damaged during the rescue. At noon, the *Augusta*'s magazine exploded, utterly destroying her. While the British fleet would eventually arrive in Philadelphia, the strong defenses delayed them long enough to force the British army to wait for spring to resume their military operations. The delay proved ultimately disastrous for the British as the French joined the war on the side of the Americans during the winter.

Relic of the USS *Constellation*

On March 27, 1794, President George Washington signed an act that led Congress to authorize the construction of six frigates, thereby creating the United States Navy. The six ships, constructed in six different cities, were the *Constellation, Constitution, Congress, Chesapeake, President,* and *United States.*

The United States Frigate *Constellation* was a ship of "firsts:" she was the first of the six vessels completed, the first put to sea, and the first to successfully engage and capture an enemy vessel.

Constructed at the Harris Creek Shipyard in Fells Point, Baltimore, Maryland, the *Constellation* was a three-masted, square-rigged frigate manned by a crew of 340 with a 38-gun main battery. She measured 164 feet in length and 41 feet across the beam.

Under the command of Captain Thomas Truxton, the *Constellation* engaged the French in battle in 1799, capturing *L'Insurgente,* a 40-gun frigate known to be the swiftest in the French fleet. In 1800, *La Vengenance* fell to *Constellation* in a five-hour battle. Stunned by her thirteen-knot speed, chagrined French sailors dubbed the *Constellation* the "Yankee Racehorse."

The *Constellation* would serve in the Barbary Wars against Tripoli and in the War of 1812 against Great Britain. In 1840, she would successfully circumnavigate the globe. By 1853, the *Constellation* could do no more. She was taken to the Gosport Navy Yard in Norfolk, Virginia, and dismantled.

Very rare shipwreck cane from the USS *Constellation*. Oak shaft with solid gold mounts. The inscription reads, "USFr. Constellation, Commodore Truxton, Baltimore," on the side panels. On the top of the handle is inscribed, "James Gray 1853 Richmond." The ferrule is brass, measuring 2-1/2" long. Only two examples are known at the time of this writing. *Courtesy of Richard R. Wagner, Jr.* $4500-5500.

Relic of the USS *Constitution*

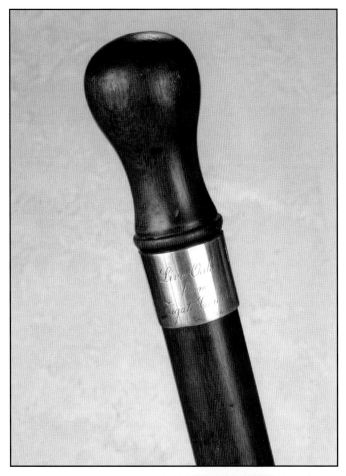

Relic cane from the United States Navy Frigate *Constitution*. This knob handled cane is made entirely from a single piece of heavy wood, live oak. The 1" coin silver collar is marked "Live Oak from the U.S. Frigate, Constitution." The base of the shaft is protected with a 2-3/4" brass and iron ferrule. Handle: 2-3/4" x 1-2/3". Overall length: 32-1/4". *Courtesy of Henry A. Taron, Tradewinds Antiques.* $1300-2500.

During an illustrious career, the USS *Constitution* hunted pirates and slave traders off the coast of Africa; fought the British Navy in the War of 1812; circumnavigated the globe; hosted Pope Pius IX at Gaeta, Italy, in 1849—the first Pope to set foot on United States territory; trained nineteenth century Naval Academy cadets; outran a steam powered tugboat that was supposed to return her from Newport, Rhode Island, to Annapolis, Maryland, in 1865—she sailed into port at Hampton Roads under her own power ten hours ahead of the steam tug; was exhibited at the Paris Exposition in 1878-1879; and remains the oldest ship in the United States Navy today.

The USS *Constitution* was built between 1794 and 1797 at Edmond Harrt's Shipyard in Boston, Massachusetts, and launched on October 21, 1797. It had taken roughly two thousand trees from all over the original states to build her. She was fitted with cannons from Rhode Island and copper fastenings provided by Paul Revere himself. The hull measured 204 feet in length from the billet head to the taffrail and 43-1/2 feet in width, had a 220 foot high mainmast, and carried thirty-two 24-pounder long guns, twenty 32-pounder carronades, and two 24-pounder bow chasers. The USS *Constitution* carried a crew of 450 and was designed to be able to outmatch any warship of her own size and outmaneuver her larger opponents.

On August 19, 1812, in a battle with the British warship HMS *Guerriere*, a crewman aboard the *Constitution* claimed to have seen British shot bounce off the side of the hull and the crew declared the hull was made of iron. The ship has been called "Old Ironsides" ever since. Once the maneuvering was over and the two warships began close quarters fighting, the *Constitution* disabled the *Guerriere* and ended the battle in a little over twenty minutes. This was a much-needed victory in a war that had produced far too many American defeats at that point.

An interesting uproar surrounded the *Constitution* in 1834. The ship's original figurehead was lost during the Barbary Wars and had been replaced with a simple decoration. The suggestion was made to replace it with a figurehead of the current president, Andrew Jackson. Bostonians were not fond of Jackson and the commandant of the Boston Navy Yard had his life threatened after the suggestion was made. Yet the figurehead of Andrew Jackson was installed. However, during a thunderstorm, the captain of a merchant ship rowed across Boston harbor, boarded the *Constitution*, removed Jackson's head from the figurehead, and gave it over to the Secretary of the Navy himself. Despite the uproar and initial decapitation, the figurehead was restored and adorned the ship for years.

Over time, Old Ironsides was overhauled and refurbished on numerous occasions, including in: 1807-11; 1811-12; 1833-34; 1871-77; 1907; 1927-30; 1972-75; and 1992-95. There were certainly plenty of occasions to make relic canes out of wood removed from this venerable warship.

Laurence shipwreck relic cane. "Wood from the Flagship Laurence" is inscribed on the silver knob handle. "Com Perry's Victory / On Lake Erie, Sept 10 1813 / We have met the enemy and they are ours" /"From Miss L. Pegram to George Miller Ely, New Jersey" completes the presentation inscription. *Courtesy of Richard R. Wagner, Jr.* $800-1200.

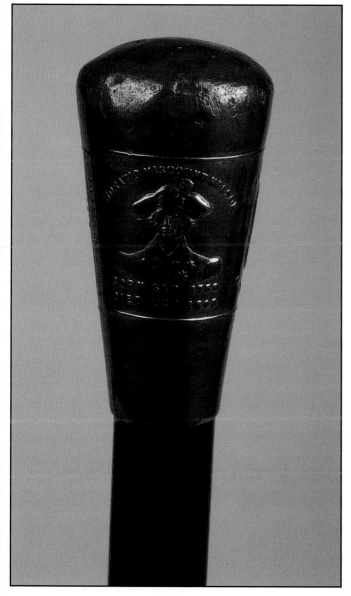

Relic cane of Admiral Nelson's flagship HMS *Foudroyant* with a copper handle, reads: "Oak and copper from vessel after breaking up/ 'Foudroyant' Nelson's Flagship Commenced 1789, Launched 1798, Wrecked 1897 Blackpool / Horatio Viscount Nelson Born Sep 1711 Died Oct 1801." *Courtesy of Richard R. Wagner, Jr.* $250-450.

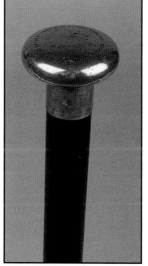

Relic cane. The metal handle reads: "Made from a part of the steering gear of Captain Hamilton's Aeroplane." The story is as follows: Robert P.G. Hamilton, b. 2/24/21, was the son of Peter Hamilton and Sally Carlson of Hibbing, Minnesota. Robert joined the RAF Hurricane Squadron and was shot down and killed in the Battle of Britain. He died near the village of Meriden where he was well known, as his fiancée lived there. She had this cane made in 1942. The base of the shaft is protected with a metal ferrule with an iron tip. Overall length: 34-1/2". *Courtesy of Ambassador Richard W. Carlson.* $775-855.

This relic cane is a single piece of laminated mahogany that originally served as a portion of a World War I warplane's propeller. The prop's original shape is evident on the shaft. A 1" brass ferrule follows the form to the blade. A silver plaque on the side reads "Mr. Thomas Harbourne, Bristol, Eng. To Robert W. Birch, Reading Penna USA Aug 29, 1921." Pistol grip handle: 2-1/2" x 2". Overall length: 35-1/2". *Courtesy of Henry A. Taron, Tradewinds Antiques.* $500-700.

Mementos of War

Boer War Prisoner's Cane

Between October 1899 and May 1902, the British battled two Boer republics of the Transvaal and Orange Free State in South Africa in Britain's last great colonial war. South African prisoners of the British forces were removed to Bermuda from June 1901 to January 1902. Prisoner of war camps were established on various islands of the Great Sound, including: Burts Island, 400 men; Darrell's Island, 1100 men; Hawkins Island, 1300 men; Hinson's Island, 120 men; Morgan's Island, 850 men; and Tucker's Island, 800 men.

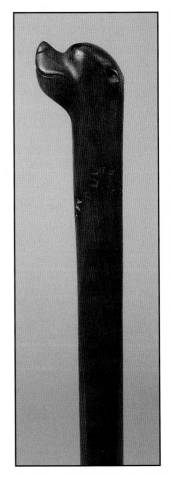

Prisoner of war cane carved from a single piece of wood, painted ferrule. Block letter carving near dog's head handle reads "J. Burcer POW Bermuda 1902" in two banners. Overall length: 33-3/4". *Courtesy of Ambassador Richard W. Carlson.* $325-360.

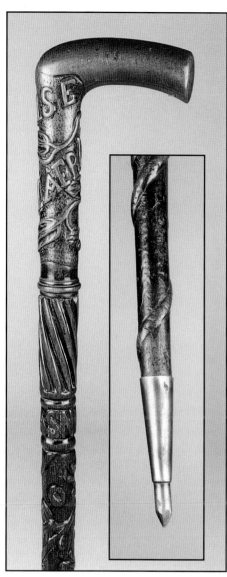

L-shaped carved wooden Franco-Prussian prisoner of war cane with a spiked metal ferrule. The carving at the top of the cane spells "Vive La Francaise," carved in a circle 10-1/2" from the top is "Nicolas," and spiraling from the ferrule upward is carved "Souvenir de Capitivite, Ingolstadt, Baviere, 1871." Along with the carved letters are leaves, pinecones, and a small animal. Overall length: 36". *Courtesy of The World of the Walking Stick.* $975-1075.

As the story goes, this French World War I stick commemorating battles was given in World War II to an American soldier by a French family to express their gratitude after the Battle of the Bulge. The shaft reads "Clezenianne Talntrux – Colmar" on one side and "Guen Trange – Metz – Vaux Nancy – Mehoncourt – Damas Aux Bois" on the other. The initials "H.T." are carved under the soldier's bust. The stick includes a variety of finely carved relief images. Overall length: 36-1/2". *Courtesy of Dale Van Atta.* $200-220.

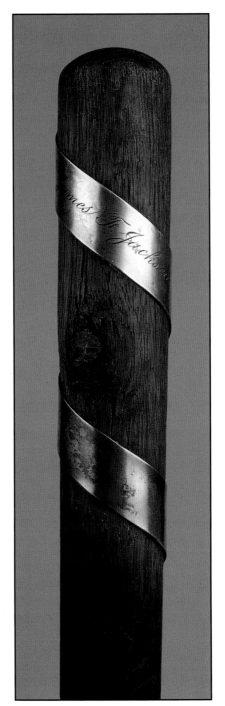

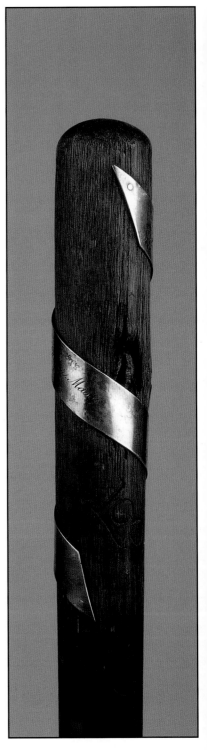

Two German prisoner of war canes: the model on the left appears to have an iron cross under a crown insignia while the cane on right has "RUSSLAND 1940" carved on the shaft. Overall lengths: 35-1/2" and 37". *Courtesy of Dale Van Atta.* $80-90 each.

Souvenirs

Prior to the era of easy travel of the latter half of the twentieth century, souvenirs were prestigious items that declared the owner had the means to be well-traveled. Souvenir canes served this purpose, especially those sticks that could only be purchased where they were made. Examples of exotic souvenir sticks are Pitcairn Island walking sticks and the British giant Jersey cabbage sticks. Victorian adventurers journeying to India and Ceylon returned with elephant head handled walking sticks. An extravagant model was made of ebony and had ivory tusks.

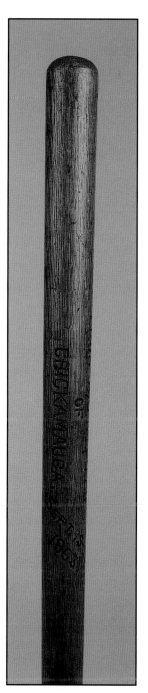

Civil War cane with a bullet visible in the shaft (which was cut from a tree with bullets embedded in it during the battle). Carved on the shaft is, "From Battle of Chickamauga / Sept. 19-20, 1863." Overall length: 33-1/2".

The battle was fought along a small stream in northern Georgia. The fighting was intense. In all, 4,000 soldiers were killed and 35,000 wounded during the bloody struggle in which the Confederates won the day. *Courtesy of Richard R. Wagner, Jr.* $850-935.

Cane made from a New Mexico cactus stalk with rubber tips at either end. This cane was produced in the 1920s. Overall length: 35". *Courtesy of Ambassador Richard W. Carlson.* $325-360.

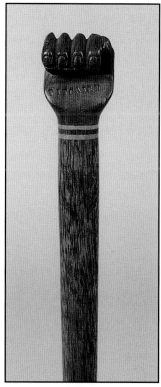

Pitcairn Island fist souvenir cane, no ferrule. Different colored woods as collar. Overall length: 36". *Courtesy of Ambassador Richard W. Carlson.* $400-500.

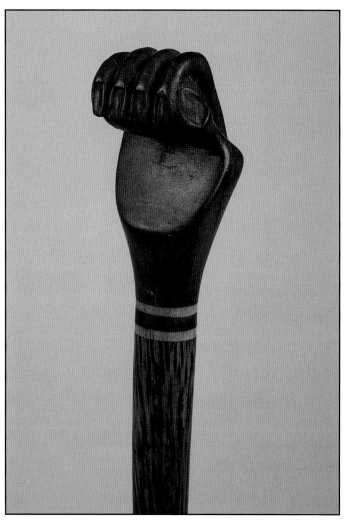

Pitcairn Island cane, red wood right fist on a
coconut wood shaft. Handle: 2-1/4" h. Stylized fist
stamped Pitcairn Island on the back. Overall length:
36". *Courtesy of Richard R. Wagner, Jr.* $400-500.

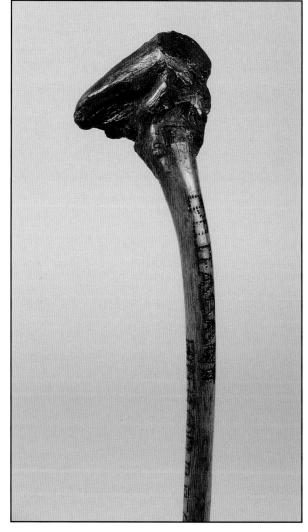

Wood souvenir stick, no ferrule, tree trunk and limb,
burned in is phrase "Pleasant Recollections of God's
Country at Greenkill." Overall length: 31". *Courtesy of
Ambassador Richard W. Carlson.* $375-415.

Celebrating the repeal of Prohibition in the United States, this jaunty little souvenir stick from the 1933 Chicago Century of Progress World's Fair sports a tapped beer barrel and a colorful stein. These are found in varying conditions; it is unusual to see an example with all its pieces and the labels, silver ribbon, and original tied braid intact. Overall length: 35-1/2". *Courtesy of Kimball M. Sterling Auctioneers.* $400-800.

1933 World's Fair cane commemorating the end of Prohibition with the images of a beer barrel and flagon. The painted wood shaft has silver paper wrapped up the length and a metal ferrule at the base. The keg spigot is missing from this example. Overall length: 37". *Courtesy of Dale Van Atta.* $400-800 complete.

Of course, visited nations soon provided Western travelers with the choice between walking sticks carved in traditional forms of the region or sticks in a Western style travelers might be most comfortable with.

During the late nineteenth century, Florida was also considered an exotic destination for many. Tourists were carting away the natural souvenirs one might expect, including Spanish moss, seashells, and alligator's teeth.

Beginning around the late 1870s, they also carried away souvenir walking sticks produced in Jacksonville, Florida, with carved alligator handles. The shafts were made of local orangewood and handles were made from a variety of materials, including bone, buckhorn, and ivory. A carved alligator was perched across the top of the handle, staring up at its new owner with an amiable, closed mouth grin.

Hailing from Jacksonville, Florida, this American souvenir folk art cane dates from around 1880. It was produced by a group of carvers working in Jacksonville producing cane sold to adventurous travelers in an age when cross country travel was a much greater challenge and a long trip was an achievement. This L-handled cane, with its finely carved alligator stained and straddling the handle, was carved from river cypress. The entire cane was lightly lacquered and the tip was protected with a bimetal ferrule. Handle: 4" x 2". Overall length: 35". *Courtesy of Kimball M. Sterling Auctioneers.* $400-800.

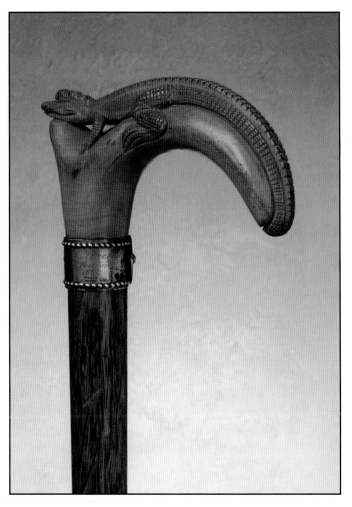

An elaborately carved wood alligator cane hailing from Jacksonville, Florida. The handle is orangewood and the alligator has tiny red bead eyes. The sterling collar's raised script reads, "Jacksonville, Fla." Additional inscriptions on the collar read, "J.B. Newcomb, E. Milton, 1896," and the seller's name is stamped as well, "Greenleaf and Crosby." The cane shaft is coconut palm wood tipped with a 1" white metal ferrule. Handle: 5" x 2-1/4". Overall length: 34-1/2". *Courtesy of Henry A. Taron, Tradewinds Antiques.* Although the estimated value in 2001 was listed at $600-800, this cane sold for $1000 at auction that year.

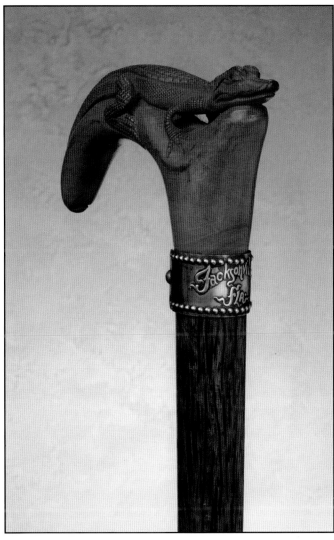

Alligator handled cane with a wood shaft that has branch tips showing, one more souvenir of an early Florida trip. The base of the shaft has a metal ferrule with iron tip. Handle: 4-1/4" l. Overall length: 35-1/4". *Courtesy of Ambassador Richard W. Carlson.* $400-800.

Collegiate Canes

University of New Hampshire college student's cane from 1925 featuring the Old Man of the Mountain natural rock formation on the handle. The wooden cane is carved with the names of classmates. Overall length: 36". The fact that the well-known rock formation collapsed on May 3, 2003, at around 7:30 in the morning in a massive rockslide, makes this cane all the more interesting. *Courtesy of Richard R. Wagner, Jr.* $350-450.

Dartmouth College student's cane well covered with names and symbols significant to the owner and friends. Dated 1909. Metal ferrule with iron tip. Overall length: 35-3/4". *Courtesy of Ambassador Richard W. Carlson.* $325-360.

During the nineteenth century, it became fashionable for students to carry school canes. Such walking sticks are usually decorated with fraternity emblems, the student's name, the names of classmates, and possibly the name of the person giving the cane to the student if it was given as a gift to mark a major academic event … such as graduation. College canes may also bear the recognized symbol of the school.

Dartmouth College graduates received graduation canes at least as early as 1898. The date the first such walking stick was presented is unclear, but the oldest example in the campus's Baker Library dates from that year. These were topped with a handle in the shape of a Mohegan Indian, the school symbol. Many are found decorated with a variety of symbols considered significant to the students and their friends and the names of each cane's recipient and their companions. The Mohegan Indian was removed as a school symbol in 1974 when the college authorities were swept up in a wave of "social conscience."

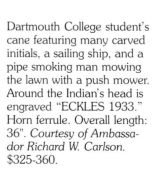

Dartmouth College student's cane featuring many carved initials, a sailing ship, and a pipe smoking man mowing the lawn with a push mower. Around the Indian's head is engraved "ECKLES 1933." Horn ferrule. Overall length: 36". *Courtesy of Ambassador Richard W. Carlson.* $325-360.

Canes were used in an innovative way at Baylor University to create the "Mace," the university's ceremonial symbol of authority. A sword, presented to Cyrus Baylor by General Andrew Jackson in honor of Baylor's bravery during the War of 1812, was donated to the university by the Baylor family in 1957. In 1974, Baylor president Abner V. McCall linked walking sticks from former Baylor president Rufus C. Burleson and General Sam Houston to the sword. Supported by a base and center pole fashioned out of wood removed from the Old Main's tower, the resulting Mace is used for special ceremonies, including commencement exercises.

However, the most *intriguing* tradition to spring from collegiate walking sticks must be the Princeton University Cane Spree. In 1865, Princeton upperclassmen decided that it was *not* fashionable for university freshmen to carry walking sticks. Decreeing that there was now a "rule" forbidding freshmen from carrying canes, sophomores attempted to relieve freshmen of their sticks one evening along Nassau Street. Freshmen saw the matter differently and a lively scrap (or "spree" to use the vernacular of 1865) ensued. This was the first of many "cane sprees." While not sanctioned by Princeton, standard times and dates were set for future, annual sprees. By the early 1870s, the sprees had moved onto campus grounds and complex rules were in place. Junior class members took to advising the freshmen on tactics, seniors did the same for the sophomores.

Midnight during October's full moon was the time, the turf in front of Witherspoon was the place. Oil-soaked broom torches provided light for the now uniformed combatants (freshmen in white, sophomores in black). Prior to the midnight melees, underclassmen of all stripes joined enthusiastically in completely disorganized attempts to relieve each other of their sticks, which became known as the "Cane Rush." As the years passed, Princeton University rules were established to tame the enthusiasms and limit the damage caused by cane sprees. Organized sporting contests including basketball, touch football, and volleyball are now spree activities. Women joined the spree during the contests between the classes of 1973 and 1974.

Political Canes

Canes for political events, rallies, parades. From left: 48-star flag pulls up out of the shaft of this metal cane with a round wood knob handle. Second cane reads "Protection 1896." The third cane features Teddy Roosevelt. The fourth is a noisemaker cane made of metal reading "Patriotism, Protection, Prosperity." *Courtesy of Ambassador Richard W. Carlson.* Flag cane: overall length: 36-1/4", $425-470. Second cane ("Protection 1896"): overall length: 38-1/2", $325-360. Teddy Roosevelt: overall length: 34-1/2", $425-470. Metal horn: horn handle: 4-1/4", overall length: 33", $325-360.

Political canes were distributed by those seeking the power and prestige of public office. Such sticks were brandished by loyal voters during parades and campaign speeches as signs of support. American political canes featuring handles or decorations promoting a particular candidate and/or agenda were first manufactured in large numbers in 1868. The vast majority of such sticks were not designed to last beyond the campaign season and were made from materials that reflect their ephemeral nature.

Bust or effigy handled sticks are the most common form of political cane. Many feature the visages of contenders for the office of President of the United States. The handles were made of base metals and frequently include the name and campaign slogan of the candidate. The most commonly found contenders are from the presidential campaign of 1896, William McKinley and William Jennings Bryan.

By 1900, a second form of political stick was produced, a tapered stick with a small round or plain metal cap handle and shaft covered with paper. The paper, colored red, white, and blue, was emblazoned with patriotic motifs and portraits of both presidential and vice presidential candidates on the upper third of the shaft.

Between 1900 and 1912, political canes were produced on carnival style sticks featuring celluloid photos of the candidates housed within the top of the rounded handle. These sticks were truly not designed to last and are rarely seen today.

A variety of political system sticks added to the excitement at political rallies and parades. In 1896, tin horn canes were fashioned as cane handles and campaign slogans were impressed into them. Tin parade torches with removable handles covering the wicks and oil reservoirs housed within the tin shafts were used to light the way for nighttime events … although in an age when straw hats were all the fashion for hot weather, one wonders how safe these torches would have been. However, prior to the electric light, torch light political parades were quite popular.

Flag canes were also produced. Usually the flag was wrapped around a short wooden shaft that was attached to the underside of the walking stick handle or ferrule. The flag was housed within the hollow shaft of the cane. Once removed, the handle or ferrule could be inverted and fitted into the shaft opening.

After 1912, political canes were used less frequently, as canes in general were beginning to fall out of common use. However, political campaign canes appeared for the candidacies of Franklin D. Roosevelt, Dwight Eisenhower, John Kennedy, Barry Goldwater, Jimmy Carter, and Gerald Ford, though these campaign sticks were manufactured in far smaller numbers than their earlier counterparts.

Franklin Roosevelt's bust also appeared on walking sticks offered as souvenirs at the Chicago World's Fair, "A Century of Progress" International Exposition in 1933-34. Another stick sold at the Chicago World's Fair sported a wooden beer barrel-shaped handle, complete with a wooden tap, poised over a small wooden goblet attached to the shaft with wire. This stick was commemorating the 21st Amendment to the United States Constitution, implemented in 1933, repealing Prohibition. It was brightly painted and is difficult to find with all its pieces intact.

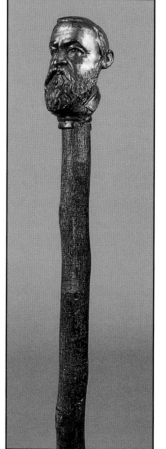

Garfield political cane on a branch shaft, with a silver plate handle. Handle: 2-3/4" l. Overall length: 37". *Courtesy of Ambassador Richard W. Carlson.* $350-385.

Democratic Party political cane reads around the sides in a banner, "The Party of the People" with the donkey symbol on top. Silver handled cane with silver ferrule. Overall length: 36". *Courtesy of Ambassador Richard W. Carlson.* $175-190.

Pewter Republican Party elephant handle cane on a thin reed shaft. This symbol of the GOP (Grand Old Party) was sold by vendors at Republican political events and conventions during the late nineteenth century. Overall length: 35". *Courtesy of Ambassador Richard W. Carlson.* $275-475.

Left and above:
Elegant three color gold, agate, and tortoiseshell cane, possibly French, c. 1870. The handle is fashioned of hammered gold and topped with an inlaid 1" cabochon agate. Below the hammered upper surface of the handle, the handle's smooth sides are pink gold with a yellow gold strap and white gold buckle as a collar. The shaft is a highly figured tortoiseshell veneer over wood and is protected at the tip by a 1" solid yellow gold ferrule with an iron tip. Wearing this cane would have made a real fashion statement. Handle: 1-3/4" x 1-1/3". Overall length: 37". *Courtesy of Henry A. Taron, Tradewinds Antiques.* $4500-6500.

An elegant gold knob handle with a white sapphire set into the top of the handle. The knob handle is inscribed, "1844, Presented To Field M. Citron from his friends." The shaft is rosewood. Handle: 2-1/2" h. x 1-1/2" w. *Courtesy of Richard R. Wagner, Jr.* $4000-5000.

Gold L-shaped handle with open cartouches on either side of the handle, in which are inscribed, "Gratitude" and "1886," with a monogram on the handle's end. Overall length: 34-3/4". *Courtesy of Dale Van Atta.* $400-800.

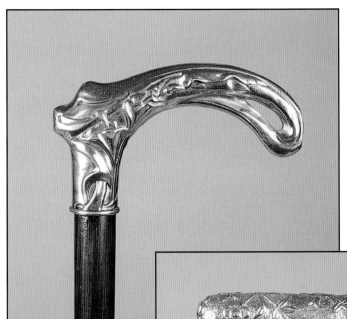

Gold Art Nouveau handle embossed with
trumpet-shaped flowers growing on a vine,
hallmarked. Hardwood shaft with 1/2" gold tone
ferrule, c. 1890. Handle: 3-3/4" w. x 2-1/4" h.
Overall length: 34-1/2". *Courtesy of The World
of the Walking Stick.* $1250-1375.

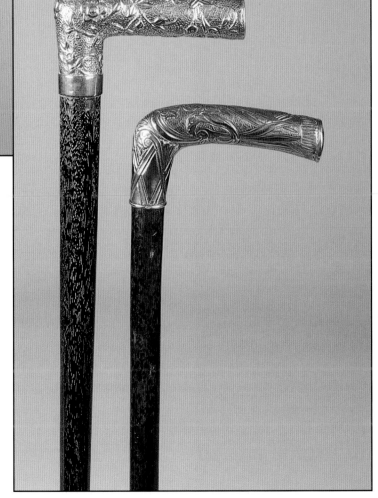

Left: L-shaped silver
handle decorated all over
with leaves and flowers.
Hardwood shaft. Handle:
4" l. x 2" h. Overall length:
33-1/2". *Courtesy of The
World of the Walking Stick.*
$525-580.
Right: 18k gold chased Art
Nouveau L-shaped handle
with a Tigerwood shaft,
c. 1900. Overall length:
35-1/4". *Courtesy of The
World of the Walking Stick.*
$1100-1500.

Elegant silver knob handle cane with ivory
ferrule, relief decoration featuring men and
women in colonial garb at play, Handle:
7-1/4" l. Overall length: 36-1/2". *Courtesy of
Ambassador Richard W. Carlson.* $425-470.

Left and below:
Silver handle in the Rococo style with a monogrammed cartouche and fancy scrollwork depicting a child playing drums on the bottom quarter of the handle. Malacca shaft with brass ferrule. Probably Continental, c. 1890. Overall length: 36-1/2". *Courtesy of The World of the Walking Stick.* $650-715.

Silver handled cane on malacca shaft with monogram on knob handle reading CHW, metal ferrule with iron tip. Handle: 2" l. Overall length: 35-1/2". *Courtesy of Ambassador Richard W. Carlson.* $325-360.

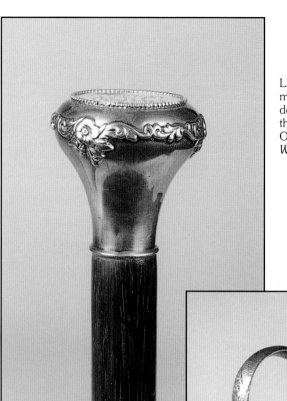

Large Gorham silver handle with monogram on top, circled by repoussé decoration of flowers and leaves near the top. Hardwood shaft, c. 1870. Overall length: 32". *Courtesy of The World of the Walking Stick.* $500-725.

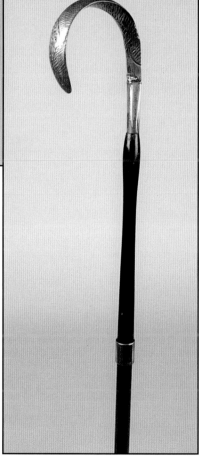

Silver crook handle cane with hammered decoration and silver low collar, slim, light weight, tiny silver cap ferrule. Handle: 4" h. Overall length: 36-1/2". *Courtesy of Ambassador Richard W. Carlson.* $225-250.

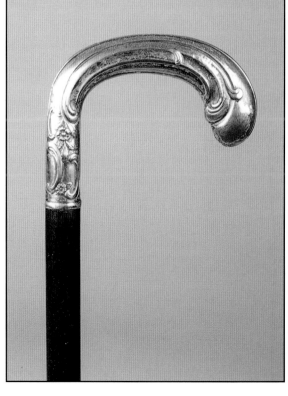

Silver Art Nouveau crook handle engraved with flowers, hallmarked 800. Mahogany shaft with 1-1/8" metal ferrule, Continental, c. 1890. Handle: 4-1/8" w. x 3-1/4" h. Overall length: 35-1/2". *Courtesy of The World of the Walking Stick.* $625-690.

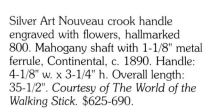

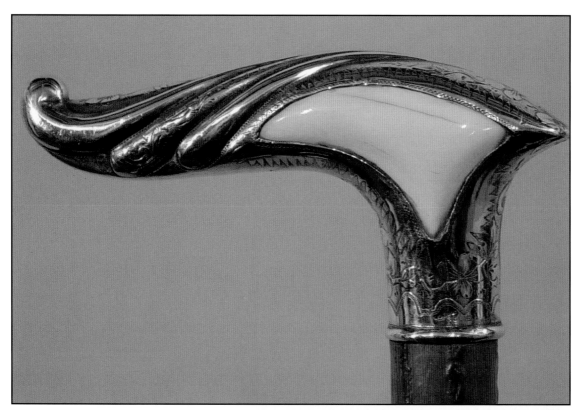

Silver and ivory handled dress cane, probably American, c. 1900, silver tau handle with ivory inserts in etched silver frame, over a scarred shaft and horn ferrule. Handle: 4-1/2" x 2-1/2". Overall length: 32-1/2". *Courtesy of Kimball M. Sterling Auctioneers.* $300-500.

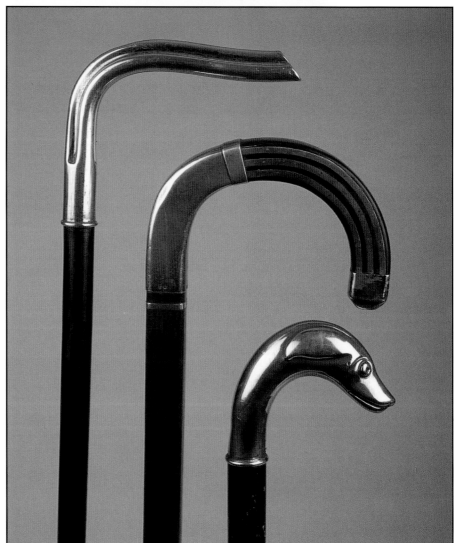

Three silver Art Deco era canes (c. 1925-1935+): an L-shaped handle, crook handle, and a dog figural handle. Silver handles are generally on black shafts. The square shaft is snakewood, which is very heavy and durable. All examples shown are sterling or 800 silver. *Courtesy of Richard R. Wagner, Jr.* These canes range in value from $300 to $500.

Tiffany canes, both marked "Tiffany & Co. 18K": crook handle, 18k gold collar on snakewood. Overall length: 35". $400-600. Silver L handle (came in at least two sizes), dark wood shaft. Overall length: 35-1/2". $1100-1300, the larger example is valued a little higher. *Courtesy of Richard R. Wagner, Jr.*

Art Deco silver and wood handle, the upper portion of the handle is octagonal and is overlaid with silver in alternating panels, the very top coming to a peak. Mahogany shaft with 1" horn ferrule, c. 1925. Handle: 2-3/4" h. x 1-1/2" w. at widest. Overall length: 35-1/4". *Courtesy of The World of the Walking Stick.* $1200-1320.

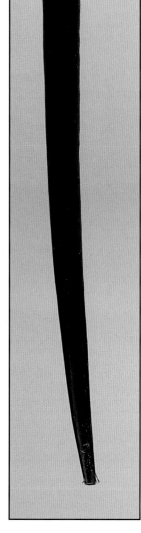

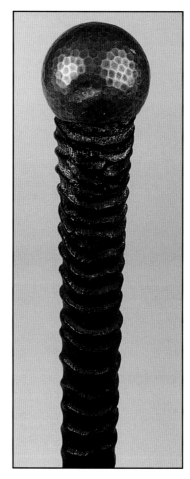

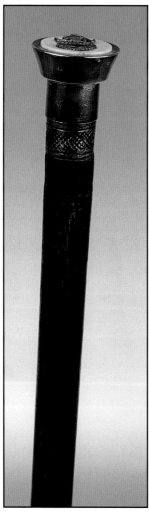

Left and above:
Ibex horn cane shaft with hammered silver ball handle. The tip of the horn is cut off to form the base of the shaft. Overall length: 32". *Courtesy of Dale Van Atta.* $260-285.

Above and right:
United States Navy silver handled cane featuring anchor and "USN" initials insignia on top, possibly the cane of a Chief Petty Officer. Short metal ferrule. Overall length: 33-1/2". *Courtesy of Ambassador Richard W. Carlson.* $310-340.

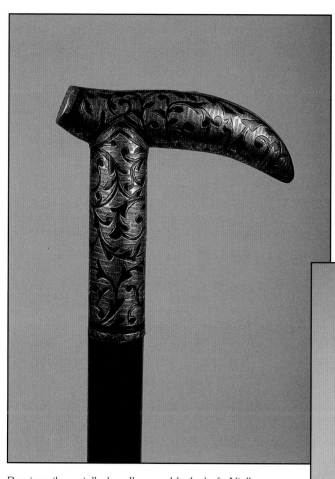

Russian silver niello handle on a black shaft. Niello work, which was done in Russia and France predominately, was produced by making patterns in the silver that were inlaid with copper and lead. Much workmanship was involved in successfully executed handles. *Courtesy of Richard R. Wagner, Jr.* $700-900.

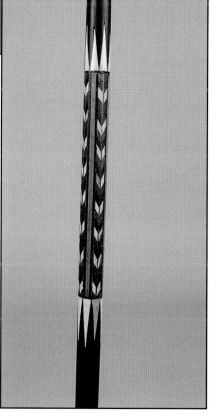

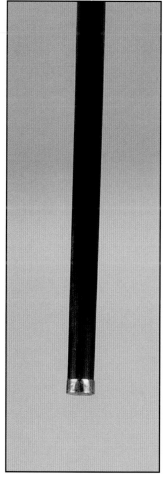

Above and right:
Copper handle, ornately molded, on cane with an inlaid wood shaft and tiny copper ferrule. Handle: 1-1/2" l. Overall length: 35-1/2". *Courtesy of Ambassador Richard W. Carlson.* $360-400.

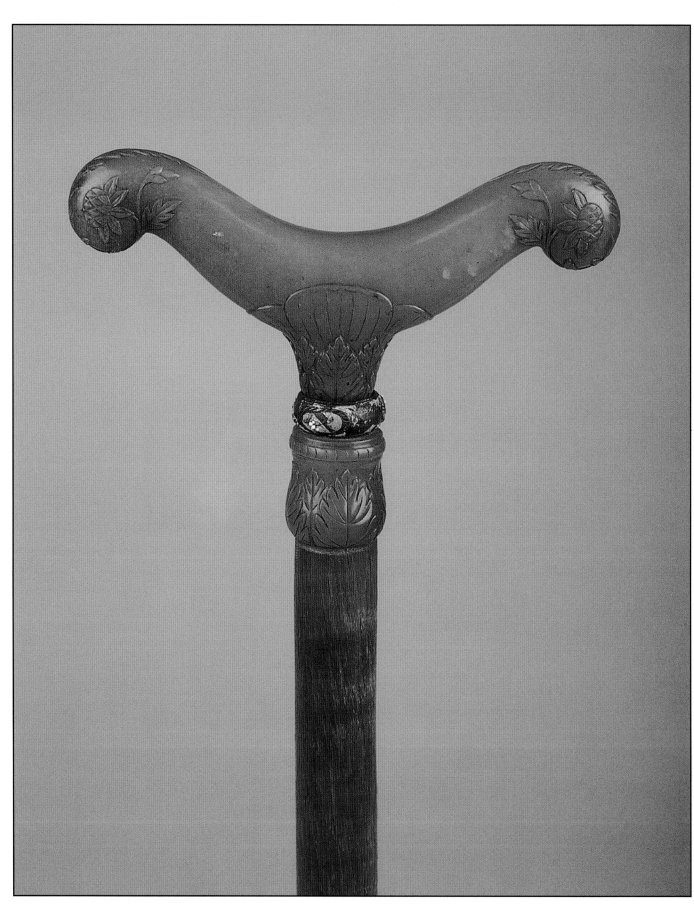

Jade, light green crutch handle carved with flowers. This is an eighteenth century example from Mogul India, featuring a metal band with remnants of enameling and a shaft made of Indian rhino horn. *Courtesy of Richard R. Wagner, Jr.* $5000-7000.

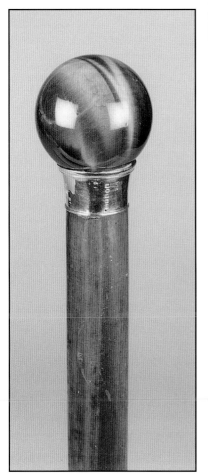

Patterned Tiger's Eye ball handle, 18k gold collar, hallmarked –
London, 1868 and stamped with the initials HS. Malacca shaft with
3/4" black horn ferrule, English. Handle: 1-3/4" d. Overall length:
38". *Courtesy of The World of the Walking Stick.* $995-1095.

Right and above right:
Multicolored agate ball handle with a detailed one-
piece cameo carving of the head of a Roman
Legionnaire on top. Silver collar, partridge wood
shaft with 5/8" metal ferrule. Late nineteenth century.
Handle: 1-1/2" d. Overall length: 35-7/8". *Courtesy of
The World of the Walking Stick.* $1550-1705.

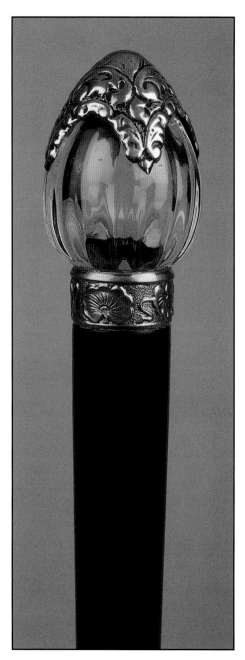

Egg shaped carved rock crystal and silver handle on an ebony shaft. This dress cane is also called a "jeweled cane." *Courtesy of Richard R. Wagner, Jr.* $700-1200.

Clear rock crystal short straight support handle. 18k hallmarked gold collar, stamped "Brigg 7 Charles Street, Berkeley Square" on back and "Ione May 23, 1906" on the front. Figured ebony shaft with 1-1/8" light colored horn ferrule, English. Handle: 1-1/2" h. x 1-1/4" at widest. Overall length: 36-3/4". *Courtesy of The World of the Walking Stick.* $1500-1650.

Blue disk glass handled cane, no ferrule. Silver collar. Handle: 2-3/4" d. x 3" h. Overall length: 38". *Courtesy of Ambassador Richard W. Carlson.* $275-300.

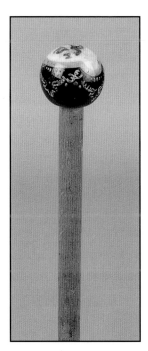

Ceramic ball handled cane with overglaze decoration, thin shaft. Handle: 1-1/4" d. Overall length: 34-1/2". *Courtesy of Ambassador Richard W. Carlson.* $225-250.

Cloisonné handles. From left: L-shaped cloisonné handled walking stick. Handle: 3-1/2" h. x 4" w. Overall length: 34". Round knob handle on black wood shaft. Handle: 3-1/4" h. Overall length: 38". Tapering handle on dark wood shaft. Handle: 3-1/4" h. Overall length: 34-1/4". *Courtesy of Richard R. Wagner, Jr.* $400-600 each.

Decorative enameled handle ringed with marked metal band and topped with an impressive, large cabochon rose quartz. Malacca shaft, black horn ferrule. Handle: 2-1/2" x 1". Overall length: 35-1/2". *Courtesy of Kimball M. Sterling Auctioneers.* $1300-1600.

Pale green guilloche enamel elongated mushroom handle with silver bands at the top and bottom. The silver is bottom stamped "925" and hallmarked. Also stamped with import marks, figured ebony shaft with 1-1/2" black horn ferrule, c. 1906. This piece was imported from the Continent to London by Asprey. Handle: 2-1/4" h. x 1-1/4" at widest. Overall length: 36". *Courtesy of The World of the Walking Stick.* $1250-1375.

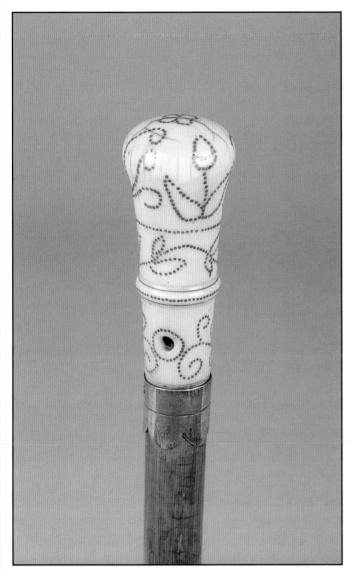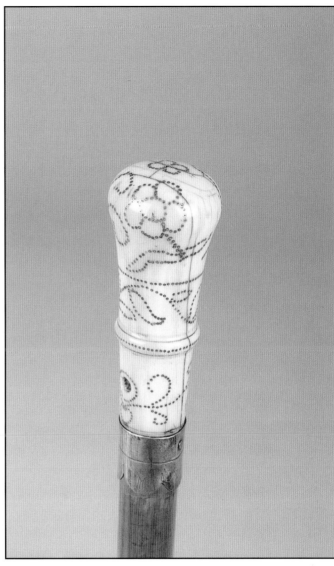

English ivory pique handle decorated with floral silver inlay and period eyelet
holes. 1" silver collar, malacca shaft. Handle: 3-3/4" h. x 1-5/8" at its widest. Overall
length: 35-1/2". *Courtesy of The World of the Walking Stick.* $3525-3880.

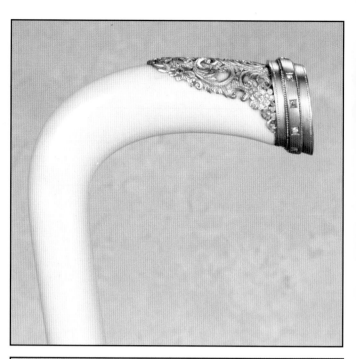

Complete with its own carrying case, this truly elegant all-ivory cane detailed with gold and diamonds was sure to turn heads when worn. The cane was created from a single piece of elephant tusk, its L-shaped handle capped with a 2" long 18k gold mount engraved with a starburst containing a mine-cut 1/4 karat diamond in its center. The raised ring around the cap is inlaid with ten small rose cut diamonds. A gold sleeve with "C" scrolls and flowers completes the end cap. The shaft is carved with simulated thorns and ends with a 1-1/4" bronze and iron ferrule. The tag within the case indicates that this cane was sold in Uruguay, although it likely was manufactured in Continental Europe and purchased by A. Rossello for sale. Handle: 3-1/2" x 1". Overall length: 33-3/4". *Courtesy of Henry A. Taron, Tradewinds Antiques.* $12,000-15,000.

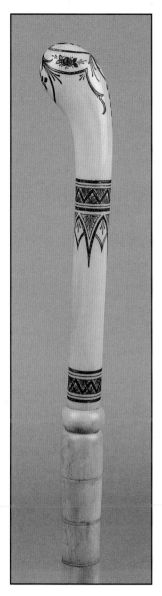

Heavy ivory pistol grip handle, segmented shaft ivory cane, incised and inked design on handle. Overall length: 33-1/2". *Courtesy of Ambassador Richard W. Carlson.* $425-470.

Three canes dating from c. 1800: an elephant ivory knob handle and two stag horn handles. Elephant ivory knob handle, silver mounted eyelet and collar, spiny branch shaft, brass ferrule measuring 2" long. Overall length: 33". Stag horn handle, bamboo shaft, 3-3/4" long ferrule, Overall length: 35-1/2". Stag horn with spine, brass eyelets and ferrule, the ferrule measuring 2-1/2" long. Shaft twisted by vine. Overall length: 37". *Courtesy of Richard R. Wagner, Jr.* $300-400 each.

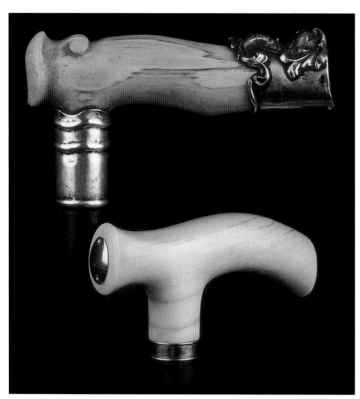

Metal mounted ivory handles: these are more desirable and expensive than many plain ivory handles. *Courtesy of Richard R. Wagner, Jr.* The silver mounted example has a dolphin on the handle and an ebony shaft, and ranges in value from $400 to $700, depending on the silver work. The mounted 18k gold example on a snakewood shaft is by Tiffany, $700-900.

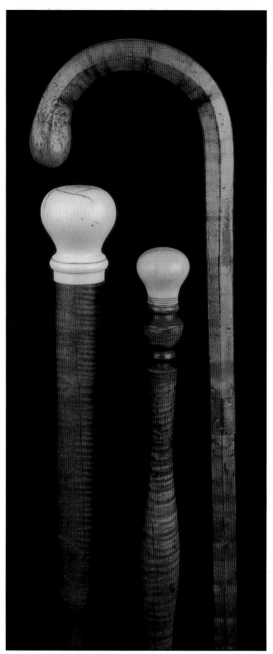

Decorated knob handle cane with reddish wood shaft, black slim collar, and small metal ferrule. Handle: 2-3/4" l. Overall length: 35-1/2". *Courtesy of Ambassador Richard W. Carlson.* $200-220.

Tiger maple canes were, at times, carved by Kentucky rifle makers; the heavier the striping, the more valuable the wood. There is confusion differentiating tiger maple and satinwood. Satinwood has a greater translucence of depth and a higher sheen. Large ivory knob handle: 2-1/4" h. x 1-7/8" d. Shaft diameter: 1-3/8". Long ferrule: 2-1/4". Hudson River walking staff with a small ivory top. Hexagonal-shaped crook handle, tiger maple with a silver collar, on some of the flat panels you see bird's-eye patterning and on others you see tiger maple patterning. *Courtesy of Richard R. Wagner, Jr.* Massive example: $400-600. Smaller example: $200-300.

Bone L-shaped handle with silver collar, black shaft, and short ferrule. Handle: 3-1/4" l. x 2" h. Overall length: 35-1/2". *Courtesy of Ambassador Richard W. Carlson.* $325-360.

Horn canes: segmented shafts on steel rods; steer's horn canes were produced in the U.S., England, and the Middle East. The example with the dots is from the Middle East. *Courtesy of Richard R. Wagner, Jr.* Generally worth $150-300 each based on quality and condition.

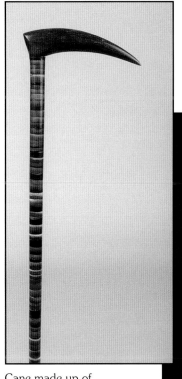

Cane made up of segmented horn, metal rod center. Handle: 4-1/2". Overall length: 35-1/2". *Courtesy of Ambassador Richard W. Carlson.* $150-300.

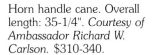

Horn handle cane. Overall length: 35-1/4". *Courtesy of Ambassador Richard W. Carlson.* $310-340.

Three antler handled canes. The cane with the stepped malacca shaft has eyelets. The silver plaque on center handle reads "Southwick." Overall lengths, left to right: 36-1/2", 36", and 34". *Courtesy of Ron Van Anda and Sandra Whitson.* $600-850 each.

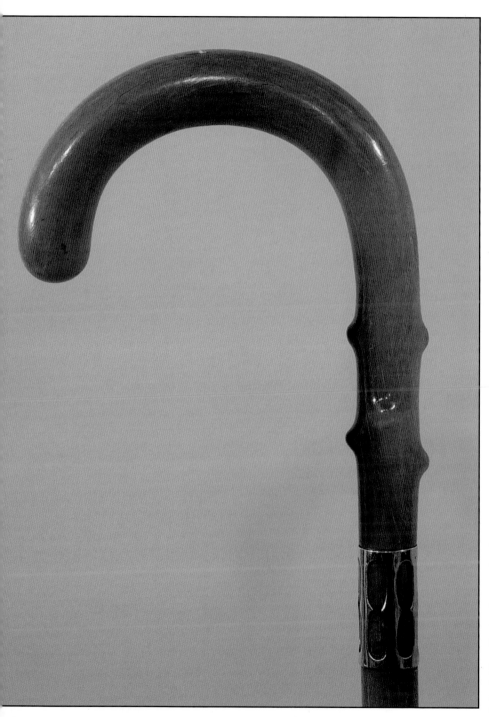

Large tooth handle with silver fittings and British hallmarks, malacca shaft, and a brass ferrule with iron tip. Handle: 4-1/2" w. Overall length: 38". *Courtesy of Ambassador Richard W. Carlson.* $675-745.

Single piece rhino horn cane with a crutch handle sporting faux twig spurs above the decorative gold collar. The shaft is finished with a gold and steel ferrule. Handle: 4-3/4" x 4". Collar: 1-1/2". Ferrule: 2". Overall length: 35". *Courtesy of Kimball M. Sterling Auctioneers.* $1400-1700.

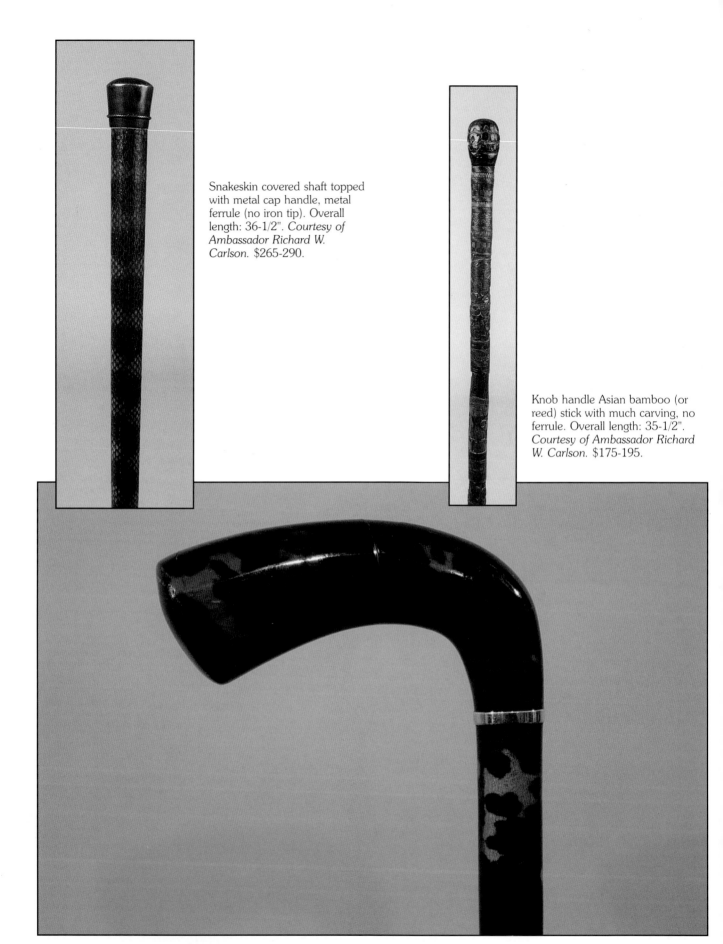

Snakeskin covered shaft topped with metal cap handle, metal ferrule (no iron tip). Overall length: 36-1/2". *Courtesy of Ambassador Richard W. Carlson.* $265-290.

Knob handle Asian bamboo (or reed) stick with much carving, no ferrule. Overall length: 35-1/2". *Courtesy of Ambassador Richard W. Carlson.* $175-195.

Highly figured tortoiseshell cane with modified pistol grip handle, narrow gold collar, and black horn ferrule. This is an elegant walking stick. Handle: 4-1/4" x 1-3/4". Overall length: 34-1/2". *Courtesy of Kimball M. Sterling Auctioneers.* $1200-1500.

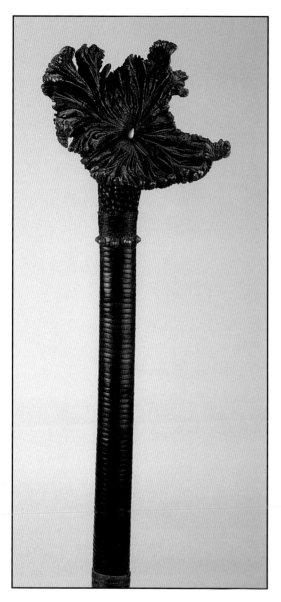

Above and right:
Tobacco handle cane with a tooth in the center of the handle. This unusual cane has a triangular shaft, leather wrap below the handle. Brass ferrule. Overall length: 37-1/2". *Courtesy of Dale Van Atta.* $250-275.

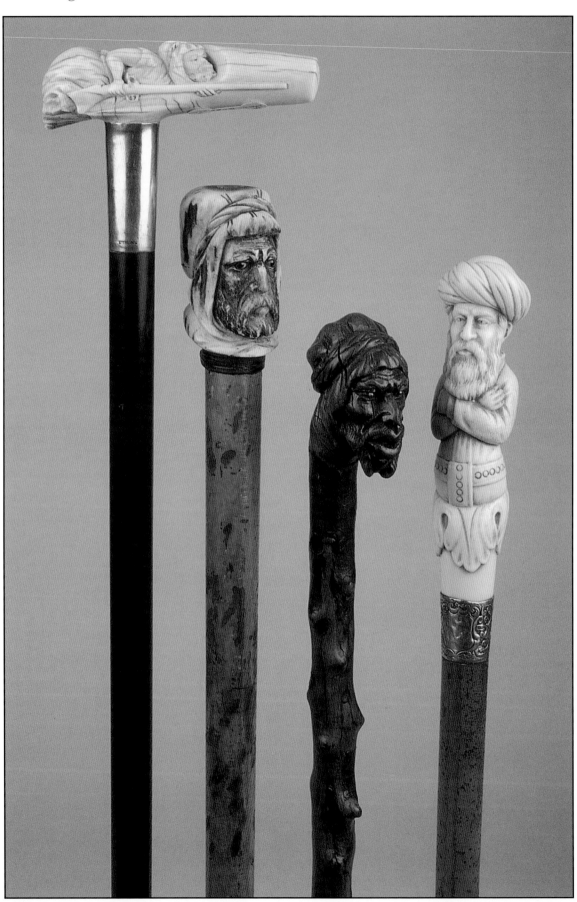

Opposite page:
We will begin our exploration of handles with figures by looking at the human form, a subject we all find endlessly fascinating by nature. Shown here are four Arabs: One in wood, three in horn/ivory. Elephant ivory L-shaped handle featuring an Arab with a rifle, on a snakewood shaft, silver mounted, $2000-2500. Stag horn with rare glass eyes with three colors in center, $900-1100. Wood: $600-700. Arab Mullah (religious person) carved in elephant ivory, silver mounted, malacca stick, $2000-2500. *Courtesy of Richard R. Wagner, Jr.*

Carved ivory Arab's head. Silver collar, oak shaft, late nineteenth century. Handle: 2" h. x 2" d. Overall length: 35-3/4". *Courtesy of The World of the Walking Stick.* $1140-1255.

Continental cane of the mid-nineteenth century featuring a detailed figural of a young girl with a fan. The cane has an ebony shaft with faux twig spurs, and a bimetal ferrule. Handle: 4-1/4" l. Overall length: 36-1/2". *Courtesy of Kimball M. Sterling Auctioneers.* $900-1200.

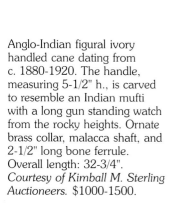

Anglo-Indian figural ivory handled cane dating from c. 1880-1920. The handle, measuring 5-1/2" h., is carved to resemble an Indian mufti with a long gun standing watch from the rocky heights. Ornate brass collar, malacca shaft, and 2-1/2" long bone ferrule. Overall length: 32-3/4". *Courtesy of Kimball M. Sterling Auctioneers.* $1000-1500.

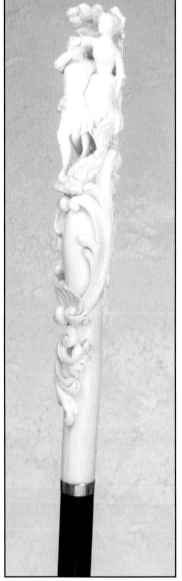

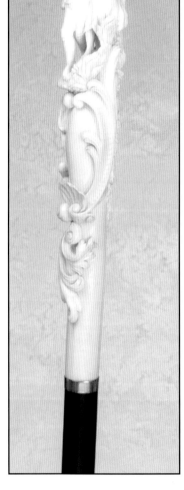

This is exquisite relief carving on an elephant ivory handle, depicting a pair of eighteenth century lovers. This is probably German work dating from c. 1890. The gallant man kisses his lady's hand in a woodland setting. The detail of the clothing, faces, the hilt of the man's sword, and their surroundings is very high quality work. The 1/4" silver collar bears the maker's initials. The shaft is ebonized hardwood finished with a horn ferrule that is worn from use. Handle: 10-1/2" x 1-3/4". Overall length: 36". *Courtesy of Henry A. Taron, Tradewinds Antiques.* $6000-8000.

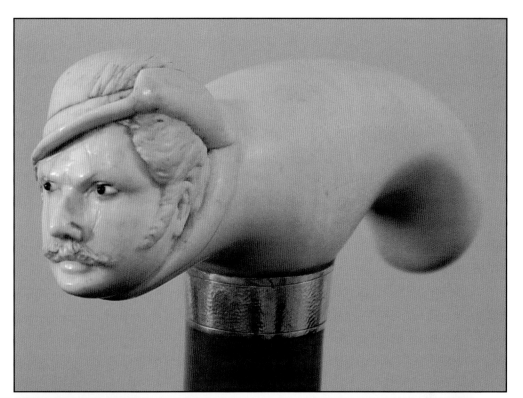

German eighteenth century tau-shaped ivory handle in the Biedermeier style. The man's head features glass eyes with two colors and a Tyrolean hat. This cane has a stippled silver collar, honey-toned full bark malacca shaft, and a horn ferrule. Handle: 5" x 1-3/4". Overall length: 35-1/8". *Courtesy of Kimball M. Sterling Auctioneers.* $1300-1800.

Three ivory handled canes with carved ladies. Lady Liberty on an L-shaped handle became popular when the French gave the United States the Statue of Liberty in the nineteenth century. The smaller cane with the bust has an elephant ivory handle mounted on a partridge wood shaft. Small ladies handle: 2-3/4" h. x 1-1/4" w.; Lady liberty handle: 4" h. x 3" w.; large ivory handle: 2-1/4" h. x 1-1/2" d. *Courtesy of Richard R. Wagner, Jr.* Smaller handles are valued at around $500. Large handle are valued in the $1200-1500 range.

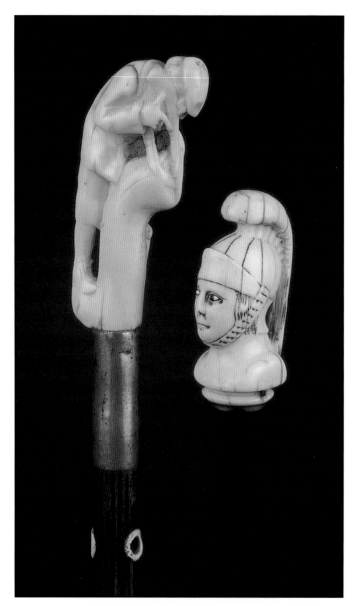

Military and hunting motifs were popular. Hunter handle with hunter aiming rifle downward, on a zebrawood shaft. Hunter handle: 3-1/4" h. x 1-1/2" w. Centurion handle with very human glass eyes mounted on a rosewood shaft. Centurion handle: 2-1/2" h. x 1-1/4" w. *Courtesy of Richard R. Wagner, Jr.* $900-1200 each.

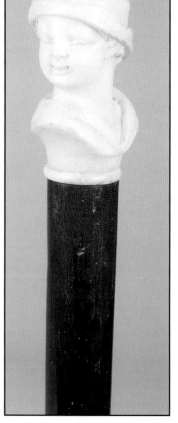

Carved ivory head of a child in profile wearing a stocking cap. Ivory collar, Maccassar shaft with metal ferrule, probably Continental, late nineteenth century. Handle: 2-1/2" h. x 1-1/2" w. at widest point x 1-1/4" d. Overall length: 35-1/4". *Courtesy of The World of the Walking Stick.* $1275-1400.

Right:
Ivory handle, man in cap with inset eyelets, metal ferrule, from New York State. Overall length: 32-1/4". *Courtesy of Ambassador Richard W. Carlson.* $625-690.

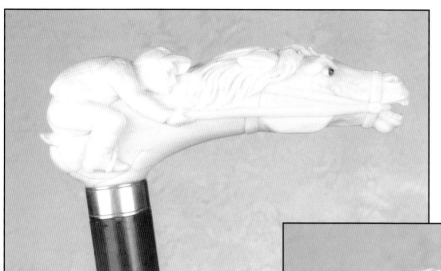

Left and below:
Ivory handle carved in the form of a jockey riding a horse at full gallop. The handle is elephant ivory and the horse has yellow glass eyes. The silver collar measures 1/2". The shaft is full bark malacca tipped with a 1-1/2" metal and iron ferrule. This is most likely an American cane dating from roughly 1870. Handle: 1-3/4" x 5-1/2". Overall length: 33-7/8". *Courtesy of Henry A. Taron, Tradewinds Antiques.* $3500-4500.

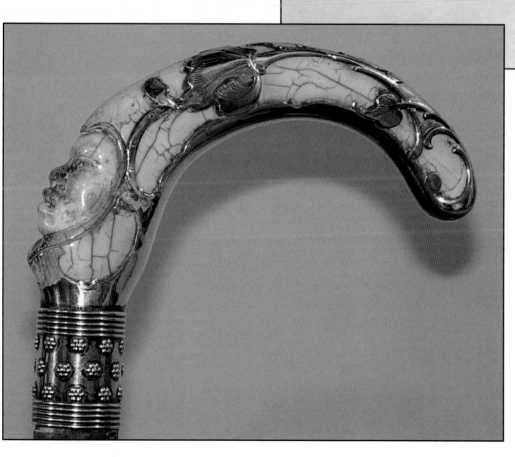

Ivory and silver handled cane, probably American, c. 1900, featuring the carving of a black man's face on one side of the handle. Silver chasing surrounds the rest of the ivory handle. Decorated silver collar, scarred shaft, and bimetal ferrule. Handle: 4-1/4" x 2-1/2". Overall length: 35-1/3". *Courtesy of Kimball M. Sterling Auctioneers.* $700-900.

This 2" tall figural gutta-percha handle (also produced in brass and silver handles) represents Dr. Syntax. The shaft is palm wood and the joint between the handle and shaft is covered with a brass collar. Overall length: 35-1/2".

William Gilpin (1724-1804), an English clergyman from Hampshire, toured the English countryside and wrote a series of books on scenery, illustrating them with aquatints. So popular was his work that he sparked the "cult of the picturesque" in England, which led to an avalanche of similarly illustrated scenic tomes. However, whenever a popular movement is inspired, someone is equally inspired to lampoon it. Thomas Rowlandson (1756-1827) wrote and illustrated the satirical adventures known as *The Tours of Dr. Syntax,* which quickly gained national attention. Determined to study the landscape, Dr. Syntax has a series of misadventures and in his single-mindeness misses much going on around him. *Courtesy of Richard R. Wagner, Jr.* $300-400.

Large porcelain handle manufactured during the mid-nineteenth century by KPM of Berlin, portraying a child with large ruffled collar and black broad-brimmed naval hat, the bust set upon a polychrome decorated, gilded plinth. Gold collar, ebony shaft, and black horn ferrule. Overall length: 38". *Courtesy of Kimball M. Sterling Auctioneers.* $1400-1800.

Porcelain handle by KPM, mid-nineteenth century, featuring the head of a woman wearing a bandana. Gold collar, rosewood shaft, horn ferrule. Handle: 2" x 2". Overall length: 35-3/4". *Courtesy of Kimball M. Sterling Auctioneers.* $1000-1200.

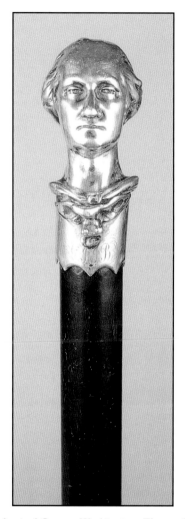

Silver bust of George Washington. Ebony shaft with 1-3/8" metal ferrule, late nineteenth century. Handle: 2-3/4" h. x 1-3/8" w. x 1-3/8" d. with the initials L.L.R. on the front and the initials J.L.N. on the back. Overall length: 34-1/4". *Courtesy of The World of the Walking Stick.* $1550-1705.

Large figural Art Nouveau tau-shaped silver handle in the form of a cherub resting on the head of a lion and decorated with leaves and foliage. Bamboo shaft with brass ferrule, Continental, c. 1890. Handle: 2-3/4" h. x 4-3/4" l. Overall length: 36-1/2" h. *Courtesy of The World of the Walking Stick.* $1500-1650.

Left and below:
Rhino horn: crook with simulated bamboo carving on multi-colored wood (rosewood). Overall length: 35" Carved figural Hindu deity. Overall length: 36". *Courtesy of Richard R. Wagner, Jr.* Rhino horn: $300-400. Hindu deity: $600-800.

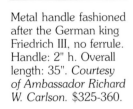

Metal handle fashioned after the German king Friedrich III, no ferrule. Handle: 2" h. Overall length: 35". *Courtesy of Ambassador Richard W. Carlson.* $325-360.

Metal handled cane with a man smoking a cigar and wearing cap. This cane has a boot for the ferrule, made of the same metal as the handle. Overall length: 33-1/4". *Courtesy of Ambassador Richard W. Carlson.* $325-360.

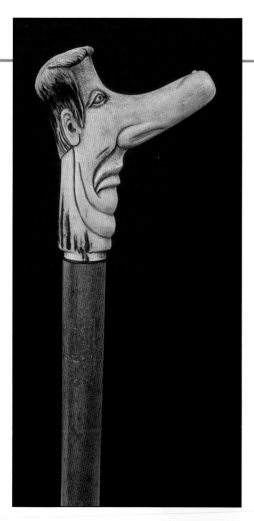

Comic face carved into an antler horn on a malacca shaft over a bone ferrule. Handle: 4" l. Overall length: 36". *Courtesy of Ambassador Richard W. Carlson.* $425-470.

Red knob handle with Asian faces, eyelets, very thin collar (white), horn ferrule. Handle: 1-3/4" d. Overall length: 35-1/2". *Courtesy of Ambassador Richard W. Carlson.* $300-330.

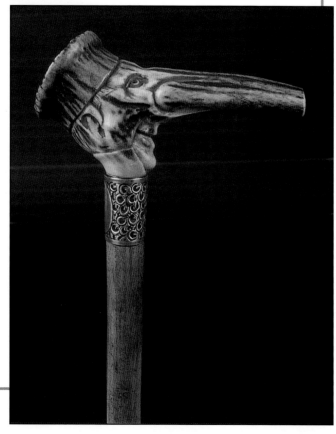

Face carved from an antler with the base of antler as a hat, silver collar with an empty oval ready to receive a presentation inscription or a monogram, metal ferrule with iron tip. Handle: 3" h. x 6-1/2" l. Overall length: 34-1/2". *Courtesy of Ambassador Richard W. Carlson.* $475-525.

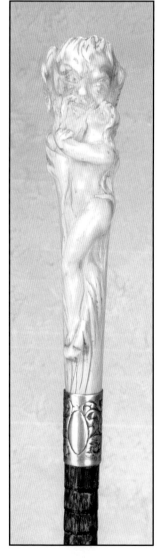

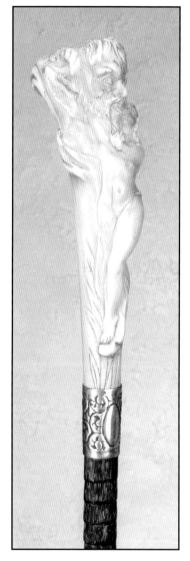

Erotic ivory handle cane carved with a nude and Satan. The elephant ivory handle is carved with a leering, horned devil complete with pointed ears and wagging tongue. The nude woman's arms encircle the demonic head. A decorated silver collar complete with empty cartouche measuring 1-1/4" covers the joint between the handle and the stepped partridgewood shaft. This is most likely a Continental cane produced around 1860. Handle: 5-3/4" x 1-3/4". Overall length: 36-1/4". *Courtesy of Henry A. Taron, Tradewinds Antiques.* While the estimated value for this cane was $2500-3500, the final auction sale price exceeded $5000 in 2003.

Red coral cane handle, possibly originating in Italy, c. 1890, relief carved with the head of Pan above a classic amphora surrounded by foliate and classical designs. Thin gold collar, light malacca shaft, and metal ferrule. Handle: 1-5/8" h. Overall length: 34-3/4". *Courtesy of Kimball M. Sterling Auctioneers.* $1400-1600.

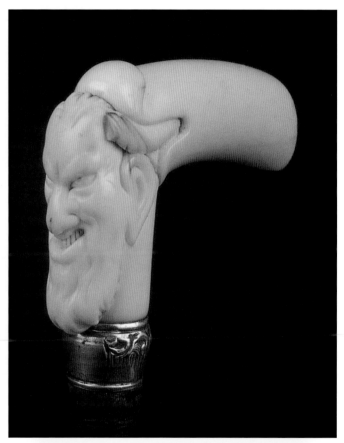

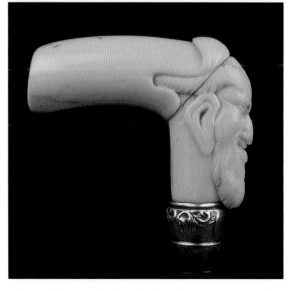

Walrus ivory devil or satyr handle with silver mounts on a bamboo shaft. This motif is not often seen but is very desirable. Handle: 2-3/4" h. x 3-1/2" w. *Courtesy of Richard R. Wagner, Jr.* $700-1200.

Bone clasped hands handle with silver collar and studs inset in wood below. Metal ferrule with iron tip. Bone handle: 2-1/4" l. Overall length: 35". *Courtesy of Ambassador Richard W. Carlson.* $725-800.

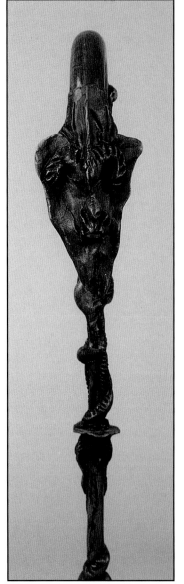

Spooky American folk art cane from New Orleans with crook handle and applied material making faces and snakes down the shaft and at the handle tip—perfect for Mardi Gras celebrations it would seem. There is no metal ferrule, just an upside down face. The shaft below the wood crook handle is metal covered with the molded material forming the decorations. There could be something malevolently magical about this stick. Overall length: 35-1/4". *Courtesy of Ambassador Richard W. Carlson.* $750-825.

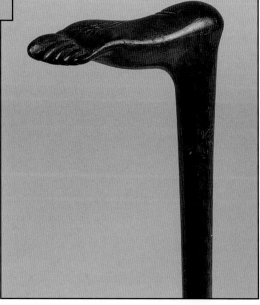

Carved foot serves as handle for this single piece cane with a horn ferrule. Overall length: 36". *Courtesy of Ambassador Richard W. Carlson.* $275-300.

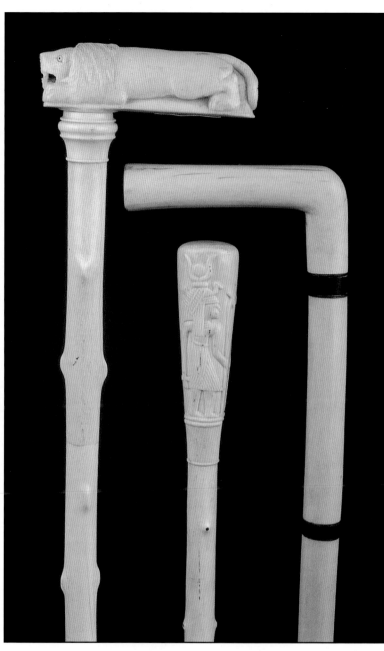

Now, we'll transition from human forms to animal figures on handles. Here are three segmented ivory, primarily Anglo-Indian canes, one in an Egyptian motif. The black banding is generally buffalo horn. One example has a lion, one is plain, and one features the Egyptian motif. *Courtesy of Richard R. Wagner, Jr.* $800-1200 each.

Moving down the ladder from man to monkey figural stained ivory handle carved as a monkey in a top hat, bearing the inscription "CHEEKY MONKEY" across the base. Dated 1875, this piece is believed to be political, referring to India seeking independence from Great Britain. Mahogany shaft, black horn ferrule. Handle: 4-3/4" x 1-1/4". Overall length: 35-3/4". *Courtesy of Kimball M. Sterling Auctioneers.* $1500-2000.

Four carved wooden dog handles. Two factors affect the value of all figured handles: 1) how well they are carved (how representational they are of the subject depicted); 2) all such canes carved from one piece of material are worth more. The bulldog is carved with horn. All have glass eyes. Occasionally these items are signed, which increases the value. *Courtesy of Richard R. Wagner, Jr.* $300-600 each.

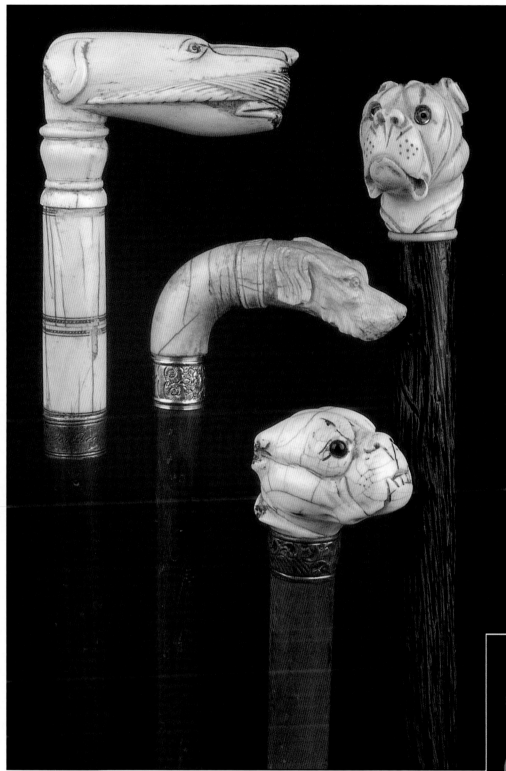

Carved ivory dogs: two bulldogs, two hunting dogs—one with a pheasant in his mouth (this is a common motif). Large deco dog with pheasant handle: 4-3/4" h. x 3-1/4" w.. Crook handle: 1-1/2" h. x 3-1/2" w. Larger bulldog handle: 1-3/4" h. x 2-1/4" w. Smaller bulldog with uplifted ears: 2" h. x 1-7/8" w. *Courtesy of Richard R. Wagner, Jr.* Value in ivory is dependent on the size of the ivory and quality and extent of the carving. These range from $400-650.

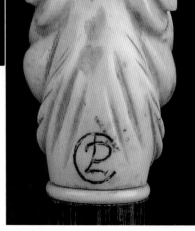

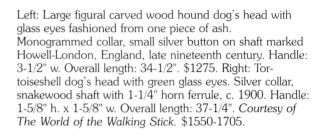

Left: Large figural carved wood hound dog's head with glass eyes fashioned from one piece of ash. Monogrammed collar, small silver button on shaft marked Howell-London, England, late nineteenth century. Handle: 3-1/2" w. Overall length: 34-1/2". $1275. Right: Tortoiseshell dog's head with green glass eyes. Silver collar, snakewood shaft with 1-1/4" horn ferrule, c. 1900. Handle: 1-5/8" h. x 1-5/8" w. Overall length: 37-1/4". *Courtesy of The World of the Walking Stick.* $1550-1705.

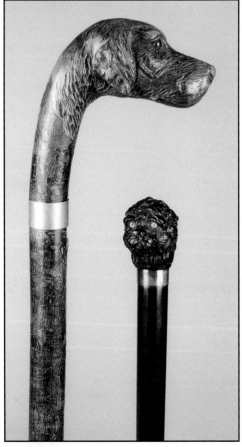

Left and below:
Carved wood dog's head with large glass eyes. Small ivory collar, hardwood shaft with 1-1/8" ivory ferrule, late nineteenth century. Handle: 3-3/4" h. x 2-3/4" d. x 2" w. Overall length: 37-1/4". *Courtesy of The World of the Walking Stick.* $475-525.

Left: Silver crook handle with dog's head at the end of the crook. The handle is hallmarked. Malacca shaft with 1-1/2" light colored horn ferrule, c. 1900. Handle: 4-1/2" x 3-5/8" h. Overall length: 36". *Courtesy of The World of the Walking Stick.* $875. Right: Crook handle walnut cane with 5/8" worn metal ferrule. Mounted on the end of the crook is a hall-marked and monogrammed silver end piece in the form of the familiar man in the moon crescent. On the shaft is a decorative silver plaque with a man and woman kissing beneath the benignly smiling moon, c. 1900. Overall length: 36-1/2". *Courtesy of The World of the Walking Stick.* $975-1075.

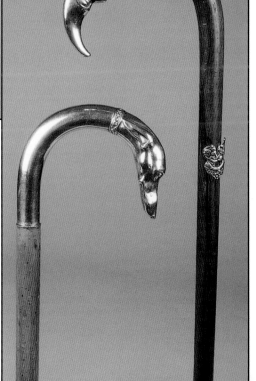

Carved wood handle in the form of two puppies sitting together, both with glass eyes. Mahogany shaft with 7/8" metal ferrule, late nineteenth century. Handle: 3-1/2" h. x 2-1/4" w. Overall length: 35-3/4". *Courtesy of The World of the Walking Stick.* $1650.

Left: Half crook handle with a sterling silver fox mounted at the
end of the crook, the fox has red eyes. Silver collar around
fox's neck is decorated with oak leaves and acorns, hallmarked,
hardwood shaft with 1-1/8" bullet-type metal ferrule, c. 1900.
Overall length: 35-5/8". *Courtesy of The World of the Walking
Stick.* $660-725. Right: L-shaped cane fashioned from one
piece of stepped partridge wood with a 1" metal ferrule.
Mounted at the end of the cane is a beautifully modeled silver
dog with red eyes and a bowtie, hallmarked. Possibly French,
c. 1900. Handle: 1-1/2" l. x 1" h. Overall length: 35". *Courtesy
of The World of the Walking Stick.* $925-1020.

Crook handled bone dog handle cane with collar.
Overall length: 35-1/2". *Courtesy of Ambassador
Richard W. Carlson.* $275-300.

Horn handle with dog's head and applied eyes, horn ferrule. Tau-shaped staghorn handle depicting bulldog with glass eyes emerging from log. Silver collar with German hallmarks and stamped 800. Stepped hardwood shaft with a 1-1/2" blond horn ferrule, German, late nineteenth century. Handle: 4" l. x 1-3/4" h. Overall length: 33". *Courtesy of The World of the Walking Stick.* $350-385.

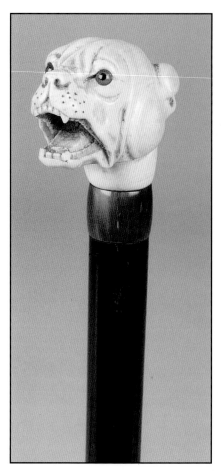

Carved ivory snarling dog's head with glass eyes, barrel-shaped horn collar, ebony shaft with 1-1/8" horn ferrule, late nineteenth century. Overall length: 32". *Courtesy of The World of the Walking Stick.* $1600-1760.

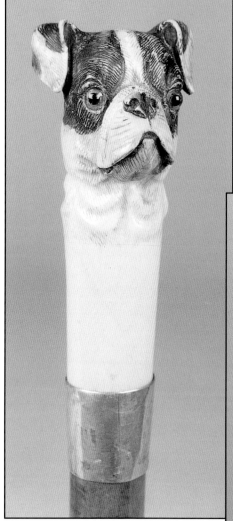

Above and right:
Ivory Boston terrier (?) handle with glass eyes, silver color marked with initials on back, A.C.W., malacca shaft, horn ferrule. Overall length: 34-1/2". *Courtesy of The World of the Walking Stick.* $2300-2530.

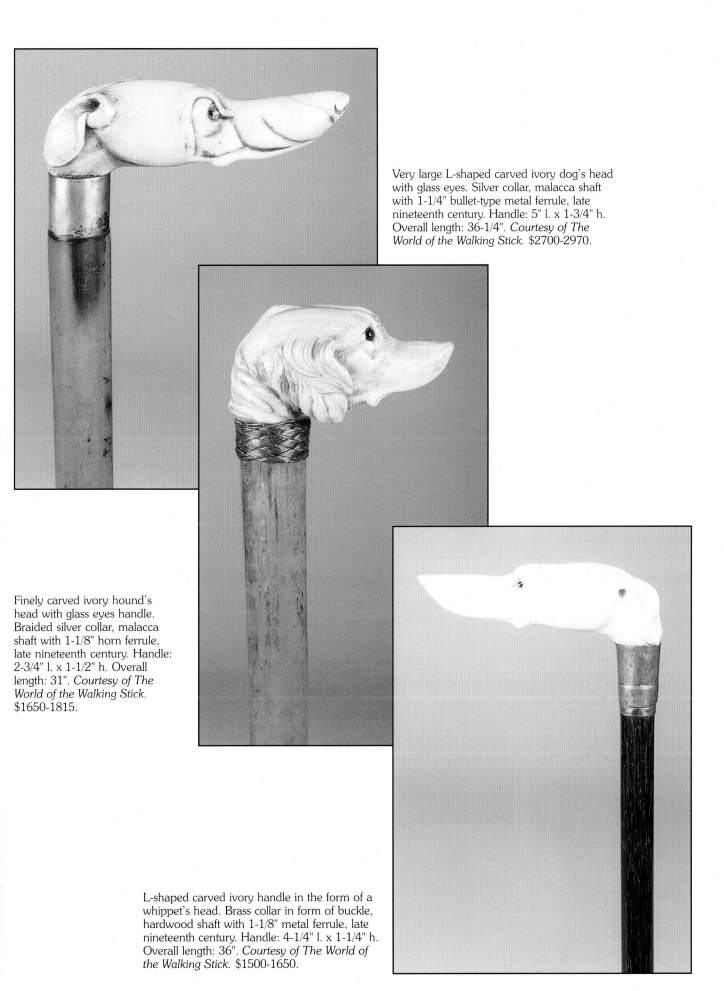

Very large L-shaped carved ivory dog's head with glass eyes. Silver collar, malacca shaft with 1-1/4" bullet-type metal ferrule, late nineteenth century. Handle: 5" l. x 1-3/4" h. Overall length: 36-1/4". *Courtesy of The World of the Walking Stick.* $2700-2970.

Finely carved ivory hound's head with glass eyes handle. Braided silver collar, malacca shaft with 1-1/8" horn ferrule, late nineteenth century. Handle: 2-3/4" l. x 1-1/2" h. Overall length: 31". *Courtesy of The World of the Walking Stick.* $1650-1815.

L-shaped carved ivory handle in the form of a whippet's head. Brass collar in form of buckle, hardwood shaft with 1-1/8" metal ferrule, late nineteenth century. Handle: 4-1/4" l. x 1-1/4" h. Overall length: 36". *Courtesy of The World of the Walking Stick.* $1500-1650.

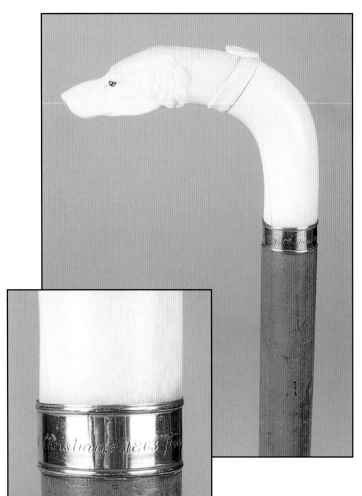

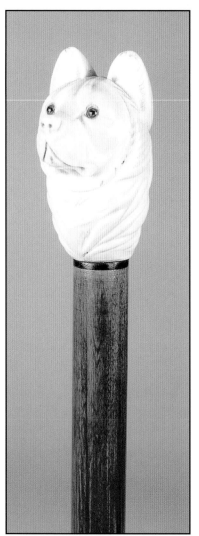

Carved ivory dog's head with pointed ears and glass eyes. Small black wood collar, hardwood shaft with 1-5/8" horn ferrule, late nineteenth century. Handle: 3" h. x 2-1/8" at its widest. Overall length: 35-1/2". *Courtesy of The World of the Walking Stick.* $1750-1925.

Semi-crook carved ivory floppy-eared dog's head with ivory collar and glass eyes. There are age lines on the ivory. Gold collar engraved "Geo. G. Coffey, Christmas 1863 to J.W.C.", malacca shaft with 1-3/4" metal ferrule, American. Handle: 3" h. x 4-1/4" l. x 1" d. Overall length: 35". *Courtesy of The World of the Walking Stick.* $895-985.

Right:
Tau-shaped carved ivory in shape of reclining dog on a dried wood log with its head resting on its front paws. Silver collar with English hallmarks, monogrammed WSB, amber color full bark malacca shaft with 1-1/2" metal ferrule, late nineteenth century. Handle: 5-1/2" l. x 1-1/2". Overall length: 36-1/2". *Courtesy of The World of the Walking Stick.* $1975-2175.

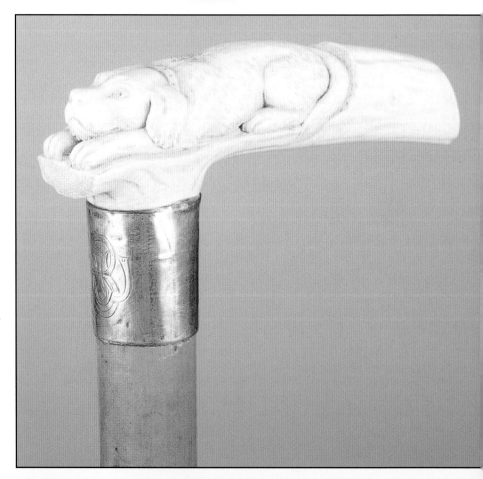

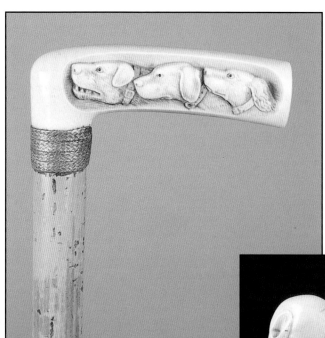

L-shaped ivory handle with relief carvings of three different dogs' heads on the left side. Each dog's head has inlaid black eyes. Coiled copper-colored collar, malacca shaft with 7/8" brass ferrule, late nineteenth century. Handle: 4-1/2" l. x 1-5/8" h. Overall length: 33-1/4". *Courtesy of The World of the Walking Stick.* $1350-1485.

Ivory handle dog's head with tongue hanging out, silver collar, metal ferrule. Handle: 4" l. Overall length: 35-1/2". This is an unusual, beautiful, and playful piece of work. *Courtesy of Ambassador Richard W. Carlson.* $1100-1210.

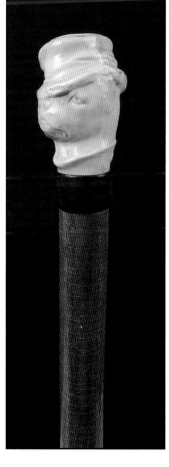

Composite molded light material handle with mold seam visible forming head of dog wearing a hat, malacca shaft, leather collar, bone ferrule. Overall length: 35". *Courtesy of Ambassador Richard W. Carlson.* $375-415.

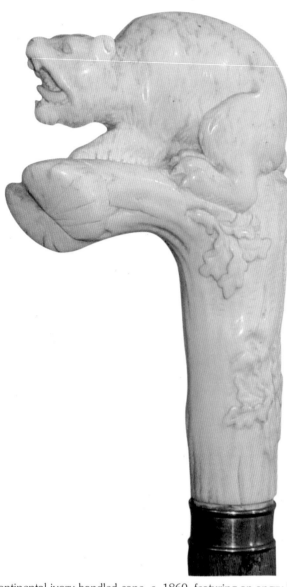

Continental ivory handled cane, c. 1860, featuring an angry bear on a branch. Brass collar, hardwood shaft with twig spurs, and worn bone ferrule. Handle: 3-1/2" x 2-1/4". Overall length: 33-3/4". *Courtesy of Kimball M. Sterling Auctioneers.* $900-1200.

Carved wooden cat with glass eyes and red painted ribbon around her neck with a bow tied in the back. She is sitting in an erect position with her tail wrapped around her paws. Decorative silver collar, hardwood shaft with 1" metal ferrule, late nineteenth century. Handle: 4-1/2" h. x 1-1/2" d. Overall length: 35". *Courtesy of The World of the Walking Stick.* $1350-1485.

Six ivory carved lions. One Deco, signed Japanese model, two with lions eating snakes (the snake eating motif is used in Europe, England, and Japan), all on different shafts ranging from hardwood to snakewood. Large L-shaped lion handle: 1-1/2" h. x 3-1/2" l. Japanese signed Deco lion handle: 1-3/4" h. x 2" w. Lion/snake handle: 4" h. x 2" w. Second lion/snake handle: 4" h. x 1-7/8" w. Small lion on pedestal handle: 2" h. x 1-3/4" w. Small L-shaped lion handle: 1-1/2" h. x 2-3/4" w. *Courtesy of Richard R. Wagner, Jr.* These range in value from $500-700 each.

Lion with shield on wood shaft, metal ferrule with iron tip. Handle: 6-1/2" l. Overall length: 40-1/2". *Courtesy of Ambassador Richard W. Carlson.* $625-690.

Tiffany cane with a silver handle fashioned in the form of nineteenth century political cartoonist Thomas Nast's rendition of the eagle. The back of the handle features the original owner's monogram. The handle is also marked "Tiffany and Co. Maker, Sterling" on the lower rim. The shaft is malacca with a thread handle mount common to Tiffany. The shaft ends in a 2-1/4" horn ferrule. This cane dates to c. 1895. Handle: 3-3/4" x 2-2/3". Overall length: 35". *Courtesy of Henry A. Taron, Tradewinds Antiques.* $5000-7000.

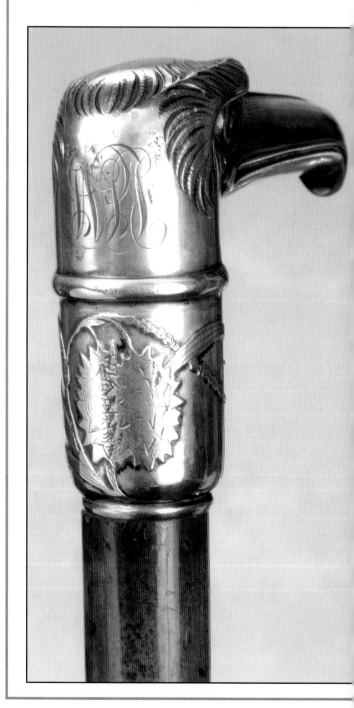

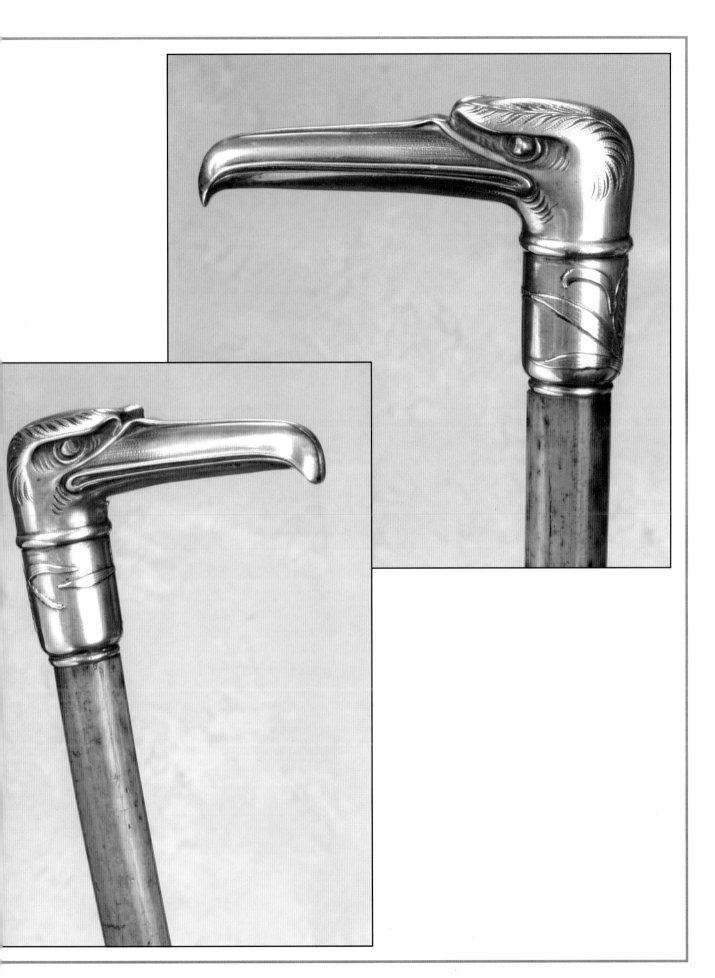

Opposite page:
Three bird handled canes. Left: folk art carved bird with carving down the shaft. This is a single piece of wood with no ferrule. Handle: 4-1/2" w. Overall length: 39". Middle: Toucan handle, metal collar, painted ferrule. Handle: 4-1/2" w. Overall length: 35". Right: Parrot tops a slender shaft with a longer metal ferrule at the base, and a metal collar. Ferrule: 2-1/4" l. Overall length: 37-1/2". *Courtesy of Ambassador Richard W. Carlson.* Together, these avian canes are valued at $400-440.

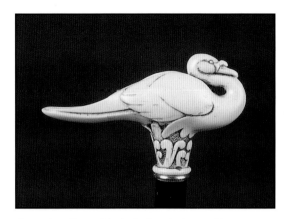

Swan handle on black shaft with thin gold collar, brass ferrule covered with a rubber tip. Overall length: 36-3/4". *Courtesy of Ambassador Richard W. Carlson.* $275-300.

Carved wood handle depicting two parrots with glass eyes, each perched on a tree trunk opposite each other. Hallmarked silver collar, mahogany shaft with 1-1/2" horn ferrule, late nineteenth century. Handle: 5-3/4" h. x 3-3/4" at widest. Overall length: 38". *Courtesy of The World of the Walking Stick.* $1350-1485.

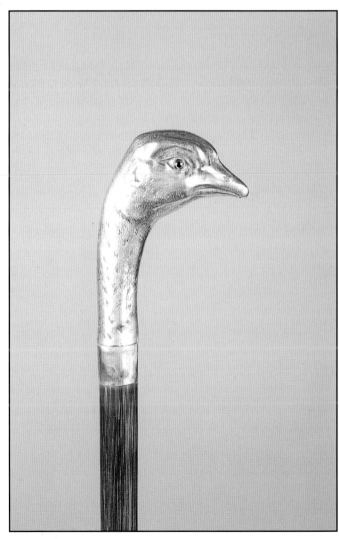

Sterling silver ostrich head handle with glass eyes, Birmingham hallmarks, dated 1931. (The subject matter of this cane is quite rare.) Also stamped AC Co. Ld. On base of handle. Partridge wood shaft with 1" metal ferrule, English. Overall length: 35-1/2". *Courtesy of The World of the Walking Stick.* $975-1075.

L-shaped silver handle in the form of an eagle's head holding a large nut or a piece of fruit in its beak. The handle is marked with the maker's initials and the number 800. Ebonized hardwood shaft with 5/8" metal ferrule, late nineteenth century. Handle: 3-3/4" w. x 2-1/2" h. Overall length: 33-1/2". *Courtesy of The World of the Walking Stick.* $975-1075.

Examples of eagle handles. Finely carved eagle with glass eyes overlaid with silver. Both the handle and shaft are birch; bark remains on the shaft. Handle: 2" h. x 4" w. Silver eagle handle on thorn wood with thorns ground off, leaving lighter marks where the thorns had been. Handle: 3" h. x 3" w. *Courtesy of Richard R. Wagner, Jr.* Birch eagle: $800-1000; silver eagle: $700-900.

Ivory handle claw and egg motif cane, brass collar and ferrule. Handle: 3-1/4" h. x 2-1/2" w. Overall length: 37-3/4". *Courtesy of Ambassador Richard W. Carlson.* $425-470.

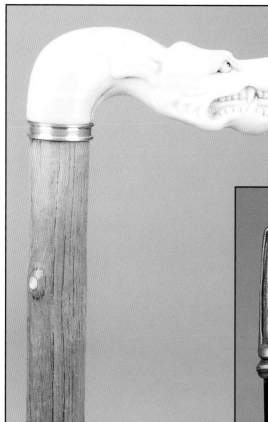

Carved ivory dragon's head with glass eyes. Silver collar, hickory shaft with mother-of-pearl insets in the knots. The handle is probably a Chinese export piece for the American market, late nineteenth century. Handle: 3" l. x 1" h. x 1" w. Overall length: 35". *Courtesy of The World of the Walking Stick.* $1350-1485.

Three gargoyles or griffins, which are not common motifs. Square L-shaped gargoyle handle in silver with black shaft; brown gutta-percha handle on a malacca shaft; griffin biting shaft in white metal, Britannia. *Courtesy of Richard R. Wagner, Jr.* Silver handle: $400-600; gutta-percha handle: $400-600; white metal handle: $500-600.

Ivory dragon handle with inset eyes, metal collar, metal ferrule with iron tip. Handle: 2-3/4" l. Overall length: 35". *Courtesy of Ambassador Richard W. Carlson.* $625-690.

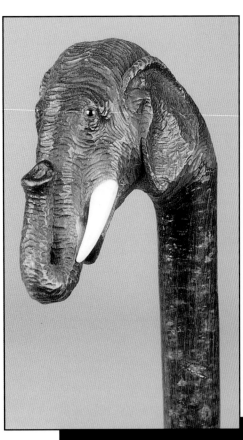

Large carved wood elephant head with glass eyes and ivory tusks. Fashioned from a single piece of ash with a 1" ivory ferrule. Late nineteenth century. Overall length: 36-1/4". *Courtesy of The World of the Walking Stick.* $1050-1155.

Elk are often seen carved on handle. These two ivory elk handles could have been produced for the Elk's Club but that is not known. Large ivory L-shaped handle on an ebonized shaft. Handle: 5" h. x 3" w. Smaller ivory handle on a snakewood shaft. Handle: 1-1/2" h. x 4" w. *Courtesy of Richard R. Wagner, Jr.* Large L-shaped handle: $600-700; smaller L-shaped handle: $600-700.

Brass elephant handle cane with rubber no skid ferrule. Handle: 4-1/2" l. x 3-1/2" h. Overall length: 36". *Courtesy of Ambassador Richard W. Carlson.* $150-165.

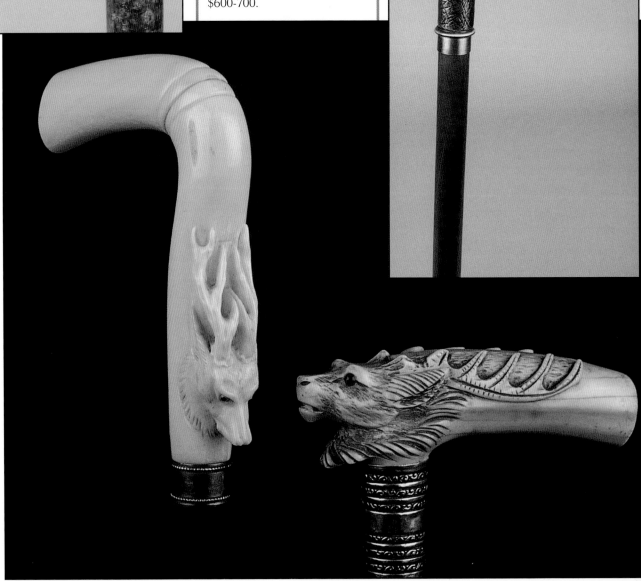

Two ivory fox handles. The fox and grapes motif is often seen. L-shaped handle is elephant ivory mounted on a partridge wood shaft. The knob handle is walrus ivory, the fox has glass eyes, and is mounted on a bamboo shaft. L-shaped handle: 3-1/4" h. x 3-1/4" w. Knob handle: 4" h. x 1-3/8" w. *Courtesy of Richard R. Wagner, Jr.* $300-500 each.

L-shaped carved ivory handle depicting canine with an eagle in his mouth. Small goldtone collar, ebony shaft (missing ferrule), late nineteenth century. Handle: 4-1/4" l. x 2-1/8" h. Overall length: 34". *Courtesy of The World of the Walking Stick.* $2950-3245.

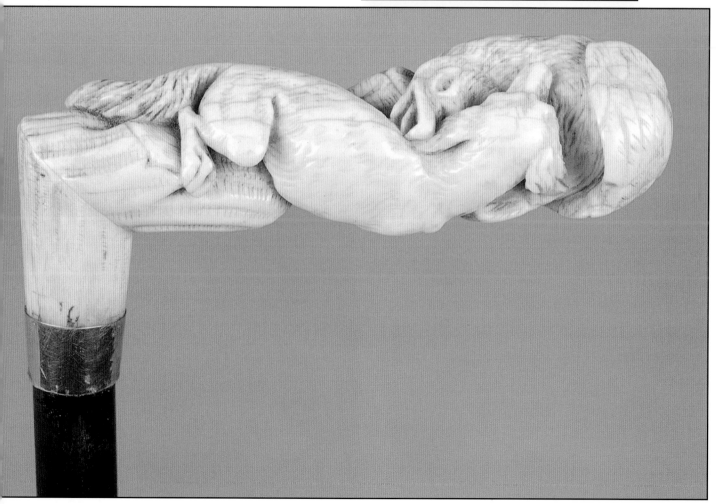

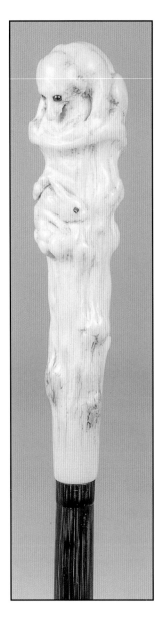

Carved ivory handle depicting a fox on top of a tree trunk looking down at a rabbit emerging from its hole. Stepped partridge wood shaft with a 1" ferrule, Continental in origins, late nineteenth century. Handle: 5-3/4" h. x 1-1/4" w. x 1-1/2" d. Overall length: 35-5/8". *Courtesy of The World of the Walking Stick.* $1975-2175.

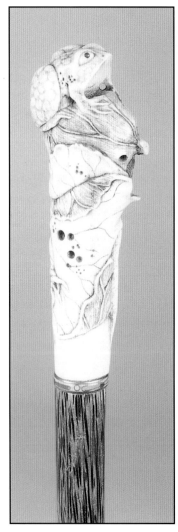

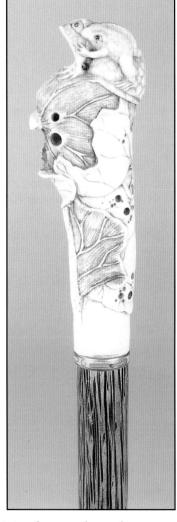

Japanese carved ivory handle depicts two frogs, mother and child, atop a gourd surrounded by leaves and foliage with half hidden crab sitting under a leaf, the gourd and some leaves inked in black. Small inlaid collar, beautifully striated hardwood shaft with 1-3/4" ivory ferrule, c. 1900. Handle: 4-1/2" h. x 1-1/2" at widest. Overall length: 34-1/2". *Courtesy of The World of the Walking Stick.* $1575-1735.

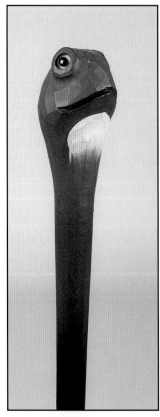

Amusing carved and painted frog head cane with inset eyes. Overall length: 36-1/4". *Courtesy of Ambassador Richard W. Carlson.* $125-140.

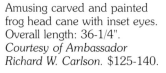

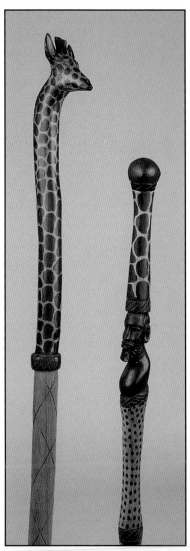

Two African motif staffs featuring a giraffe and an African man, well-carved and brightly painted. Overall lengths: Giraffe: 47"; Man: 43". *Courtesy of Ambassador Richard W. Carlson.* $50-55 each.

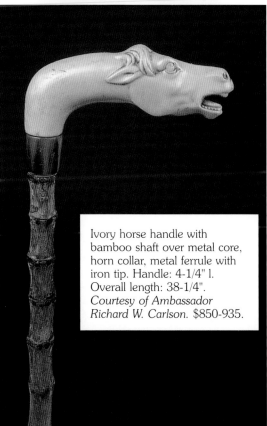

Ivory horse handle with bamboo shaft over metal core, horn collar, metal ferrule with iron tip. Handle: 4-1/4" l. Overall length: 38-1/4". *Courtesy of Ambassador Richard W. Carlson.* $850-935.

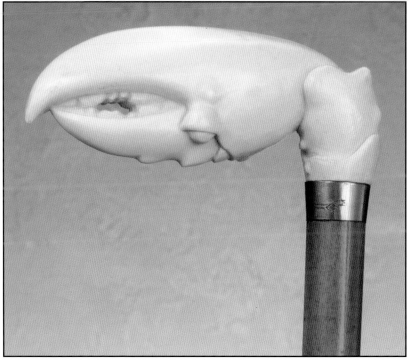

Elephant ivory handle carved as a large and realistically detailed lobster claw, probably produced in England, c. 1890. The joint between the handle and the tan malacca shaft is a gold collar measuring 2/3". The shaft tip is protected with a 1-1/4" horn ferrule. Handle: 5-1/4" x 2-1/4". Overall length: 37". *Courtesy of Henry A. Taron, Tradewinds Antiques.* $1800-2800.

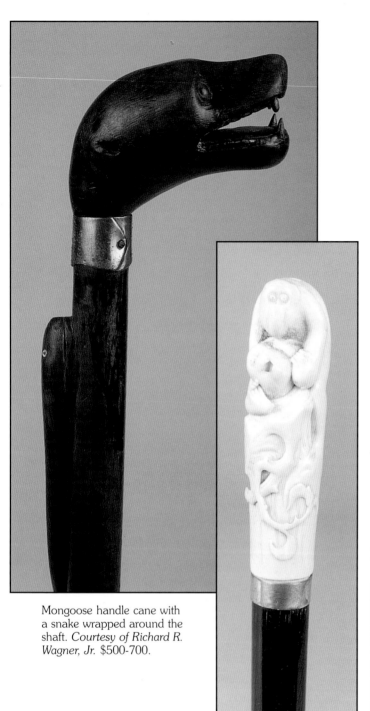

Mongoose handle cane with a snake wrapped around the shaft. *Courtesy of Richard R. Wagner, Jr.* $500-700.

Carved Japanese ivory depicting two howler monkeys, silver collar, malacca shaft, late nineteenth century. Handle: 4-1/2" h. Overall length: 37". *Courtesy of The World of the Walking Stick.* $1350-1485.

Below:
Snake handles: snakes have proven to be a very popular walking stick motif. Walrus ivory carved as a snake, this is a modern example from Indonesia with amber eyes and a crooked snake carved palm wood shaft. $350-450. Elephant ivory Japanese T handle with a bug on either end of the handle, the snake is wrapped around a log on the rosewood shaft. Handle: 4-1/2" l. $600-800. Hollow silver snake handle featuring green glass eyes, mounted on a black wood shaft. Handle: 3-1/2" w. x 2-1/2" h. $600-800. Austrian bronzed, poly-chrome snake on a cabbage wood shaft dating from the late nineteenth century. $350-550. *Courtesy of Richard R. Wagner, Jr.*

Left: Art Nouveau large silver handle in the form of a serpent with its mouth open wide to bare its deadly fangs. Its long tail coils around a silver post. The handle is hallmarked. The silver is beautifully chased, showing the scale-like pattern of the skin. Malacca shaft with 1-3/8" horn ferrule, c. 1900. Handle: 5-1/8" l. x 3-3/4" h. Overall length: 33". *Courtesy of The World of the Walking Stick.* $1595-1755. Right: Art Nouveau silver handle in the same serpent form, hallmarked at the base. Snakewood shaft, c. 1900. Handle: 4-5/8" l. x 3-1/2" h. Overall length: 34-1/2". *Courtesy of The World of the Walking Stick.* $1595-1755.

Sterling silver handle in the shape of cobra entwined in a branch. Cobra has two blue stones on back. Thin lightweight branch shaft. Handle: 5" l. Overall length: 35-1/2". *Courtesy of Ambassador Richard W. Carlson.* $475-525.

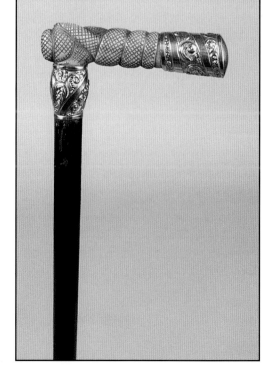

L handle with ivory and gold cap and gold collar: handle fashioned in shape of snake, a K in the opening on the collar for a monogram, metal ferrule. Handle: 4-1/2" l. Overall length: 35-1/2". *Courtesy of Ambassador Richard W. Carlson.* $825-900.

Amber handle with silver collar and small silver ferrule. The handle is formed to look like linked chain and measures 8-3/4" long. Overall length: 36-1/2". *Courtesy of Ambassador Richard W. Carlson.* $375-415.

Below:
Elaborately carved antler handle featuring many sea turtles, small silver collar, metal ferrule. Handle: 6-3/4" l. Overall length: 31-3/4". *Courtesy of Ambassador Richard W. Carlson.* $975-1075.

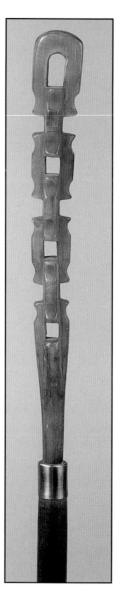

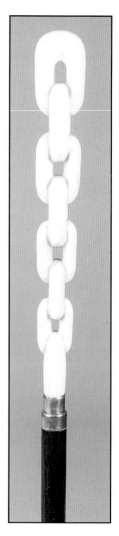

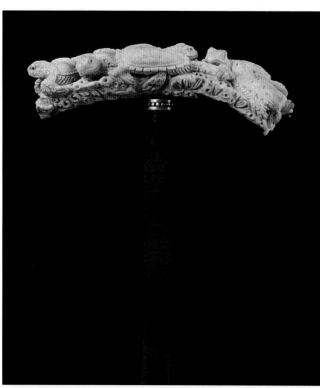

Carved ivory handle in the form of linked chain, the interlocking square links graduate in size from a narrow base. Silver collar, ebony shaft with 1-1/4" ivory ferrule, c. 1900. Handle: 7-3/4" h. x 1-1/8" at widest. Overall length: 37". *Courtesy of The World of the Walking Stick.* $1550-1705.

The Walking Stick's Universal Appeal

The very utility of the walking stick ensures that wherever people have ready access to appropriate raw materials, they will make them. Because these sticks are frequently constant companions and considered important aids to the users, they are decorated with the regional motifs of the native inhabitants, improving the appearance of the stick and the user alike. As people move from one area to another, they take their walking sticks and regional decorative motifs with them, spreading artistic concepts and cultural ideas around the world. In this chapter we will touch upon some of the walking sticks produced around the globe.

Nepal shaman's cane. This is a striking double staff cane with carved hands holding a man's body. It dates from the nineteenth century. *Courtesy of Brant Mackley Gallery.* $600-1200.

The Idea of the Stick

Diffusion is defined as the spread of cultural ideas and occurs in two different ways. Primary diffusion occurs when large groups of people move from one area to another, either through migration or military conquest. For example, Norwegian immigrants coming to the United States in the 1850s were moving to the frontier and could carry few personal items with them. However, many Norwegians felt it was important to bring their handsomely crafted canes with them. In this way, Norwegian concepts of beauty and workmanship were transferred across the sea to the wilds of Minnesota.

Secondary diffusion is the spread of an idea from culture to culture, region to region, without any large population movement. The adoption of the white cane as a tool of independence and symbol for the blind spread in this way. While the blind had always found canes useful in navigation, it was not until the twentieth century that the concept of using a particular cane as a symbol for the blind, alerting others to their presence, developed.

In 1921, James Biggs of Bristol, England, claimed to create the first white cane. Blinded in an accident, Biggs, an artist, felt threatened by the ever-increasing automobile traffic around his home. He painted his walking stick white to make himself more noticeable to drivers. In 1931, a national white stick campaign was launched in France. The movement quickly spread in England and North America.

Another example of diffusion in action occurred among woodcarvers in Devrek, Turkey, after World War I. During the First World War, Ali Ziya Efendi was captured by the British and held as a prisoner of war. During his internment, he noted that British officers used walking sticks as symbols of authority. In Devrek, canes had been seen solely as walking aids for the elderly. Upon returning home to Devrek after the war, Ali Ziya described the canes he had seen and their symbolic use to others. At that point, Devrek woodcarvers began producing sophisticated sticks decorated with motifs from Anatolian culture.

With that change in direction, the production of elegant walking sticks became central to the economy of Devrek. Now, walking sticks are produced by master carvers, the techniques are passed down from one generation to the next, and Devrek canes have received international recognition.

Devrek Cane Manufacture & Decoration

Suitable red dogwood trees are cut down during the months of December through February when the wood is dry. Branches are separated and allowed to season for a year. Bread ovens are used to straighten inappropriate bends in the wood and lathes are used to refine the shape of the shaft. Saws are used to create decorative grooves and files sand the shafts smooth.

Shafts are frequently decorated with an entwined snakes motif. Other decorative motifs include snake or horse heads, duck feet, and sparrow hawks. Flaws in the wood of the shaft are filled with varnish when the shafts are painted. Once the shafts are complete, handles of walnut, precious stones, silver, nacre, bone, tortoiseshell, or mountain goat hooves are applied.

Devrek cane masters have also been known to produce walking sticks with hidden compartments. They have manufactured sword and gun canes from time to time as well.

The first exhibition of Devrek canes occurred in 1933. In 1984, the first Devrek Cane Festival was held. Recognized past Devrek cane masters include: Aziz Salman; Andon Usta; Hakki; Celik Ahmet; Hasan and Abdullah Usta. Contemporary cane masters include: Munteka Celebi; Murvet Okur; Tansel Isik; Cemal Salman; Rasit Korum; Murat Ayvaci; Bulent Korum; Rasit Devrek; Ismet Durbak; Hikmet Incirli; Gursel Incirli; Ozcan Erdogan; Tuncer Bicmen; and Ali Akarsu. (Yucel 1999)

Opposite page:
Delaware/Lenape Mësingw [false face] dance cane with a face effigy. It was made in the mid-nineteenth century. Overall length: 29-1/2".
Courtesy of Brant Mackley Gallery. $3000-5000.

Global Walking Sticks & Customs

Native Americans had canes in many forms for many uses. Here are only a few generalized descriptions. Tribal leaders and shamans carried staffs as symbols of their authority. It was traditional among the peoples of the Six Nations to carve a hickory condolence cane upon the death of a chief. This cane was passed on to the new chief at the time of his installation. Planting sticks featured carvings of the "corn maiden" on top and pointed ends at the base for planting seeds. Story sticks bore carvings that recorded the histories of the people. Talking sticks were wonderful for keeping council meetings civil as only the individual holding the talking stick could speak. (Perhaps this concept should be universally adopted.) Coup sticks were carried into battle by warriors. A warrior touched his opponent with the stick before killing him. Notches carved into the shaft of the coup stick recorded the number of opponents the owner had "counted coup" against. The oddly named and peculiarly carved "booger bones" stick was used to ward off unwanted visitors.

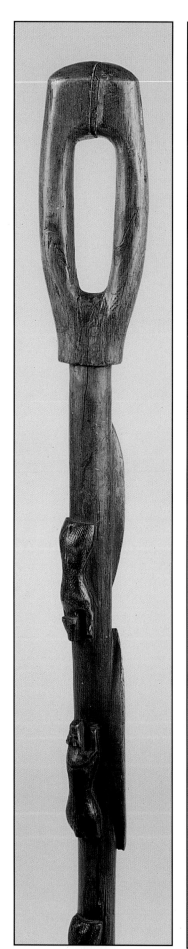

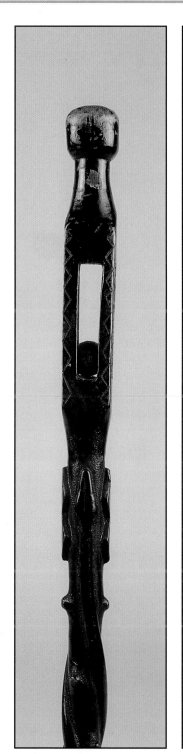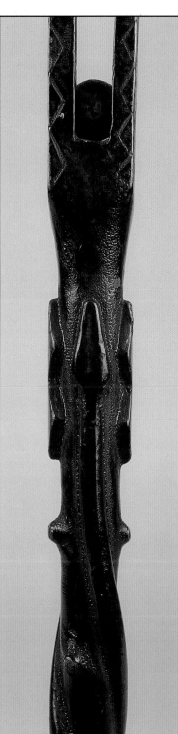

Iroquois Indian snake with ball in cage cane, used to scare snakes and spiders from long
houses. Nineteenth century. *Courtesy of Brant Mackley Gallery.* $400-1500.

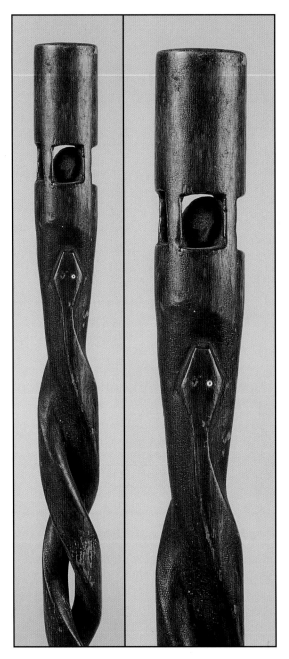

Second Iroquois Indian snake with ball in cage cane, used to scare snakes and spiders from long houses. Overall length: 36-1/2". *Courtesy of Brant Mackley Gallery.* $400-1500.

Iroquois Indian walking stick with a human face on the end of the handle. Overall length: 39". *Courtesy of Ron Van Anda and Sandra Whitson.* $2500-3500.

Great Lakes Woodlands Indian stick made
from a single piece of white ash with a
flattened and gently curving handle and twin
tendrils woven around the shaft in parallel
and fastened near the base. This walking stick
was produced by either the Ojibwa or
Patawatami tribes during the late nineteenth
or early twentieth century. Handle: 4" x
5-1/3". Overall length: 34-1/3". *Courtesy of
Kimball M. Sterling Auctioneers.* $600-800.

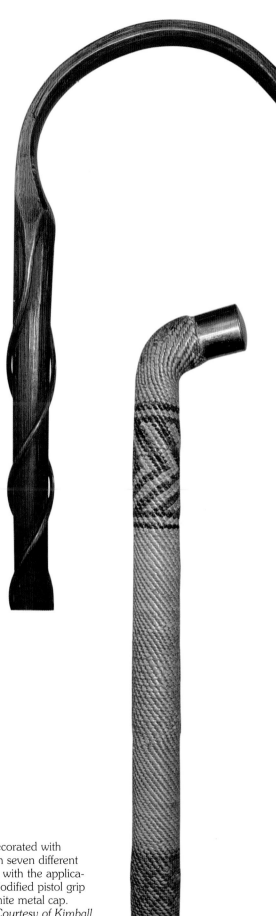

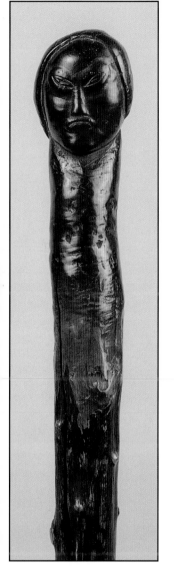

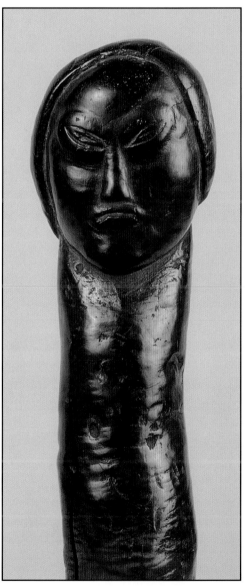

Above and right:
Possibly Eskimo hand
carved branch cane. Overall
length: 35". *Courtesy of
Ron Van Anda and Sandra
Whitson.* $2500-3500.

Native American cane decorated with
intricately woven hemp in seven different
decorative motifs created with the applica-
tion of vegetable dyes. Modified pistol grip
handle finished with a white metal cap.
Overall length: 34-1/2". *Courtesy of Kimball
M. Sterling Auctioneers.* $700-1000.

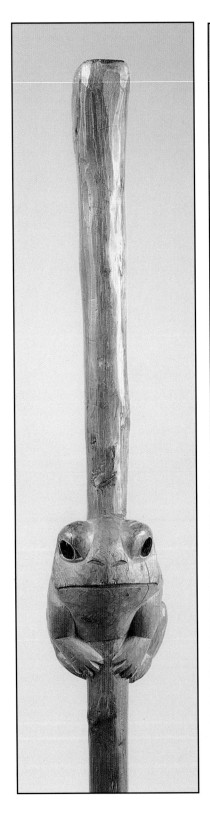

Chiefs of the Northwest Coast First Nations, in British Columbia, carried highly decorated ceremonial staffs as symbols of office. Standing shoulder high, these staffs were adorned with carved and painted figures such as whale crests and herons' heads above the waist level. They were carried during all public events. These staffs were also known as "speaker's staffs" when they were held by someone speaking on the chief's behalf. It has been assumed that these staffs of office developed among the First Nations peoples independent from European influence. Research into this issue is ongoing.

Some examples of First Nations canes combine aboriginal heraldry with European decorative motifs. Historical photographs depict First Nations men wearing canes in the European fashion.

Frog staff (featuring two large carved frogs) of the Northwest Coast Indians, used as a talking staff or a chief's/shaman's staff. Tlingit tribe, c. 1870s. Overall length: 45". *Courtesy of Brant Mackley Gallery.* $16,500.

Charles Edenshaw (b. 1835, d. 1920) was well known as a Northwest Coast First Nations aboriginal artist. His personal walking stick featured a handle with an ivory beaver, his family's crest. Edenshaw's cane was a heavy, functional, no-nonsense stick designed for regular use on the streets of Massett where he lived. Edenshaw produced elaborately decorated canes very different from his own for sale to interested customers outside the tribe. One of Edenshaw's canes was inspired by an image he had seen in *The Illustrated London News,* an impressive depiction of P.T. Barnum's elephant, Jumbo, then enthralling audiences on a tour of North America. This image made enough of an impression on Edenshaw that he carved an elephant head handled cane.

Jumbomania

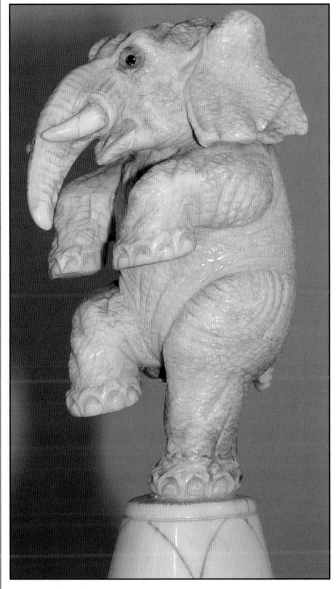

American ivory handle cane featuring that most famous of performing pachyderms, Jumbo, the star of the Barnum and Bailey Circus who gained notoriety across the United States and Canada performing a variety of feats. Paraded with a baby elephant to increase the image of his enormous size, Jumbo was billed as the largest elephant in the world (would you expect anything less from P. T. Barnum?). Well-carved handle with two color glass eyes, an ebonized shaft with faux twig spurs, and an ivory ferrule. Handle: 4-1/8" x 2". Overall length: 35-1/4". *Courtesy of Kimball M. Sterling Auctioneers.* $2400-3000.

Jumbo the elephant was captured on the plains of Abyssinia in 1861. After several stops, he found a home briefly at the London Zoo. There his trainer, Matthew "Scotty" Scott, taught Jumbo to accept a many-seated "*howdah*" on his back and take marveling children for rides. Among the enthusiasts who rode Jumbo then were Winston Churchill, Theodore Roosevelt, and Phineas T. Barnum. Part of Jumbo's mighty size may be attributed to the peanuts and English buns given him by his admirers.

P.T. Barnum, the entertainment entrepreneur who had once displayed the upper half of a monkey's skeleton attached to the lower half of a fish as the "Fejee mermaid" and billed Joice Heth, an elderly African-American woman, as George Washington's 161-year-old nanny, purchased Jumbo from the London Zoo in 1882 to become a star attraction in the newly established Barnum and Bailey Circus. Britons, including Queen Victoria herself, were enraged by the sale. However, by April 9, 1882, Jumbo arrived at the Manhattan Battery pier. With typical Barnum fanfare, the elephant was paraded down Broadway in a wagon hauled by sixteen horses, several hundred strong men, and a battery of circus elephants. Thus began Jumbo's showbiz career.

Jumbo toured North America for four years as part of the Barnum and Bailey Circus. To enhance the impression of great size, Jumbo was featured with a baby elephant. Gingerbread replaced English buns as Jumbo's favorite treat from fans. It was estimated that sixteen million adults and four million children paid to see the elephant billed as "The Towering Monarch of His Mighty Race." In the United States, and back in England, Jumbo products were sold to an adoring public, including: canes, hats, bracelets, earrings, cigars, fans, trading cards, and anything else that could have the elephant's image applied to it.

It was reported that Jumbo died in a railroad accident in 1885, heroically sweeping the baby elephant he toured with off the tracks before the end. Reports say Jumbo died after wrapping his trunk around the waist of his weeping trainer, drawing "Scotty" in for a final embrace. Following the tragedy, Jumbo's skeleton went to the Smithsonian Institution, his stuffed hide to the Tufts College Barnum Museum of Natural History, and his name to the general public to define anything colossal. (Wilson 2002)

African walking sticks have been seen as symbols of authority all the way back to the Pharaoh in Egypt. Carvings on African walking sticks reflect the power of the wearer, religious beliefs, and important matters in daily life. Early African-American slaves carved folk art sticks with heads and faces on the handles reminiscent of African motifs. In Ghana at the beginning of the rainy season, a festival is held featuring brightly colored umbrellas to glorify the Ashanti chieftains. Each Chieftain wears traditional handwoven robes and carries a gilded cane of office.

African Nguni stick, c. 1850, carved to resemble bone at the handle. The collar is of woven iron and copper wire. No ferrule. Overall length: 43-1/4". *Courtesy of Ambassador Richard W. Carlson.* $425-470.

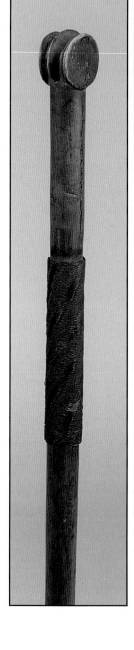

Simple, lightweight, old African cane with a head carved as the handle, all of one piece of wood. Handle: 3" h. Overall length: 37". *Courtesy of Ambassador Richard W. Carlson.* $260-285.

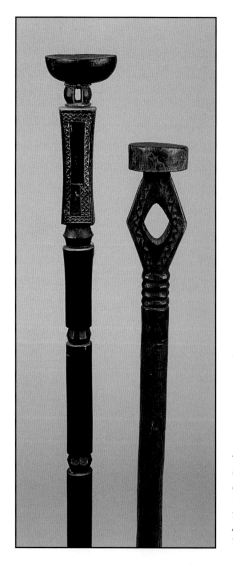

Two African canes. Left: from the Belgian Congo; right: from the Zulu, produced during the 1880s, bearing the initials "T.H.M." on top. Left: overall length: 40"; right: overall length: 42-1/2". *Courtesy of Ambassador Richard W. Carlson.* Together, these canes are valued from $700-770.

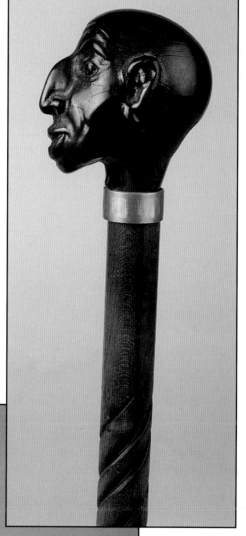

South African cane, silver collar, spiral carved wood shaft, 1920s. Overall length: 35-1/2". *Courtesy of Dale Van Atta.* NP (**N**o **P**rice)

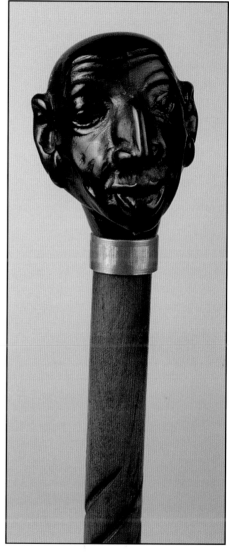

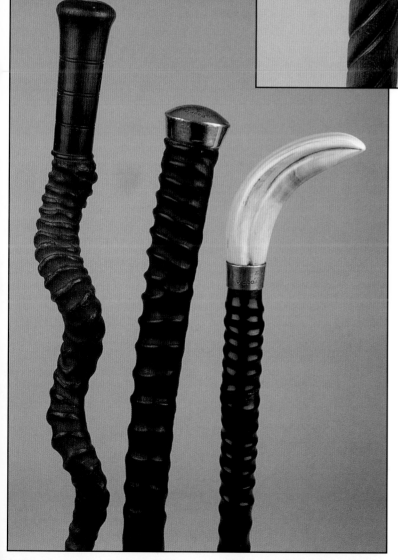

Three canes from Africa: two of Oryx horn and one of Kudu horn, polished Oryx and unpolished shafts. Boar's tusk handle reads, "taken from a Oryx killed by a lion near Karia Shevel Octo. 23, 1896." The rolled gold handle cane reads, "Prof. Dr. H. G. Barbour Psychology 1924-25 from the appreciating South African students." The third handle, the Kudu horn cane with two horns, has mother-of-pearl inset into the handle. *Courtesy of Richard R. Wagner, Jr.* Plain cane: $300-400. More decorative examples: $900-1500.

The Walking Stick's Universal Appeal 165

Below and right:
Two African canes: the example on the left features a colored ivory handle in the form of a woman and child. The example on the right has very early wood with great patina; there is a mirror inset on the stomach of this woman, which probably has a fetish inside. Copper wire is wrapped around the woman's neck on the cane to the right. *Courtesy of Richard R. Wagner, Jr.* Colored ivory handle, woman and child: $1000-1500. Woman with mirror, period piece: $700-1000.

Two North African figural handles, both probably representing police officers with belts and fez. The heavier model has a snake wrapped around the shaft. *Courtesy of Richard R. Wagner, Jr.* $500-700 each.

Robert Norris (d. 1791) wrote in his memoirs of his eighteenth century adventures in Africa that he had encountered the king of Dahomy. Norris stated the king was interested in obtaining European goods of all description, including walking sticks. After three days when Norris had little more to do by his own account than purchase slaves and ivory, he was summoned for a festival. During the festival, women paraded past displaying the king's wealth. Over one hundred of them carried walking sticks with gold or silver handles.

In Panama, men of rank on San Blas Island carry walking sticks called *orsualas*. Policemen, chiefs, and village officials all carry these sticks as symbols of the authority of their offices. Shaman-healers carry sticks entwined with carved snakes. Other sticks are used for religious ceremonies.

In mountain farming regions of Europe, mountain hatchet canes with ax-shaped handles were in use as early as the fifteenth century as symbols of authority. These hatchets are highly decorated and the handles are frequent made of brass. Such hatchets continue to be presented to individuals on special occasions and most examples found in collections today are of twentieth century manufacture.

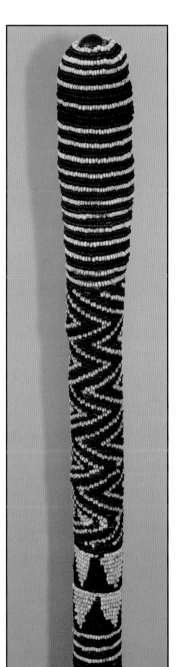

African beadwork cane, possibly produced by the Massai during the early to mid-twentieth century. It sports several bead designs in dark red, white, and blue. It also features a brass brad in the handle and a brass ferrule. Overall length: 33-1/2". *Courtesy of Kimball M. Sterling Auctioneers.* $200-400.

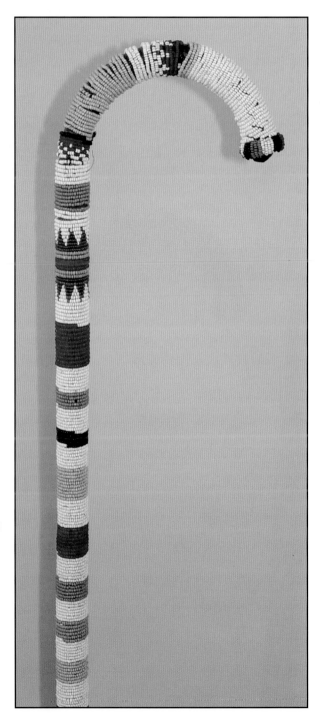

African beadwork crook handled cane, possibly produced by the Massai during the early to mid-twentieth century. This colorful cane features a variety of beadwork designs and colors. A leather knob finishes the crook handle and a broad brad covered leather ferrule protects the bottom of the shaft. With beaded canes, both the complexity of the work and how much of the beadwork has survived over time intact go far toward determining the value. Overall length: 34-1/2". *Courtesy of Kimball M. Sterling Auctioneers.* $200-400

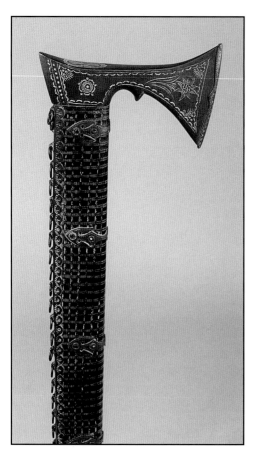

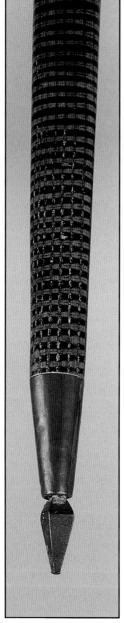

Above and right:
Mountain hatchet cane with rings down the side and a spiked ferrule at the tip. Handle: 6" l. Overall length: 32". *Courtesy of Ambassador Richard W. Carlson.* $425-470.

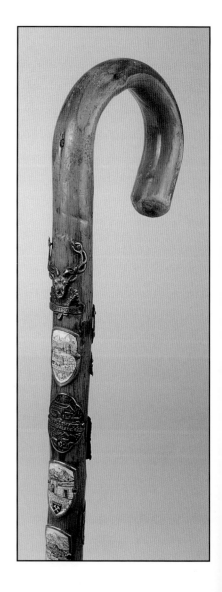

Bavarian traveler's cane with many medallions of different cities and sights. It has a serious pointed metal ferrule (with a spiked end) for negotiating rough terrain. Overall length: 35-3/4". *Courtesy of Dale Van Atta.* $450-495.

Asian walking sticks are frequently manufactured from bamboo with ivory, mahogany, or mother-of-pearl handles. Carvings adorning Asian sticks frequently feature monkeys, birds, elephants, and lizards. Walking sticks of recent manufacture in China feature dragon's head motifs or rattan sticks.

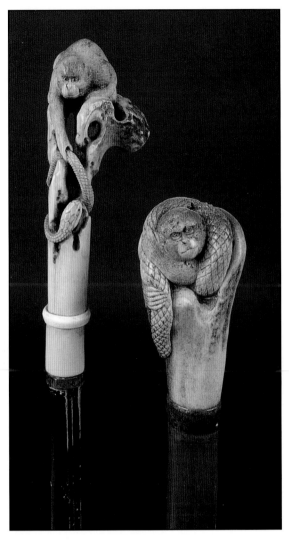

Japanese motifs, monkeys having bad days with snakes, on bamboo shafts with small metal collars, small metal ferrules. Handles: 5-3/4" and 3-1/2" h. Overall lengths: Left: 35"; right: 34-3/4". *Courtesy of Ambassador Richard W. Carlson.* Left: $475-525; right: $525-580.

Right and below:
Japanese wood knob handled walking sticks featuring a skull and snake motif. The stick with skull and snake in mother-of-pearl has portions of the snake appearing in four places. Overall length: 35-1/2". The second example has an ivory skull and snake. Overall length: 36". Both feature branch wood shafts. *Courtesy of Richard R. Wagner, Jr.* $500-750 each.

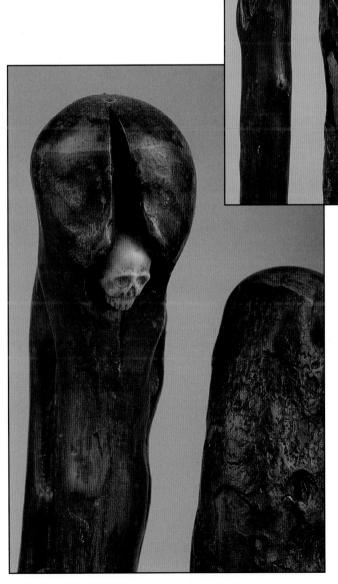

Japanese carved cane with insects on the shaft and a snake on the
handle (such sticks are found with shafts carved in many different
motifs). *Courtesy of Richard R. Wagner, Jr.* The quality of the
carving determines the value. These range from $150-400.
Signatures increase the value slightly.

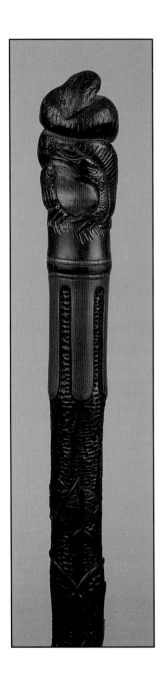  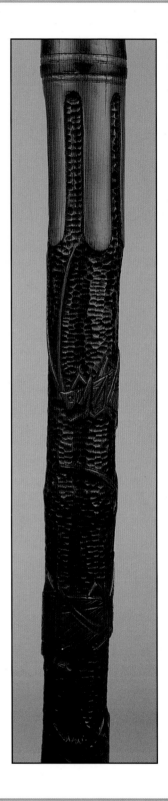

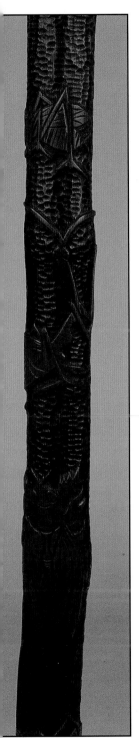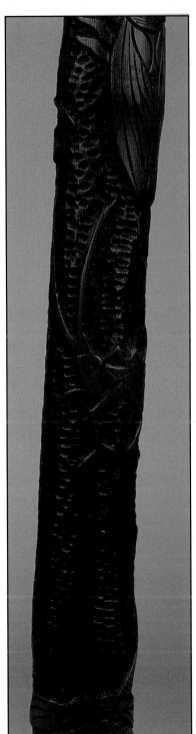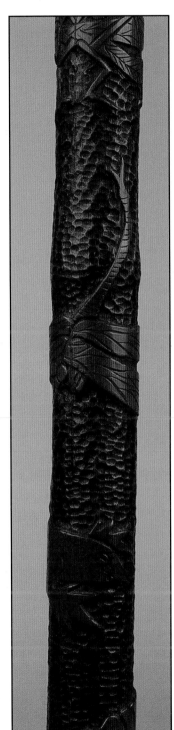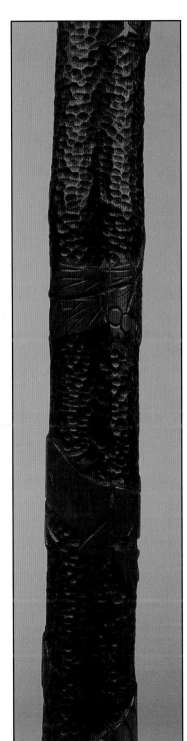

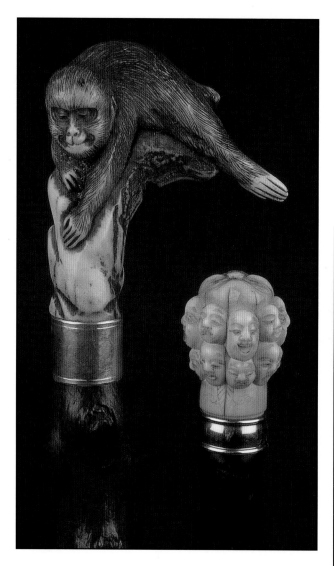

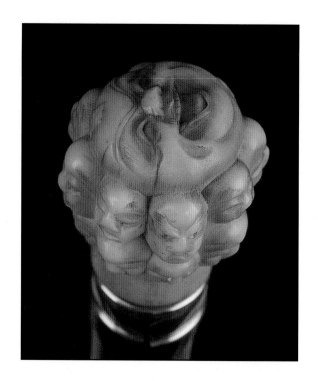

Two Japanese stag and ivory canes, one has a monkey and the other is a "thousand faces" motif. These have bamboo shafts. Other handles of this type are mounted on hardwood shafts. Thousand face handle: 1-1/2" h. x 1" d. Monkey handle has brown coloration on the handle: 2-3/4" h. x 2" w. *Courtesy of Richard R. Wagner, Jr.* Japanese carvings are always well done and the value is based on how much work there is on them. Poorly carved stag horn examples are much less expensive than ivory. These examples are around $400 each; elaborate examples run up to $1000.

Red dragon cane from the People's Republic of China. Overall length: 37-3/4". *Courtesy of Dale Van Atta.* $100+.

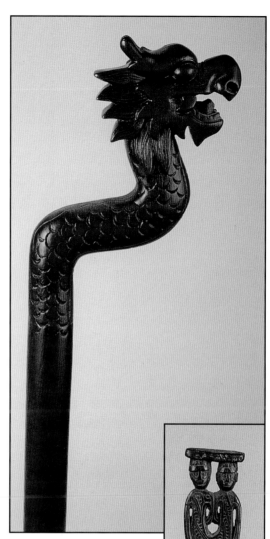

Right:
Moving around the globe … two figures top this cane from New Guinea. No ferrule. Overall length: 39-1/4". *Courtesy of Ambassador Richard W. Carlson.* $375-415.

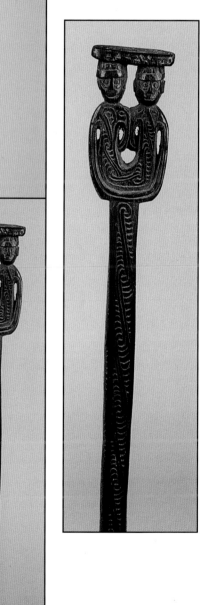

Two elaborately carved canes from the People's Republic of China. The cane on the right is a smoker's cane. There is a small mouthpiece leading out of the back of the handle. Overall lengths: 41-1/2" and 37-1/2". *Courtesy of Dale Van Atta.* $100+ each.

Indian sandalwood cane carved with a monkey at the handle and other
animals below with flowers. *Courtesy of Richard R. Wagner, Jr.* $500-600.

Burmese sandalwood cane made from a single length of wood, finely carved, c. 1880. The handle displays a mythical beast with ivory eyes and bared fangs. The detailed shaft carving has many high relief figures, including leaves and flowers, wild animals, dogs, rodents, snakes, tropical birds with long tail feathers, and numerous geometric shapes. The base of the shaft sports a 7/8" bright gold ferrule. Overall length: 36". *Courtesy of Henry A. Taron, Tradewinds Antiques.* $1800-2800.

Folk Art Sticks

Elaborate folk art cane found in Nebraska, dating from the nineteenth century. It is carved with soldiers on either side of the handle, and United States presidents down the shaft, beginning with Washington, Jefferson, Madison, and Monroe, and continuing with all the presidents up to Harrison. Overall length: 37".
Courtesy of Ron Van Anda and Sandra Whitson. $15,000-25,000.

Folk Art Sticks   177

Folk art walking sticks were created by nonprofessional artists; independent craftsmen working alone for personal pleasure or profit. Both scrimshaw and glass canes are considered folk art, along with canes made from more common materials. Folk art canes were produced for the artist, for family and friends, or for sale privately by the artist to interested parties.

Folk art sticks are generally created by a lone artist working with a single length of raw material. More often than not, folk art canes have neither collars nor ferrules. Working with a single length of wood eliminates the need for a collar, as there is no joint between the handle and shaft. The carver expected the shaft to be sturdy enough to withstand dirt, rock, and mud without the aid of a ferrule.

Folk art canes were generally made with native wood from the carver's region and often included maple, walnut, cherry, ash, hickory, willow, elm, birch, pine, poplar, and cedar. Carvers chose from tree branches, roots, saplings, and vines.

The purpose of the folk art stick is to highlight the skills of the craftsman, drawing attention to the quality of his work. The decorative carving used to accomplish this task usually covers the handle and continues on down the shaft as well to form an integrated piece of art. Folk carved canes also reflect their owners' personalities, often boldly, since the carvers often were also the owners or knew the owners personally. These canes are very personal reflections of the maker and the owner. The designs found on folk art canes are also frequently important to the artist. They may reflect favorite pastimes, pivotal events in the carver's life, or organizations and allegiances held dear. Designs also reflect the owner's passions: naturalists and hunters alike carried canes with elaborate carvings of animals and birds; great lovers carried folk art canes with handles fashioned in the shape of a woman; a gambler's stick might display dice.

Folk artists frequently learned their craft in an apprenticeship with an older, experienced artist in the community. In this way, traditional carving techniques and decorative motifs were passed down from one generation to the next. In the end, the folk art walking stick as an artifact provides insights into the resources of an artist's region, the aesthetics values of an artist's community, and the beliefs held dear in a particular time and place. There is much to be learned from the careful examination of well-crafted folk art walking sticks.

German folk art man regurgitating man handle carved from one piece of blackthorn, nineteenth century. Overall length: 35". *Courtesy of The World of the Walking Stick.* $1450-1595.

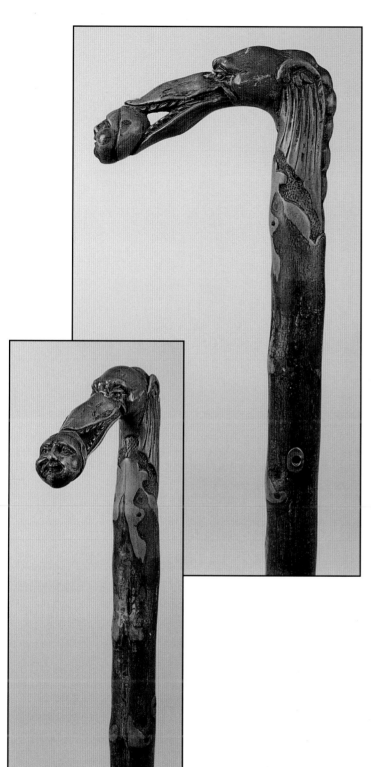

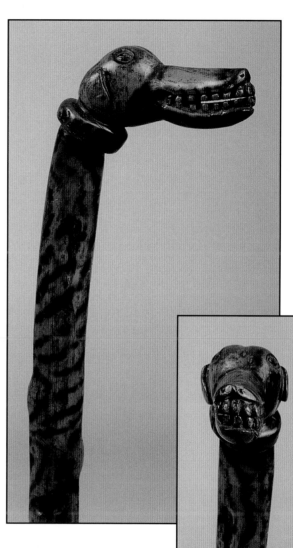

Left:
Folk art cane featuring a carved beast with a man's head in its mouth. Eyelets (brass) and short, flat disk ferrule nailed to the base. Overall length: 35". *Courtesy of Dale Van Atta.* $560-615.

Above and right:
Folk art smiling dog with a serious mountaineer's ferrule. Handle: l. 5" l. Overall length: 32-1/2". *Courtesy of Ambassador Richard W. Carlson.* $475-525.

Folk Art Sticks 179

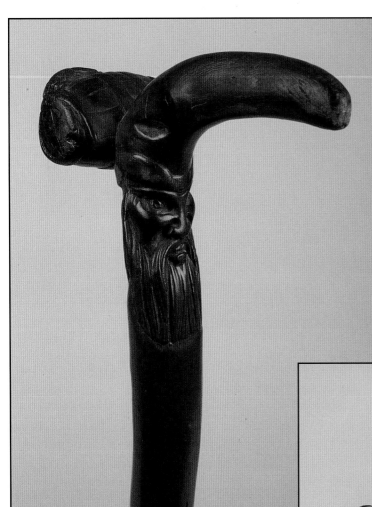

Carved bearded man on the underside of the crook with a keg behind his head and an animal on top of the keg. *Courtesy of Richard R. Wagner, Jr.* $500-700.

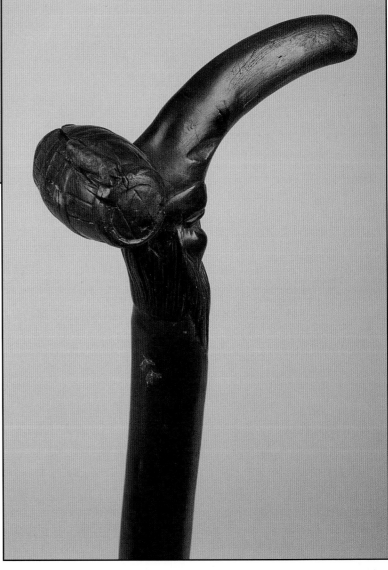

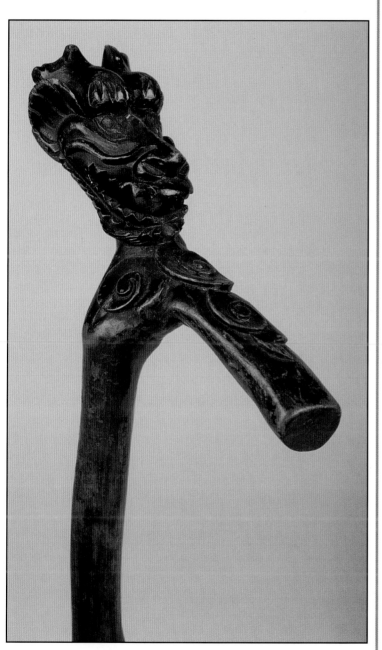

Chinese folk art cane on a branch barked
shaft, dragon handle with ball in its mouth.
Courtesy of Richard R. Wagner, Jr. $500-700.

**Left, below
and following page:**
Nineteenth century Ohio folk art
cane, elaborately relief carved
with vines, fruit, animals, and
birds. Among the fauna are an
eagle, horse, chicken, and deer.
Overall length: 35". *Courtesy of
Ron Van Anda and Sandra
Whitson.* $9500.

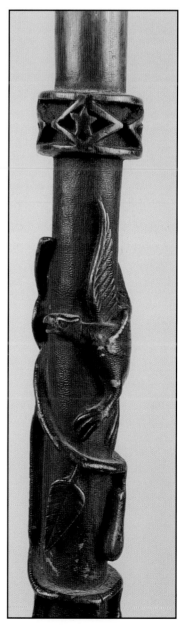

Folk Art Sticks   181

More of the nineteenth
century Ohio folk art
cane shown on the
previous page.

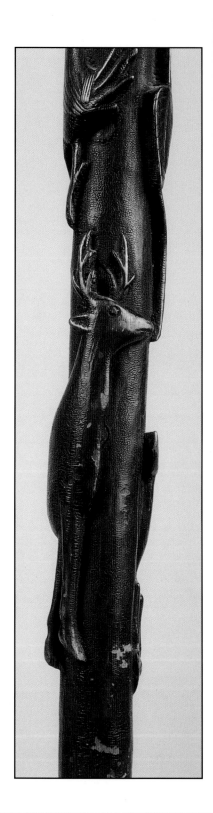

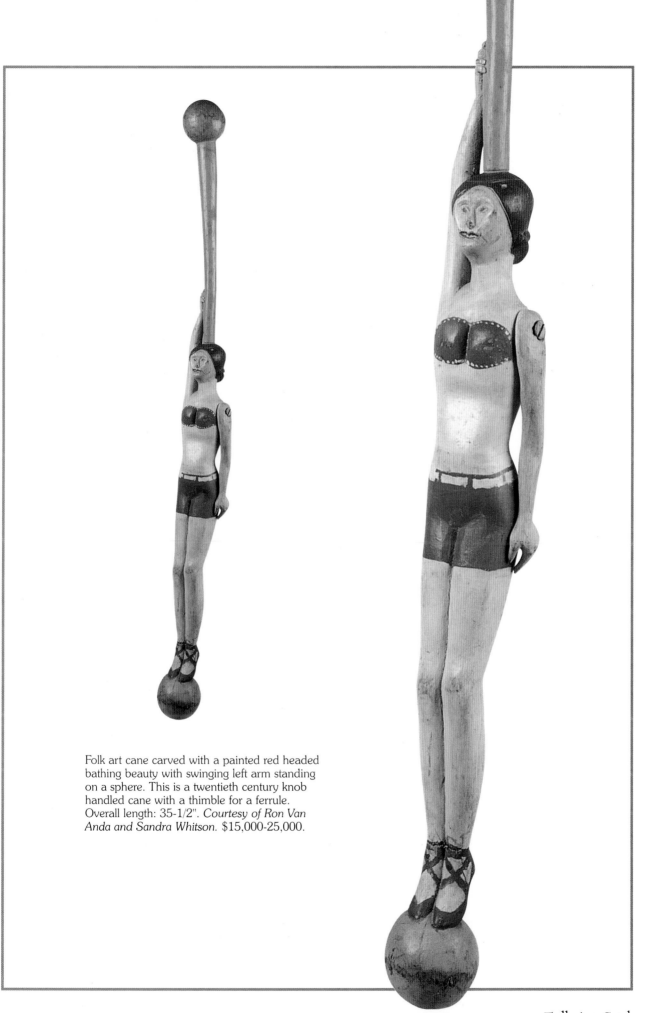

Folk art cane carved with a painted red headed
bathing beauty with swinging left arm standing
on a sphere. This is a twentieth century knob
handled cane with a thimble for a ferrule.
Overall length: 35-1/2". *Courtesy of Ron Van
Anda and Sandra Whitson.* $15,000-25,000.

Crooked stick with human face on the end of the stick. Possibly Native American. Overall length: 32". *Courtesy of Ron Van Anda and Sandra Whitson.* $3500.

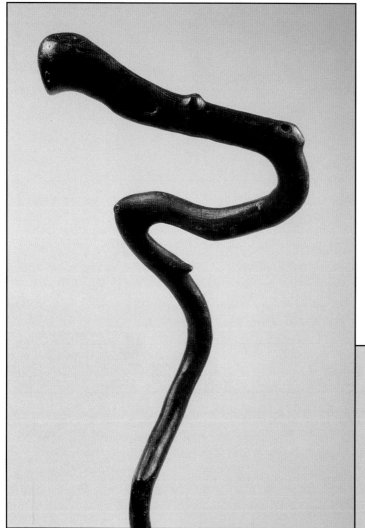

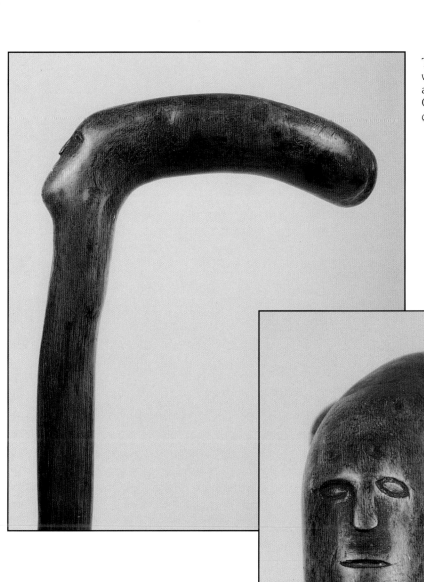

This is possibly a Native American walking stick, with a carved face at the near end of the handle at its juncture with the shaft. Metal ferrule. Overall length: 35". *Courtesy of Ron Van Anda and Sandra Whitson.* $600-800.

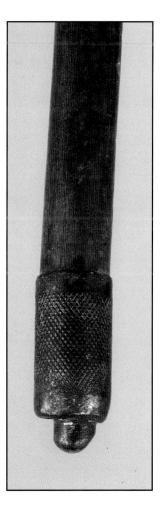

Folk Art Sticks   185

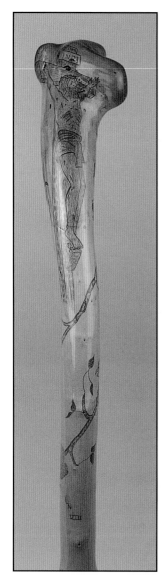

Cruciform painted cane, from Charleston, West Virginia. Overall length: 39". *Courtesy of Dale Van Atta.* $170-190.

A very large folk art cane made from wood deformed by a vine with the bark remaining on the shaft. The shaft is carved with the following inscription: "W. H. Taft, March 4, 1909." The story goes that this stick was given to Teddy Roosevelt by Taft as Roosevelt left office. It would be the proverbial "big stick." Overall length: 38-1/2". *Courtesy of Dale Van Atta.* $800+ for the genuine article.

Two folk art sticks with whimsy balls inside, knob handles, no ferrules. Seaman's work most likely dating before 1890. Overall lengths: 38" and 41" long. *Courtesy of Ambassador Richard W. Carlson.* $575-635 each.

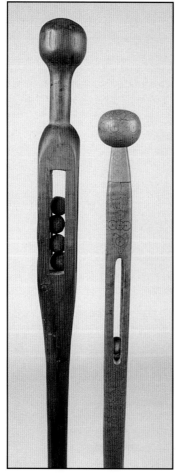

American folk art cane from the southern "Tobacco School," carved from a single length of wood, c. 1880. The heavily carved cane features carved and stained tobacco leaves, figural carvings including the head on the handle, a frog, alligator, and bird, and symbols including a heart and a shield. Overall length: 36-1/2". *Courtesy of Kimball M. Sterling Auctioneers.* $1400-2000.

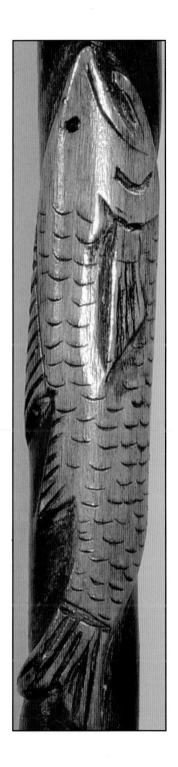

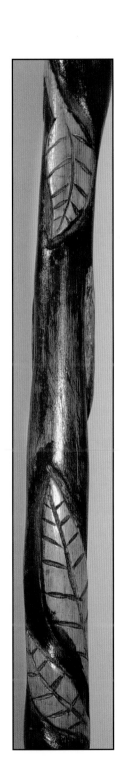

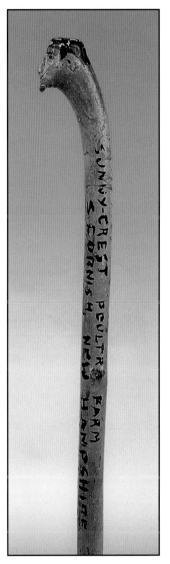

Folk art advertising stick with a man's face handle, painted wood, and message on side reading "Sunny-Crest Poultry Farm, S. Cornish, New Hampshire, July 14, 1935." Overall length: 34". *Courtesy of Ambassador Richard W. Carlson.* $310-340.

American slave market cane carved with the figural head of a smiling slave and featuring the advertisement "Smith & Allen Slave & Livestock Sales Lexington, KY" on the shaft. Dating from the early nineteenth century, this is an important, sobering, and unsettling artifact from the history of the United States. The oak figural handle is carved in the form of a smiling African-American man and features painted eyes and teeth. The oak handle and shaft are joined with a large brass collar measuring 2-1/8" above the original black over-painted brass eyelets and circular wrist strap holes. A 3" black painted brass ferrule that is significantly worn from repeated use protects the base. Overall length: 35-3/4".

Lexington was the center of Kentucky's slave trade. When feeding, clothing, and housing became too expensive for a cash-strapped landowner, slaves were often hired away or sold to other Kentucky slaveholders or to others in the market further "down the river" in the Deep South. Auctions scheduled for court day were common events throughout Kentucky during the antebellum period. By 1860, one out of every five Kentuckians was an African-American slave. No doubt Smith & Allen did brisk business. The association of slaves and livestock on the cane shaft is not coincidental; both were considered the sole property of the landowner who purchased them. The benignly smiling face on the cane handle would have been reassuring to those attending a Smith & Allen auction. Slaveholders feared resistance and uprisings from those they kept in bondage. *Courtesy of Kimball M. Sterling Auctioneers.* $10,000-15,000.

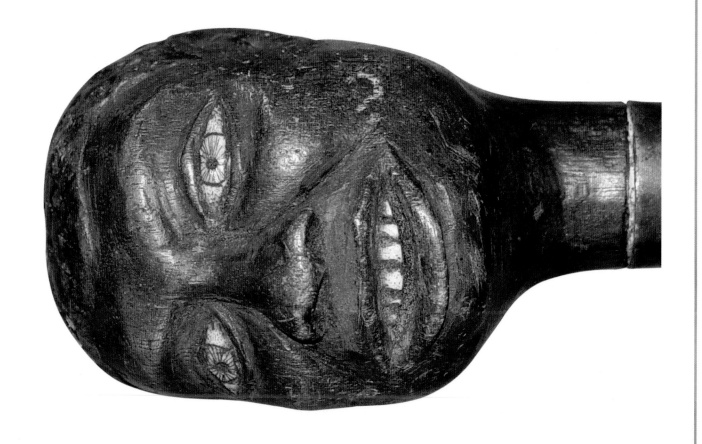

Folk Artists

For further insight into the lives and motivations of folk artists, here are brief sketches of the lives and works of several known artists. Frank Feathers is well known among folk art walking stick collectors today. His walking sticks will sell for as much as five thousand dollars or more today.

Frank Feathers

Frank Feathers created his walking sticks during the late nineteenth and the first half of the twentieth centuries while traveling through the Maryland countryside. Drifting from place to place, Feathers supported himself by performing odd jobs around farms or by selling his carvings, including walking sticks, wall sconces, spoons, utensil handles, newspaper racks, and comb cases. Occasionally, he would carve his initials into canes he completed. Decorative motifs common to Feathers's work include large letters (up to two-inches high) spiraling down cane shafts and forming sentiments such as "hope, love, peace, victory." He also carved acorns, flowers, and horse's heads. When he stayed at a farm, Frank Feathers preferred to sleep in barns and take his meals there, shying away from the company of others.

Feathers told many colorful stories about his life. During the 1930s, Frank Feathers dropped out of sight for several years, reappearing in the Pennsylvania countryside. He claimed to have walked to the West Coast and back. However, a relative who knew Feathers politely stated that he decorated his life in the same way he decorated his carvings. Frank Feathers died of a stroke in Frederick, Maryland, in 1951.

To see four examples of canes carved by Frank Feathers, turn to page 224 of my book *Canes: From the Seventeenth to the Twentieth Century.*

Luster Willis

Luster Willis (b. 1913, d. 1990) was a southern folk artist born near Terry, Mississippi. Willis reached adulthood during the Great Depression. With work hard to find, he turned to carving to make a living. Lacking money for formal classes, Willis was self-taught. Also lacking funds for supplies, he turned to the materials close at hand and began carving folk art walking sticks. His walking sticks were made of cedar because it was a soft wood that was easily carved. He sold walking sticks ranging in price from twenty-five cents to six dollars and made his living during the Depression years in this way.

Willis's sticks have the feel of African ceremonial sticks, each featuring the carving of an individual at the top of the cane. Among his more recent works were a self-portrait and images of Malcolm X and Gerald Ford.

Hugh Williams

Twentieth century carver Hugh "Big Daddy" Williams created folk art sticks in New Orleans from a van he lived in parked at the end of Clairborne Street. Williams's path to carving notoriety was an unusual one. Early in life, his nose had been shot off. Locals felt sorry for the man and purchased him a prosthetic nose. At the time, however, there were no prostheses made for African-Americans and Williams was unhappy with the white nose. He carved himself a mahogany nose instead and glued it to his sunglasses.

The mahogany nose drew a lot of attention. Soon, people were examining his other carvings, including his walking sticks. Williams carved walking sticks for the black Mardi Gras. Among his stick decorations were erotic women, alligators, snakes, and leaves. In time, jazz and blues musicians around the country sought out Williams's canes.

David Allen

David Allen was born in 1925 in Louisiana. He picked up a pocketknife found under the house ten years later and started whittling toys. By age fifteen, Allen, an African-American, had carved his first cane from a gum stick. However, Allen's life, and various careers in logging, carpentry, and plumbing, came between him and carving until the late 1960s. Retiring with health issues, Allen returned to carving walking sticks, with a preference for hickory saplings. Sapling roots were used to create a variety of imaginative handles featuring reptiles, mammals, and human faces. Knots in the shaft were incorporated into designs ornamenting the shaft, including various geometric patterns, four leaf clovers, black and white designs, and snake motifs. At times, rhinestone eyes were added. For fancy sticks, Allen would add a high gloss sealer as a finishing touch.

In the early 1980s, David Allen continued an old tradition among folk artists; he took his neighbor, Bennie Holyfield, in as an apprentice carver. Holyfield had expressed a keen interest in cane carving and had also whittled toys in his youth.

David Allen's work began to be noticed in Louisiana in 1979, when he showed his work at a festival in his hometown. In 1981 and 1985, Allen received national recognition when invited to participate in the Festival of American Folklife, sponsored by the Smithsonian Institution and held on the Mall in Washington, D.C. One of his canes also appeared on display in the museum.

While at the Smithsonian, Allen was interviewed about his connections with African art. Although Allen had never seen African motifs himself, his work strongly reflects an African heritage. His work had coiled snakes, serpentine fluting, geometric incisions and symmetrical positioning of carved figures, as well as polished finishes, all attributes of African carving.

From the four examples of these talented individuals' lives, we have seen that folk art walking sticks were at times traded in barter for food and lodging. Relying on raw talent and a sharp knife, an artist could survive hard times carving walking sticks, gathering his raw material from the local forests and selling his work within his own community. As in the case of Hugh Williams, if that work was unique in some way, it might attract a following among a community that transcends a single region. In Williams's case, blues and jazz musicians far from New Orleans seek out his work. Finally, the carvings found on folk art sticks will reflect the influences and motifs prevalent in the carver's community, and by extension in his or her ancestry. As in the case of David Allen, this may not be a conscious decision. However, when skills are passed from one generation to another through apprenticeships, that practice guarantees that traditional carving techniques and motifs are passed along to future generations, whether those generations are aware of their origins or not.

"Mike/Orion" American folk art cane carved by Michael Cribbons, an Irish immigrant living in Michigan and carving canes close to Lake Orion, near Pontiac, Michigan. As with virtually all of Michael Cribbons's canes, this example is carved of open, or diamond, willow wood. The irregular knobs, branches, and natural diamond-shaped outgrowths of the willow are inventively incorporated into Cribbons's work. Cribbons's trademark relief carved "Mike" and "Orion" are prominently featured, using black lettering against a stippled background field. The background field was once painted gold. Black and gold paint decorate many of Cribbons's canes. Also found on the abundantly carved shaft are the name "Col. OA. Janes," evidently the recipient of this cane—Cribbons worked from roughly the end of the American Civil War to the turn of the twentieth century (the latest known dated 1902) and produced canes for men who had served in the Civil War—as well as three snakes carved from the willow's oval pods, a bird's head, dog, fish, horse, and a star spangled diamond and cloverleaf. The knob handle and handmade lead ferrule with dentate edges are common features of Cribbons's work. The handles are often painted black and frequently are further adorned with gold stars. George Meyer hypothesizes in his book, *American Folk Art Canes: Personal Sculpture*, that given the quality of Cribbons's work, he may have carved professionally. At least one of his canes was carved for an individual who presented it to a third party. (Meyer 1992, 157; Sterling 2003, 14) *Courtesy of Kimball M. Sterling Auctioneers.* $6000-8000.

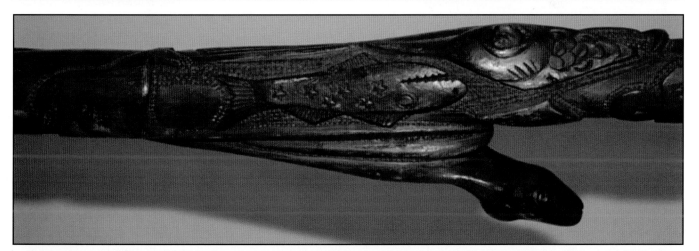

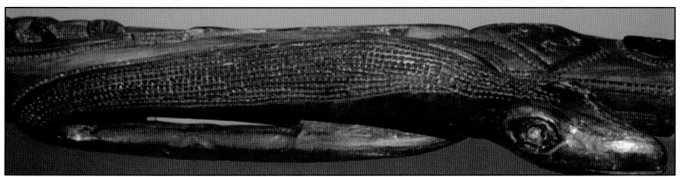

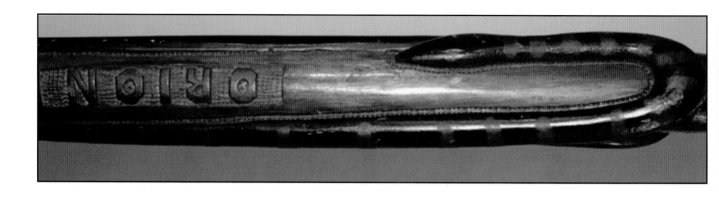

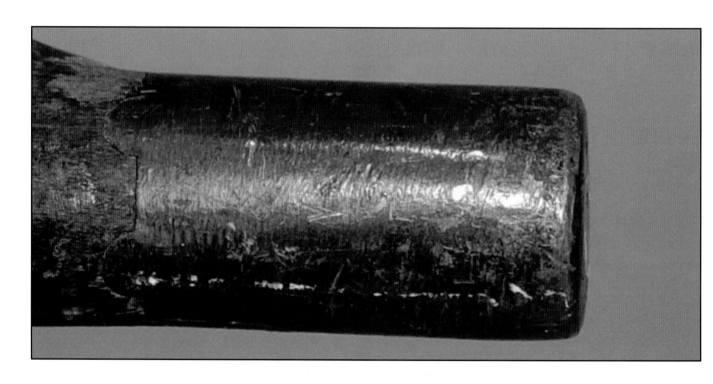

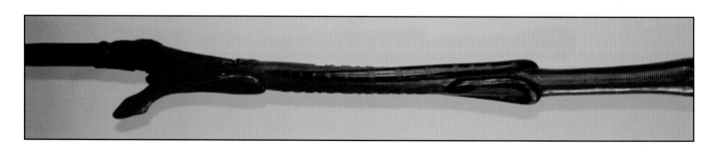

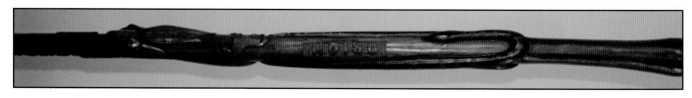

Early twentieth century American Tramp Art staff signed "Chas. E. Fox." His moniker, "Reefer Charlie," is carved into relief on the shaft, a title earned by riding the rails across the nation in refrigerator cars (reefers). The staff is carved with stars, decorative notching, and lodge symbols. The handle is carved as a man's head with long hair. Overall staff length: 47-1/2". *Courtesy of Kimball M. Sterling Auctioneers.* $800-1200.

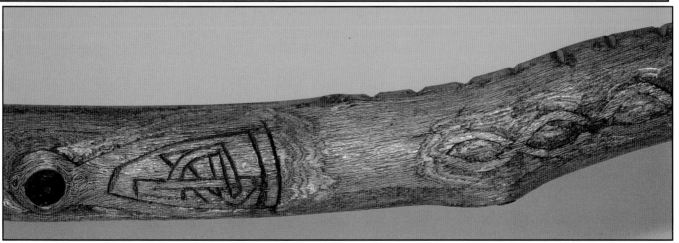

The Ever-present Snake Motif

While animal, reptile, and insect denizens of the forest all appear on folk art walking sticks, the sinuous snake is most often featured. The long, lazy S shapes of many branches used as raw material just beg to be transformed into snakes. More intricate and demanding are the carved snakes coiled around the shafts of folk art sticks. The snake motif has been used around the globe and throughout time. The symbolic significance of the snake, however, varies from place to place.

Primitive peoples around the globe have viewed snakes as symbols of fertility. Snake idols beneath beds were believed to facilitate conception and close association with snakes was recommended both for easy delivery and to ensure a child would have a pure heart.

In the Anatolian culture, as reflected in the canes produced in Devrek, Turkey, intertwined snakes are representative of life's dualities: the spiritual and physical, life and death, love and hate, good and evil, reason and emotion.

Mythology is rife with snakes. The medical community's Caduceus (a staff entwined with two snakes), symbol of healing, has its origins in mythology. In ancient Rome, snakes were seen as the physical manifestation of guardian angels. In Thebes, serpents were believed to be reincarnated kings and queens.

In the Judeo-Christian tradition, the dark and mysterious aspect of the snake holds sway, reflected in the Genesis story of Adam and Eve, with their fall from grace facilitated by a cunning serpent.

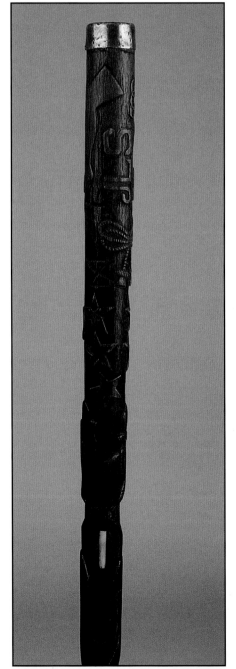

American folk art cane featuring secret society symbols, initials, and various inset materials for decoration. A large snake is entwined near the base of the cane. Small metal ferrule. Overall length: 34". *Courtesy of Ambassador Richard W. Carlson.* $425-470.

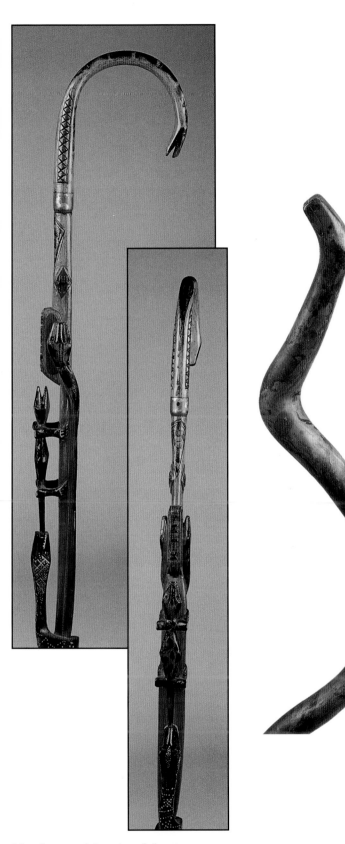

Folk art snake cane with a polychrome painted surface and a very crooked shaft ending with the snake's tail as the pointed lower tip of the cane shaft. There is no ferrule. Overall length: 34". *Courtesy of Ron Van Anda and Sandra Whitson.* $1500.

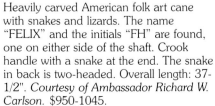

Heavily carved American folk art cane with snakes and lizards. The name "FELIX" and the initials "FH" are found, one on either side of the shaft. Crook handle with a snake at the end. The snake in back is two-headed. Overall length: 37-1/2". *Courtesy of Ambassador Richard W. Carlson.* $950-1045.

Glass Canes

Glass blowers were big men, many ranging from 175 to 200 pounds and standing six feet tall. The demands of their labors, transforming hot blobs of molten glass into beautifully shaped glassware, forced most to retire between the ages of fifty-five and sixty. As one glass worker observed, "They just ran out of wind." (Lindbeck and Snyder 2000, 22) Blowers created canes representative of their great skill and control over molten glass. Long sections of glass are difficult to handle at best. Mastering the techniques necessary to produce these beautiful objects was a challenge for apprentice and master glass blowers alike. Once produced, glass canes were carried as examples of an artist's pride in his craft. At ceremonial occasions and parades, glass blowers were commonly seen with these symbols of their expertise. Blowers at the Fostoria Glass Company in West Virginia carried their glass canes in Labor Day parades.

The appearance of glass canes coincides with the first commercial use of long rods of glass. In glasshouses, the sand, soda ash, and lime that comprised glass was considered virtually worthless. Every worker could claim the "frigger" or "whimsy" he produced as his own. Anything made between shifts or while waiting for malleable glass from the furnace was his to take, provided it was still there the following morning after cooling overnight in an annealing oven.

English, French, and American examples of glass canes are fairly common. Surprisingly, although Italians mastered glass blowing techniques early and produced a variety of complex objects as testimony to their skills, they appear to have had little interest in making glass canes.

Glass canes may be found in two general types. The first is fashioned from solid lengths of glass, frequently featuring decorative twists along the shaft and most often finished with crook or L-shaped handles. It was not unusual for the inner core of glass to be encased in an outer layer (or layers) of different colored glass. The second type of glass cane is a hollow baton with a rounded knob handle. This form was often made of clear glass and decorated with spiraling stripes of assorted colors along its length. On rare occasions, metallic or white powders were blown into these canes, coating the interior with a metallic or milky sheen. These canes were brought into the homes of glassworkers and were given as gifts or bartered in trade.

West Virginia Civil War era glass cane, hollow with a bulbous handle. Overall length: 52-1/2". *Courtesy of Dale Van Atta.* $420-460.

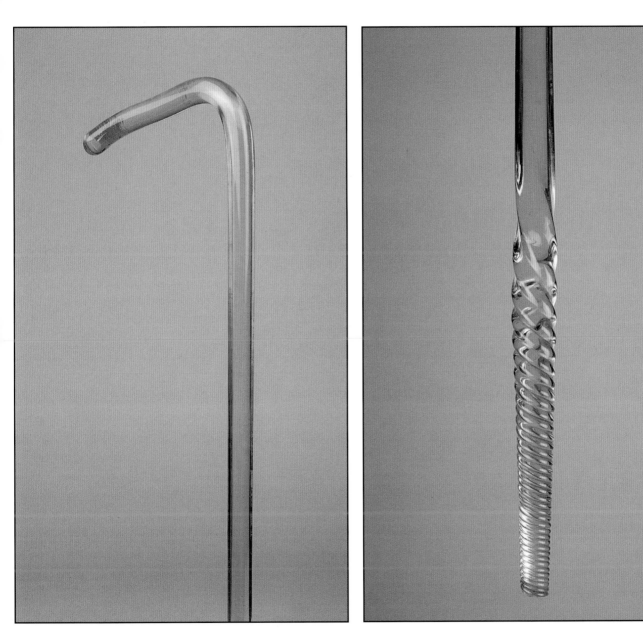

Glass cane. An interesting feature is the twist at the base of the shaft. Overall
length: 29". *Courtesy of Ambassador Richard W. Carlson.* $375-415.

Scrimshaw: the Nautical Canes

Looking back over human development, ivory has been found useful to peoples around the world for both tools and decorative items. Inland peoples used mammoth ivory, seafaring folk turned to whale bone and whale ivory. The Thules culture, originating in Alaska and spreading eastward eventually as far as Greenland, used whale ivory and bone. Whale ribs were used to create partially buried homes. Ivory was used to trade with European whalers along the Bering Sea. During the late eighteenth century, a healthy ivory carving industry developed, trading vast quantities of ivory products including walking stick handles, buttons, pastry wheels, sewing tools, billiard balls, and much more.

Above and right:
A group of nautical canes, five whalebone shafts. *Courtesy of Richard R. Wagner, Jr.* Value based primarily on the heaviness and largeness of the cane and the degree of carving and inlay work. Plain examples with nice white shafts range from $700-1200 depending on the weight of the shaft. Others are valued on the degree of carving and range from $2000-8000+. The most expensive in this group values around $2000+.

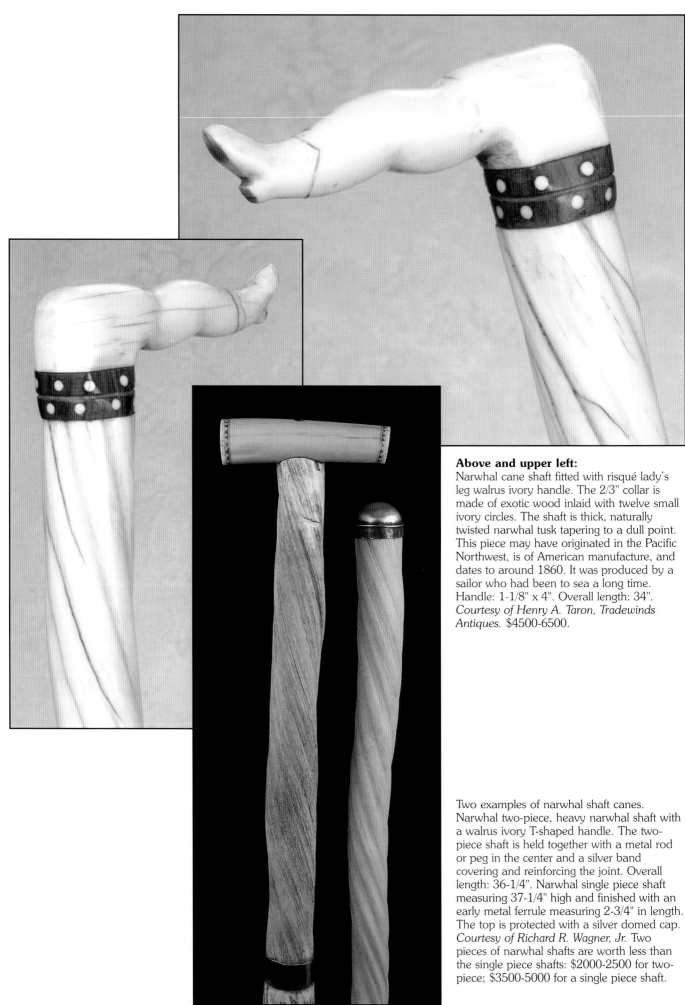

Above and upper left:
Narwhal cane shaft fitted with risqué lady's leg walrus ivory handle. The 2/3" collar is made of exotic wood inlaid with twelve small ivory circles. The shaft is thick, naturally twisted narwhal tusk tapering to a dull point. This piece may have originated in the Pacific Northwest, is of American manufacture, and dates to around 1860. It was produced by a sailor who had been to sea a long time. Handle: 1-1/8" x 4". Overall length: 34". *Courtesy of Henry A. Taron, Tradewinds Antiques.* $4500-6500.

Two examples of narwhal shaft canes. Narwhal two-piece, heavy narwhal shaft with a walrus ivory T-shaped handle. The two-piece shaft is held together with a metal rod or peg in the center and a silver band covering and reinforcing the joint. Overall length: 36-1/4". Narwhal single piece shaft measuring 37-1/4" high and finished with an early metal ferrule measuring 2-3/4" in length. The top is protected with a silver domed cap. *Courtesy of Richard R. Wagner, Jr.* Two pieces of narwhal shafts are worth less than the single piece shafts: $2000-2500 for two-piece; $3500-5000 for a single piece shaft.

However, most of the beautiful scrimshaw and nautical items available to collectors today date back to the nineteenth century whaling industry. By definition, scrimshaw is an art form produced by mariners at sea during the nineteenth century. The materials used were largely the bony leftovers of the whaling industry: sperm whale ivory, skeletal whalebone, and baleen. These are often combined with exotic materials picked up at sea or in various ports of call. On the other hand, while nautical canes used similar materials to create products, the raw materials were assembled into useful and artistic items professionally on shore to be sold to clientele seeking exotic oceanic items without enduring the rigors of shipboard life themselves.

Sailors were allowed to make their art from portions of the mammals caught at sea that were of little or no commercial value in and of themselves. At times, sperm whale teeth were polished to a high gloss and engraved with a wide variety of images, which were then darkened with lampblack (a mixture of carbon in oil) and colored pigments (homemade fruit and vegetable dyes, commercial India inks, and verdigris—the green deposit that builds up on copper and brass) to finish them. Other sailors preferred to carve relief decorations or full sculptural forms including human and animal figural sculptures, cane handles, box ornaments, finials, corset stays, and any number of other items. No matter what form the carving took, the most common tool used by sailors was the sailors' knife.

Walrus tusk was frequently used in scrimshaw. Whalers were not hunting for walrus on their voyages, however; rather walrus tusks were bartered for with peoples in Alaska, Canada, and Siberia. While sperm whale teeth provided a smooth material to work with, walrus tusk had the advantage of greater size.

Baleen is the keratin plate from the mouths of a number of different whales, but not sperm whales. Baleen is the whale equivalent of animal hooves, bovine horns, or human fingernails. Working with baleen was a challenge. While the material was flexible enough to make umbrella ribs, skirt hoops, and corset stays, it was generally considered hard to work with as it was both brittle and wiry. There are examples of baleen canes in this book that are examples of great workmanship and persistence, considering the nature of the material.

Whalers combined the raw materials from whales and the bartered for walrus tusks with a wide variety of natural materials to create impressive works of art. Among the found materials incorporated into scrimshaw canes are exotic woods, metals, tortoiseshell, seashells, and bits of cloth or braided twine. Coins from Latin America are found at times adorning scrimshaw cane handles and other items.

The whaling industry came into its own during the early nineteenth century. With this rise in business came longer voyages on larger ships filled to capacity and beyond with whaling crews. The earliest examples of engraved pictorial scrimshaw have been dated to around 1817-21. Early producers decorating sperm whale teeth were British South Sea whalers.

The first known American scrimshaw artist is considered one of the very best. Hailing from Nantucket, Edward Burdett (1805-33) began scrimhanding around 1824. Burdett's first dated piece is engraved with the year 1827. The most famous of the early nineteenth century American scrimhanders also was a Nantucket resident, Frederick Myrick (1808-62). He was the first to sign and date his work. During the 1830s and 1840s (considered the Golden Age of scrimshaw), whalers considered scrimshaw artists were natives of America, Australia, and Great Britain.

Once the techniques had been pioneered, scrimshaw caught on with sailors in ever-increasing numbers. Sailor John Martin, returning from his second whaling voyage on the ship Lucy Ann of Wilmington, Delaware, declared in 1844 that scrimshaw was produced by all hands on the ship. He said that the favorite products were walking sticks, stating, "…There are enough canes in this ship to supply all the old men of Wilmington." Harvey R. Phillips, a journal-keeper and mate aboard the Minerva of New Bedford, confirms this statement, "…every body Scrimpshonting as the term goes … that is making canes and corset boasks and getting out whale boan hoops for presenting for their wives and sweet hearts." (Frank n.d., 7)

The diversity of motifs found on scrimshaw relates to the makeup of whaling crews. Early deep sea whaling crews were made up of Caucasians from Long Island and New England, Gay Head Indians from Martha's Vineyard, and African-Americans. While at sea, captains also picked up crewmen as needed wherever they found them. In time, crews could be found that were half American and half from other nations. Among the foreign crewmen were Cape Verdeans and Pacific Islanders. Men of various nations tended to stick with their own countrymen aboard ship; however, violence between men of different nations was generally diffused by the arduous nature of the task at hand.

Not all scrimhanders were men. Some whaling captains brought their wives and children with them. Seafaring family members also produced scrimshaw in significant amounts.

Of the motifs employed, ship portraits and whaling scenes were pioneered in the 1820s. During the 1830s, motifs ranged far afield, including naval scenes, patriotic subjects, symbolic figures such as Columbia, Hope, and Britannia, portraits of famous men and women, biblical subjects, scenic displays, figures of women and family groups, and material ranging from the common to the erotic.

The most highly skilled of the scrimhanders were the ship's carpenters and coopers, woodworkers whose mechanical and artistic skills allowed them to create scrimshaw of truly outstanding quality. Sailors who displayed dexterity and ingenuity in scrimshaw gained respect among their crewmates. While many produced scrimshaw as souvenirs for family and friends on shore, some sailors exchanged scrimshaw items as gifts among themselves while other mariners worked on commission.

It should be noted again that not all sticks produced from marine materials were made by scrimhanders at sea. Walking sticks of such materials bearing nautical themes were also professionally manufactured on shore. While these are formal sticks, they are included here to make readers aware of their existence.

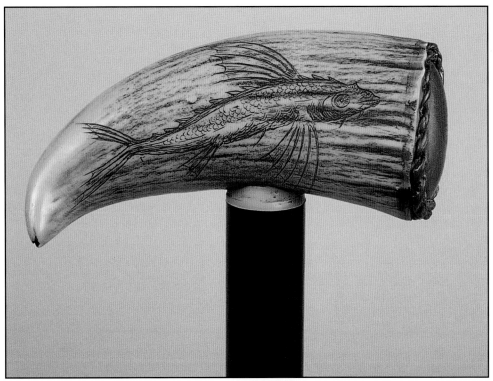

Left and below:
Scrimshaw tooth handled cane featuring a flying fish on one side and a whaling scene on the other. Small silver ferrule. The whaling scene side is initialed "J.A." in an oval. Handle: 4" l. tooth. Overall length: 36-1/4". *Courtesy of Ambassador Richard W. Carlson.* $675-745.

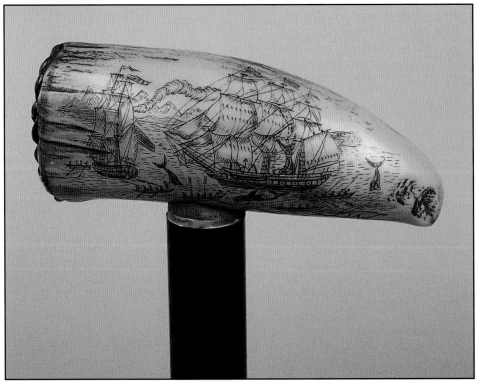

Heavy scrimhander's cane with inscribed "RC 1862" and art (anchor at end) and whale on other side, silver collar, bone ferrule. Handle: 3" h. x 5" w. Overall length: 36-3/4". *Courtesy of Ambassador Richard W. Carlson.* $725-800.

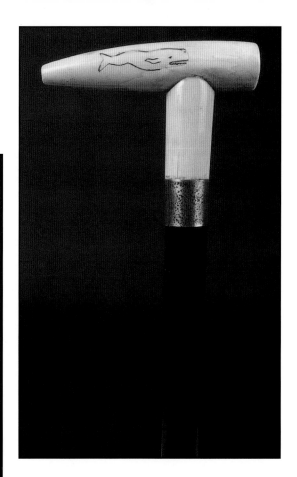

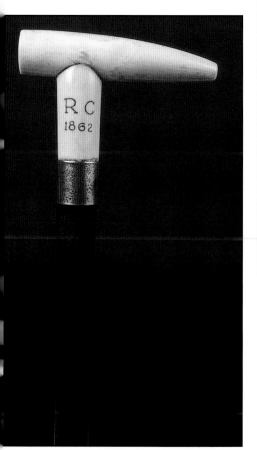

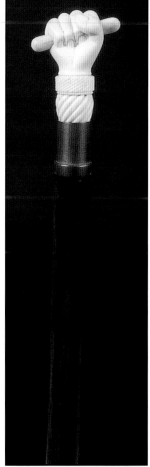

Ivory fist with stick nautical handle, metal collar, unusual small twisted metal ferrule measuring 3/4" l. Handle: 2" l. Overall length: 33". *Courtesy of Ambassador Richard W. Carlson.* $725-800

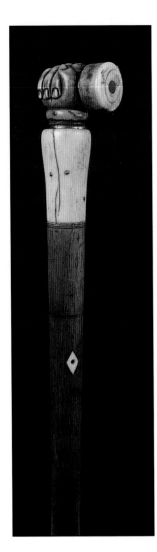

Scrimhander's fist gripping handle
with eyelet, metal ferrule. Handle:
4-1/2" l. Overall length: 37-1/2".
*Courtesy of Ambassador Richard
W. Carlson.* $625-690.

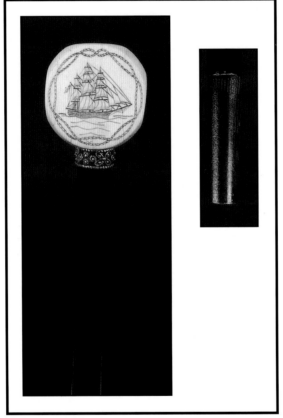

Nautical bone handle with sailing ship
incised and inked, metal ferrule with no iron
tip, silver collar. Handle: 2" x 2". Overall
length: 36-1/4". *Courtesy of Ambassador
Richard W. Carlson.* $695-765.

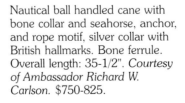

Nautical ball handled cane with
bone collar and seahorse, anchor,
and rope motif, silver collar with
British hallmarks. Bone ferrule.
Overall length: 35-1/2". *Courtesy
of Ambassador Richard W.
Carlson.* $750-825.

Scrimshaw hand holding object over
wood or vegetable ivory collar, no
ferrule. Handle: 3-3/4" l. Overall
length: 38-1/2". *Courtesy of Ambassador Richard W. Carlson.* $900-990.

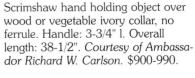

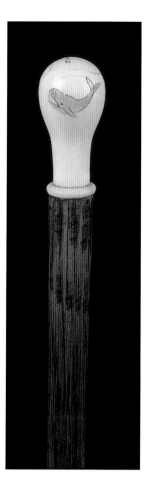

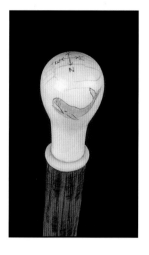

Left and above:
Nautical knob handle, whale incised and inked with compass bearings on top of handle, on wood shaft with a bone ferrule. Handle: 2" h. Overall length: 35". *Courtesy of Ambassador Richard W. Carlson.* $775-855.

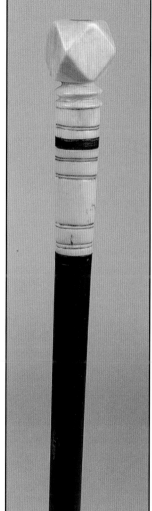

Scrimshaw cane with ivory, baleen collar, inset mother-of-pearl on top, brass inset eyelets. Overall length: 33". *Courtesy of Ambassador Richard W. Carlson.* $375-415.

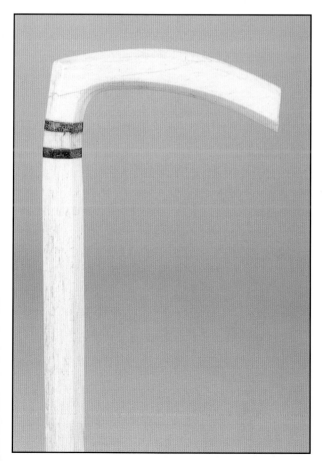

Scrimhander's knob handled cane covered in knotted cord with cord collar, metal ferrule with iron tip. Overall length: 35-1/2". *Courtesy of Ambassador Richard W. Carlson.* $225-250.

L-shaped whalebone nautical walking stick. The whalebone handle and shaft are both octagonal in shape and are separated by baleen spacers. No ferrule, American, c. 1860. Handle: 4" w. x 1-1/2" h. Overall length: 34-1/2". *Courtesy of The World of the Walking Stick.* $1375-1515.

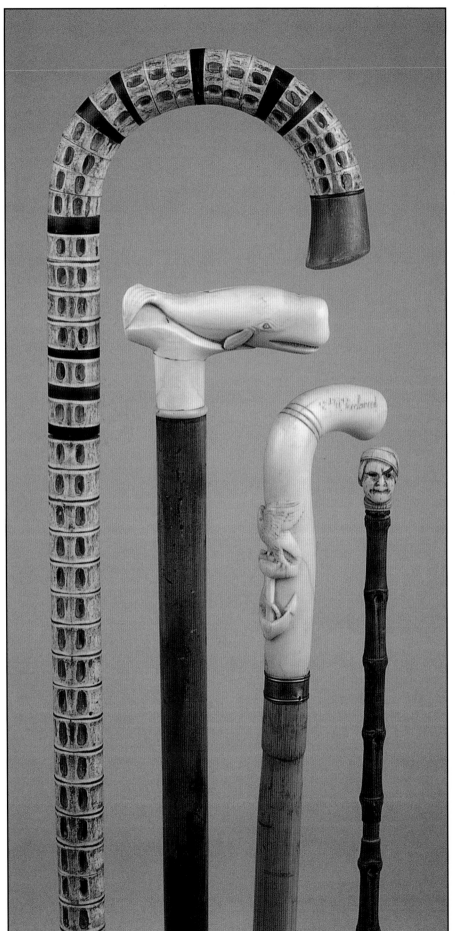

Left:
Four nautical style canes made on land. Vertebrae cane (shark or ray vertebrae with steer's horn spacers), crook handled, made on dry land in a factory, $250-400. Whale carved in whale ivory on a malacca shaft, $1000-1350. L-shaped walrus ivory handle with the name "Lockwood" engraved into it with an eagle standing on anchor insignia, white metal band, bamboo shaft, $450-650. Handle with figure of a sailor (missing his eye patch) carved from elephant ivory, thin bamboo shaft, $250-350. *Courtesy of Richard R. Wagner, Jr.*

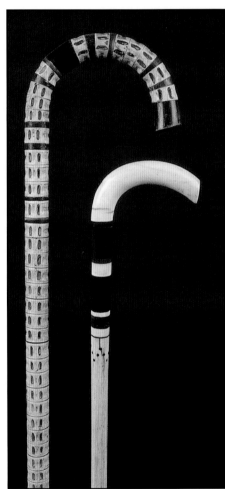

Two nautical canes, bone with baleen inlay (right) and vertebra crook handle. Overall lengths: Left: 35-1/2"; right: 36-1/4". *Courtesy of Ambassador Richard W. Carlson.* Left: $360-400; right: $475-525.

Nautical cane with a whale ivory fist handle, the fist holding a bar of black-stained tropical wood. This wood is also used as octagonal segmented spacers alternating with whale ivory spacers down the upper portion of the shaft, prior to meeting with a one-piece whalebone shaft. The upper portion of the shaft is octagonal in shape like the spacers while the lower portion is round. This is an elegant piece of work. Handle: 5" x 2-1/4". Overall length: 34-7/16". *Courtesy of Kimball M. Sterling Auctioneers.* $2600-3000.

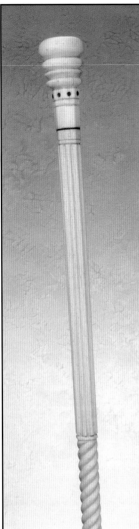

Left:
American whale ivory and whalebone nautical cane, c. 1840. The handle is produced from a single piece of whale tooth ivory. The lower portion of the handle has eight panels decorated with inlaid baleen dots. A thin baleen separator bridges the gap between the handle and the shaft. The whalebone shaft is fluted for the top 10", followed by 9-1/2" of rope twist carving, and a final 10" of smoothly tapering shaft protected at the tip by a 1-1/3" long brass and iron ferrule. *Courtesy of Henry A. Taron, Tradewinds Antiques.* $3000-4000.

Above and left:
Possibly Scandinavian in origins, this beautiful nautical narwhal cane belonged to Captain T. Johanson. Fitted above the narwhal tusk shaft is an elephant ivory handle capped in silver. The silver cap is adorned with engraved bows and leaves. The ivory handle is carved in ten panels that are scalloped at the base. A 3/4" silver collar is inscribed "Capt. T. Johanson, 6-12-07." The shaft is polished and innocent of any ferrule. This piece was professionally prepared on shore for the Captain. *Courtesy of Henry A. Taron, Tradewinds Antiques.* $4500-6500.

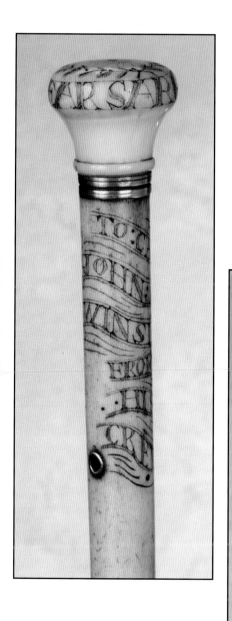

This is an impressive scrimshaw cane presented to Union Navy Captain John Winslow by his crew. The knob handle is whale ivory decorated on top with a spiral sunburst and a baleen dot in the center, highlighted in red. The sunburst is surrounded by a wreath with red berries. Around the handle's rim is written "U.S.S. Kearsarge, 1864," the initials and words separated with baleen dots. The handmade brass collar measures 1/4" and covers the joint between the handle and the whalebone shaft, which features oval brass eyelets. The scrimshaw work along the shaft reads, "To Capt. John A. Winslow From His Crew." The bone tip was considered sturdy enough to remain free of a ferrule. Handle: 1-1/8" x 1-1/3" dia. Overall length: 35-1/4". *Courtesy of Henry A. Taron, Tradewinds Antiques.* $10,000-15,000.

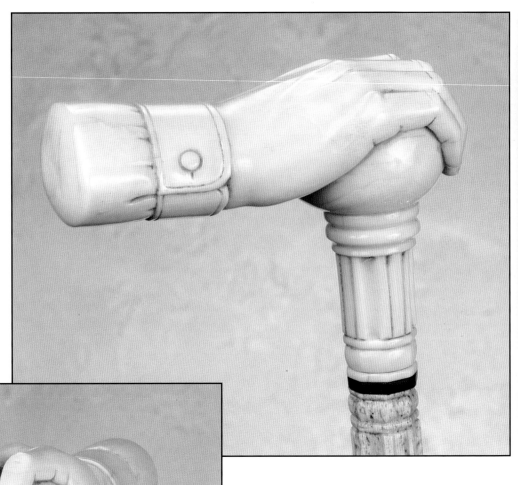

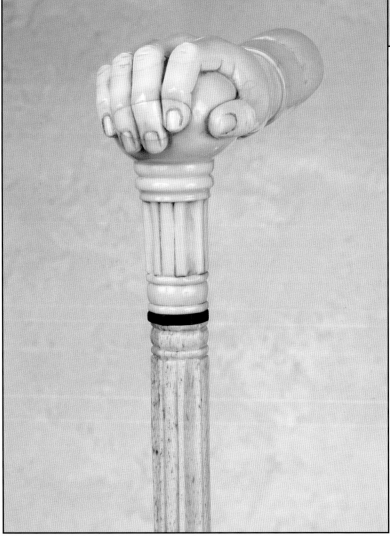

A beautiful example of a professionally made American nautical cane, c. 1850, featuring a whale ivory handle and whalebone shaft. The handle is created from a single whale's tooth and features a very well carved hand clothed in a shirt cuff holding onto a knob handle. Below the knob, the 1-3/4" piece of whale ivory is decorated with fluting and turned decoration. A thin piece of baleen separates the handle from the whalebone shaft, which is in turn decorated with deep fluting above a twisted rope decoration. Handle: 4-1/3" x 1-1/2". Overall length: 36". *Courtesy of Henry A. Taron, Tradewinds Antiques.* While this fine piece was estimated at $8000-12,000, when the hammer dropped, the bidding had stopped at $17,000.

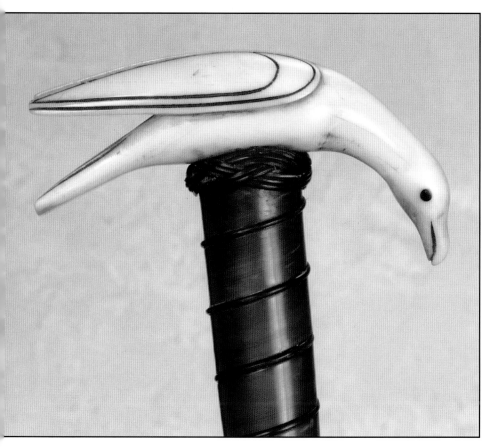

Nautical cane featuring a whale ivory seagull on a baleen shaft, the gull's wings, beak, and tail all detailed in black ink. This canes dates from c. 1850 and the country of origin is unknown. The bird's eyes are made of baleen. The woven baleen collar in the form of a turk's head knot measures 1/2". Two other knots are found along the shaft. The shaft is wrapped in wide bands of baleen veneer overlaid with thin strings of baleen. The baleen ferrule measures 1-1/2". Handle: 4-1/4" x 1". Overall length: 35-3/4". *Courtesy of Henry A. Taron, Tradewinds Antiques.* While the estimated values of this cane was listed as $6000-8000, it sold at auction in 2002 for $11,000.

Collecting Modern
Folk Art Canes

As we saw with David Allen, modern folk artists are found selling their walking sticks at regional shows on a regular basis. Attend shows in your area and study their work. Many are truly skilled artists creating innovative work rivaling or exceeding the craftsmanship employed in centuries past. These items are well worth your attention and study. They are also fine additions to any collection of folk art sticks.

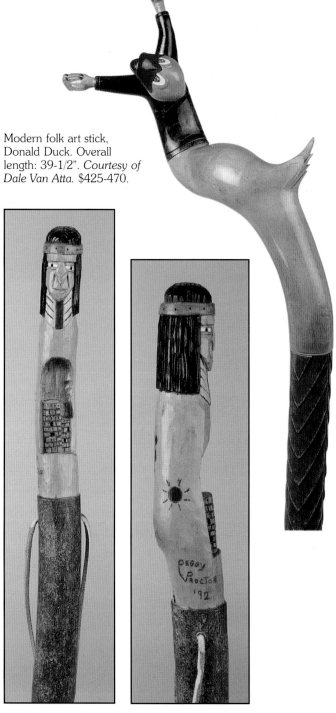

Modern folk art stick, Donald Duck. Overall length: 39-1/2". *Courtesy of Dale Van Atta.* $425-470.

Modern folk art staff with an Indian bust and cliff Pueblo houses, signed "Peggy Proctor '92." No ferrule. Overall length: 54-1/2". *Courtesy of Dale Van Atta.* $100+.

Left:
Two modern folk art sticks. Check out the work of modern artists at regional fairs. These artists are very talented and worthy of your notice. Left: L handle with flag draped down the shaft, signature burned on the base of the handle, reading: "Jack H. Floyd. Austell, GA. 12/7/93 NO. 155." Overall length: 42". Right: a root cane carved with a wild, horned animal head with a snake in its mouth for a handle. A planking effect adorns the shaft. Overall length: 37". Left: no ferrule, right rubber ferrule. *Courtesy of Ambassador Richard W. Carlson.* $425-470 each.

Sticks of Aggression, Sticks of Defense; Sticks at Play & System Sticks

This chapter covers a diverse collection of walking sticks ranging from the lethal to the whimsical. Among them are sticks with items hidden inside them in a staggering array of forms. Here is a real peek into the ingenuity of a bygone age. The sticks you will find here are a sampling of the wide variety available on the collector's market today. This is by no means an encyclopedic enumeration. It is, however, a very interesting one.

The Dark Side of Walking Sticks

Individual Attacks

Throughout recorded history, a stout stick has always been a handy means of defending oneself or ending an argument. During the last decade of the twentieth century, a study was made of violence among men in Lower Canada during the period 1800 to 1850. This study is truly pertinent to our investigation of the walking stick and its many uses. Violence between men in that time and place, when it occurred, happened fast and ended abruptly. Usually no more than two or three blows were required to end an argument. While knives, swords, and guns were available, they were rarely carried or used by civilian men. When a weapon was required, Canadian men of the first half of the nineteenth century reached for a good stout stick. They used walking sticks, whip handles, and ox-goads to make their points.

Canadian men of different social and economic classes were all either aggressors or victims in equal numbers. It seems a caning knew no class or social bounds but was a truly democratic form of attack. Men of high economic and social rank did avail themselves of an opportunity for ritual violence denied to men of lower rank, however. Wealthy men participated in duels while others did not.

While wealthy men were not subject to a greater proportion of violence, one man to another, than any other group (with the exception of dueling), these social elites were different in both their perception of violence and in the way they inflicted it on other Canadian men. Men of elite status feared that they were going to be attacked by those of lesser standing. Possibly as a response to this fear, wealthy Canadian men struck out against those of lower classes with their canes. However, the lower classes rarely ever validated this fear; they almost never attacked wealthy men. In fact, well-to-do Canadians had more to fear from each other than from those of lower socio-economic standing. And when the rich Canadian struck, his weapon of choice was almost always his walking stick. (Fyson 1999)

In the United States, one of the most famous acts of cane violence between wealthy men occurred in 1856, when Congressman Preston Brooks beat Senator Charles Sumner with his walking stick. This attack, however, did not end abruptly, as in the Canadian model.

Preston S. Brooks was a former military man and lawyer elected to the Congress from South Carolina in 1852. In 1856, Senator Charles Sumner of Massachusetts delivered a lengthy two-day speech opposing the admission of Kansas into the Union as a slave state. Sumner condemned slavery, calling it a "crime against Kansas," and denounced a proslavery advocate, Senator Andrew Butler of South Carolina, in the process. This incensed Senator Butler's nephew, Congressman Preston Brooks. After waiting for two days for an apology that was never to come from Senator Sumner, Congressman Brooks attacked Sumner at his desk in the Senate Chamber. Enraged, Brooks beat Sumner over the head repeatedly until the Senator lay unconscious on the floor. Of the attack, Brooks stated, "I struck him with my cane and gave him about thirty first rate stripes with a gutta-percha cane … Every lick went where I intended … Towards the end he bellowed like a calf. I wore my cane out completely." (Rosenweig 2002, Par. 5)

The attack was widely reported. In response, Preston Brooks received many gold-handled canes from supporters across the South to replace the one he had lost. Congressman Brooks was expelled and then re-elected to his post by his district. Senator Sumner required years to recover from that beating. Congressman Brooks died in Washington the following year.

Workhouse Sticks

By the 1820s, the Industrial Revolution was in full swing in Britain. Large factories filled with newly invented machines increasing the rate of production sprung up by the hundreds across the British Empire. Factories producing wool and cotton products, iron, steel, and steam engines all needed a steady supply of workers to meet the demands of expanding markets both at home and abroad. Children were found to be ideal laborers. They came cheap from poor parents and workhouses, they were easily intimidated, and they were found to be very nimble when working in tight and dangerous spaces. Without the benefits of health and safety regulations, working conditions were incredibly dangerous and horrific accidents were commonplace. Many children were maimed or killed in these factories.

Children as young as five were working sixteen hour days with little in the way of food, rest, clothing, or wages. Mill owners frequently used the canes they carried to discipline workers found to be obstreperous or lazy. Canes would flash when children fell asleep, made mistakes, or had enough common sense to refuse truly dangerous tasks. Industrial progress and economic gain came at an awful cost. In Britain, social reformers would begin to have an influence, passing labor reform laws creating minimum working ages and limiting working hours, in 1833.

School Discipline & Walking Sticks

There was a time when using a cane to discipline students was considered normal behavior. Harvard University President Josiah Quincy (1772-1864) held his post from 1829 to 1845 and left his walking stick behind in Quincy House. A former lawyer and past mayor of Boston, Quincy was considered a notorious disciplinarian and rumor has it the splits in his cane's shaft were the result of its repeated impact upon many disruptive students' behinds.

In New Zealand, canes were commonly used to discipline secondary school boys in the 1960s. Ethnographic studies of this practice released in the 1970s open a window to the mindset of teachers and students alike from an era when caning was commonplace.

Male teachers used canes to instill discipline and to toughen the boys in their charge. One report cited a teacher who kept a box beside his desk. At the beginning of the school year he would open the box and display canes of different lengths and thicknesses. The teacher explained to the boys that the bigger they were, the larger the cane would be that was used to discipline them. Other schools kept a caning room. Canes of various sizes lined the walls. A student was taken to the room and caned by the teacher in front of a witness, both of whom signed a book prior to proceeding with the punishment. Young men in these schools took pride from their ability to withstand the pain inflicted and each caning added prestige to a boy's reputation.

Teachers opposed to caning in New Zealand boys' schools found they could not opt out of this form of discipline. It was a part of the culture. Those who did not participate were viewed as weak by students and fellow teachers alike. Women were largely limited to teaching in primary grades as it was believed they would not be strong enough to wield a cane with sufficient authority to keep the older boys in check.

Some male teachers who were part of this system quickly discovered they were ill-equipped to deal with a classroom of girls. Caning of girls was not permissible. Without a cane, these men were mystified about how to deal with their boisterous students. On one level, caning as discipline was feared by male students and loathed by some teachers. However, caning became insidiously enmeshed into the educational system and, on another level, students and teachers alike made such an accommodation to this violent form of discipline that both sides found it difficult to relinquish.

Moving on to England, by the early 1950s British authorities had apparently had enough of one proponent of corporal punishment. In 1953, police raided the headquarters of the National Society for the Retention of Corporal Punishment. In the four hour raid, officers removed thousands of canes and other sticks designed for discipline from the premises, along with hundreds of brochures proclaiming the virtues of corporal punishment. The Society's president claimed to be supplying canes to ten thousand schools in the United Kingdom, America, and Continental Europe at the time.

Cane Defense

In the July 1903 issue of the magazine *Health and Strength*, Pierre Vigny, a self-described "professor of physical exercise specially adapted to self-defense" declared that the sturdy walking stick was the best means of self-defense. For Vigny, the malacca cane was both the most up-to-date of all walking sticks and the most formidable weapon for self-defense. He recommended working out with a malacca stick to develop supple, strong muscles and hone one's personal agility, creating an individual with elegant and graceful movements.

Vigny considered the sturdy walking stick the perfect weapon, as it is a great equalizer, eliminating an opponent's advantages in size, strength, and weight. He further stated that a properly trained individual could hold off several attackers at once as the cane could be wielded through every possible direction around you very quickly and "... whoever is hit by this weapon, which acquires an enormous force in its swinging motions, does not return to the attack again...". (Vigny 1903, 253-254)

Among the methods of self-defense described by Vigny in the article were:

1. Holding the stick in the grip of the whole hand and delivering a swinging hit;

2. Passing the stick from one hand to the other on alternate passes;
3. Holding the stick by the ferrule end while swinging;
4. Holding the stick in both hands while striking at the head, face, body, hands, and legs;
5. Using the end of the stick like a dagger. (Vigny warns that for this to be effective your blow must not be deflected by the opponent's cane or the force of the blow will be lost.)
6. And, seizing your opponent's stick if possible.

Finally, if struck, the author advises the cane wielder to return to a guard position and not to attempt to strike again immediately.

Of course, the author offered twelve lessons in his methods to interested readers. He also offered a few modified malacca walking sticks as well. These were medium-sized canes with heavy metal ball handles firmly riveted

to the shafts. The author assures his readers that the handle, while elegant, was sturdy enough not to dent during heavy use. Using this weighted bludgeon had an additional advantage, according to Vigny, as it "relieves one of the danger of carrying a revolver, and the feeling of disgust of having a dagger about one." (Vigny 1903, 253-254)

Weapons Canes

So far, we have explored how the simple, sturdy walking stick was used as a weapon. Now we shall see how weapons of other sorts were ingeniously integrated into walking stick handles and shafts. While, in reality, these weapons would be awkward to unlimber and ungainly to use in many cases (with the exception of a poacher who could slowly ready and use his weapon from a concealed location), they no doubt gave reassurance to those who carried them.

We will begin with the bludgeons and work our way through to the firearms. The simplest of the weapons canes increase the impact of a swung cane by adding a lead knob handle to the top of the shaft, covered in leather or cording. A variation on the simple, direct bludgeon places the lead knob on a flexible spring, rod, or cord secured to the shaft, giving the weighted knob a whipping action when swung. Life Preservers feature either a length of leather with a metal tip or a length of coiled steel attached to the handle and hidden in the shaft. When the handle was released from the shaft and the Life Preserver revealed, the holder was carrying a lengthened blackjack.

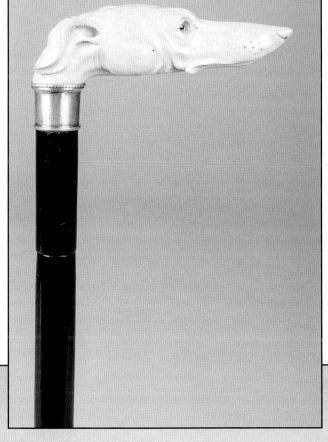

Left and below:
Life Preserver weapon cane with a carved ivory handle in the form of a greyhound or whippet's head with glass eyes. Ebonized faux bamboo shaft with 3/4" brass ferrule. The shaft conceals a 14-1/4" metal Life Preserver used to strike at ruffians, late nineteenth century. Handle: 4-1/2" w. x 1-3/16" h. Overall length: 34". *Courtesy of The World of the Walking Stick.* $2200-2420.

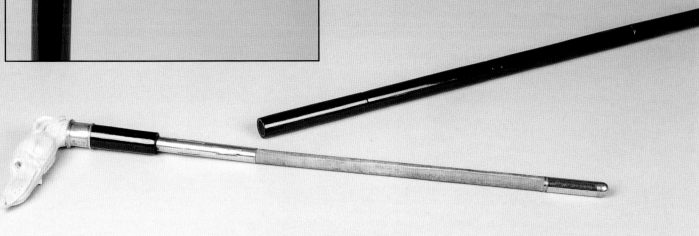

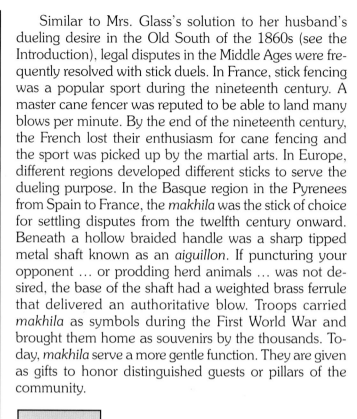

Macramé (string woven to cover lead knobs) sailor's "shore canes," defensive weapons to carry on shore: bamboo and mahogany shafts. *Courtesy of Richard R. Wagner, Jr.* $200-350 each.

Similar to Mrs. Glass's solution to her husband's dueling desire in the Old South of the 1860s (see the Introduction), legal disputes in the Middle Ages were frequently resolved with stick duels. In France, stick fencing was a popular sport during the nineteenth century. A master cane fencer was reputed to be able to land many blows per minute. By the end of the nineteenth century, the French lost their enthusiasm for cane fencing and the sport was picked up by the martial arts. In Europe, different regions developed different sticks to serve the dueling purpose. In the Basque region in the Pyrenees from Spain to France, the *makhila* was the stick of choice for settling disputes from the twelfth century onward. Beneath a hollow braided handle was a sharp tipped metal shaft known as an *aiguillon*. If puncturing your opponent … or prodding herd animals … was not desired, the base of the shaft had a weighted brass ferrule that delivered an authoritative blow. Troops carried *makhila* as symbols during the First World War and brought them home as souvenirs by the thousands. Today, *makhila* serve a more gentle function. They are given as gifts to honor distinguished guests or pillars of the community.

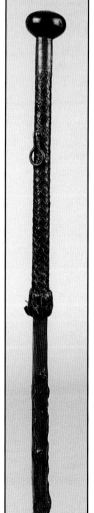

The *makhila*, a mountain cane with a weighted metal ferrule, a sharp metal shaft beneath the handle (handy for settling disputes or prodding thick-skinned livestock), and a decorated shaft (the decoration created by splitting the bark of the living plant, the healed bark creating decorative scarring). Overall length: 35-1/2". *Courtesy of Ambassador Richard W. Carlson.* $325-360.

If combatants were skilful and lucky, disputes were settled quickly with these battering weapons and neither combatant would require the services of a physician. Considering the dubious nature of medical care up to the twentieth century, these weapons were quite popular among the quick-tempered.

Bladed weapons of all sorts have been hidden within walking sticks. Stiletto blades housed within the upper or lower shaft of the cane would spring from concealment with the flick of the wrist and lock into place. A variation on the stiletto featured a blade fixed firmly to the base of the shaft. The bottom of the shaft itself was a movable sheath concealing the blade. Push the ferrule against an opponent and the base of the shaft retracted as the blade was driven home, yet never revealed to passersby.

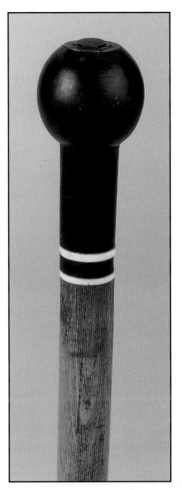

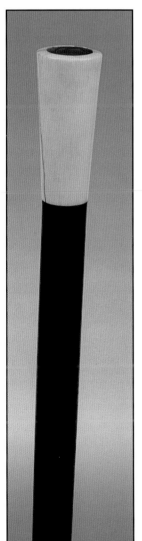

Above and right:
Wooden ball handled stiletto with a bone ferrule and bone disk collar. Overall length: 35-3/4". *Courtesy of Dale Van Atta.* $775-855.

Ivory handled stiletto. With a flick of the wrist, this blade flies out and locks in position, ready for use. The blade retracts when a small split lever on the side of blade is pushed back against the edge of the blade. Metal ferrule. Overall length: 34-1/2". *Courtesy of Ambassador Richard W. Carlson.* $525-580.

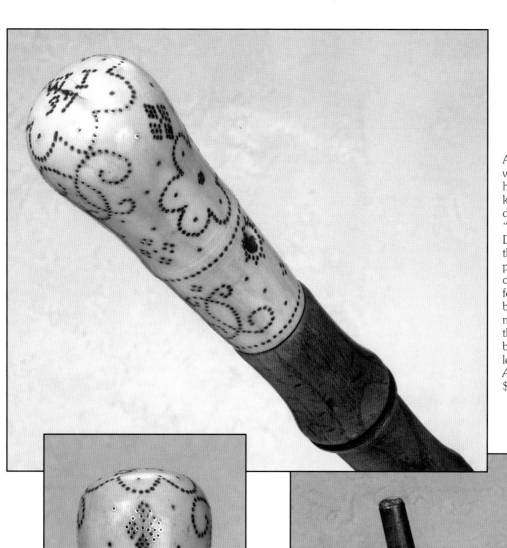

A seventeenth century pique cane with a twist, this example has a hidden blade in the base. The large knob handle is elephant ivory decorated in pique and initialed "W.I. 97" indicating the year 1697. Decorative pique work surrounds the eyelets. The shaft is hardwood, possibly chestnut, that has been carved to simulate bamboo. The ferrule at the end covering the blade measures 7-3/4" long and is made of iron. A quick twist removes the ferrule, exposing a 6-1/4" long blade. Handle: 4" x 1-1/3". Overall length: 37-1/4". *Courtesy of Henry A. Taron, Tradewinds Antiques.* $6000-8000.

Daggers and swords have long been hidden within walking sticks. European aristocracy of the seventeenth and eighteenth century, concerned that the common folk would rise against them or brigands would assault them, were among the first to order walking sticks with swords and daggers hidden within their shafts. Considering everyone was armed during this period, the fear seems reasonable. As sword carrying fell from favor during the latter half of the eighteenth century, sword canes became popular replacements. Early sword canes were produced with ivory knob handles and malacca shafts. During the nineteenth century, sword cane popularity continued to rise in Europe and the United States.

Similarly, in Japan the Samurai were banned from carrying swords in public in the 1860s. They created bamboo walking sticks known as *katanas* with sword blades hidden inside.

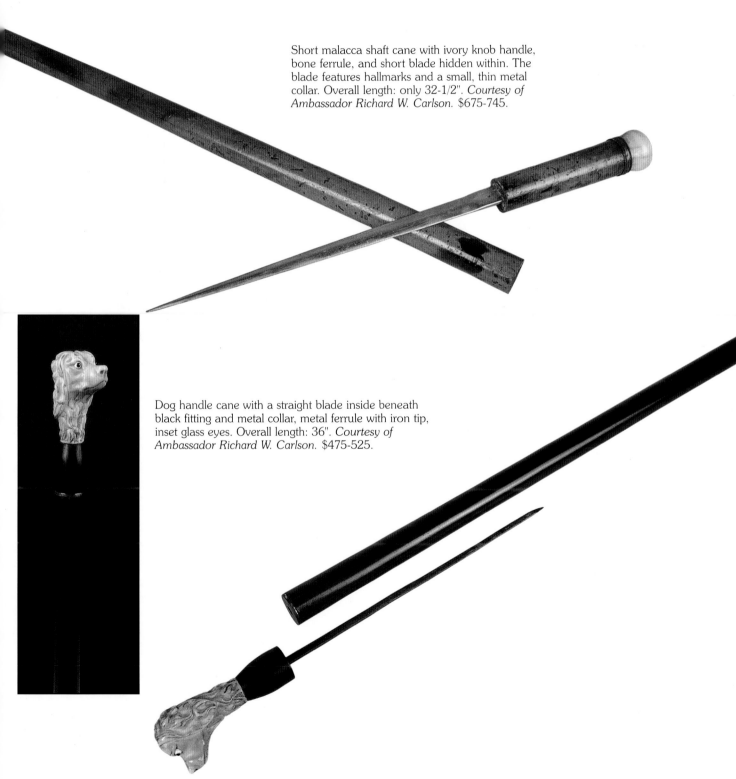

Short malacca shaft cane with ivory knob handle, bone ferrule, and short blade hidden within. The blade features hallmarks and a small, thin metal collar. Overall length: only 32-1/2". *Courtesy of Ambassador Richard W. Carlson.* $675-745.

Dog handle cane with a straight blade inside beneath black fitting and metal collar, metal ferrule with iron tip, inset glass eyes. Overall length: 36". *Courtesy of Ambassador Richard W. Carlson.* $475-525.

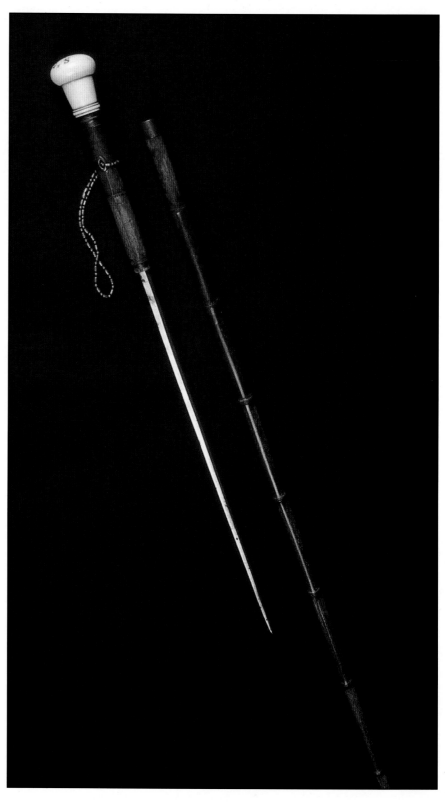

Short blade hidden in a cane, ivory handle marked "P.G.S." on top, eyelet above silver collar, four-sided blade within. Bamboo shaft, metal ferrule with iron tip. Handle: 1-1/2" h. Blade: 13" l. Overall length: 35". *Courtesy of Ambassador Richard W. Carlson.* $525-575.

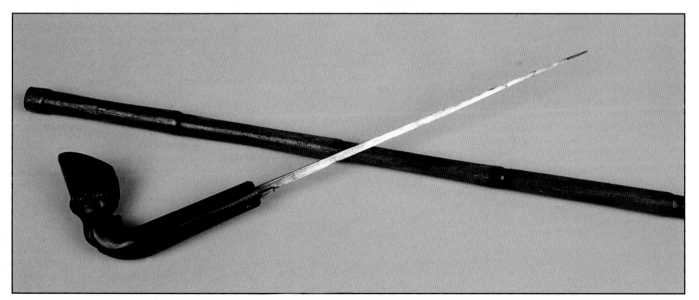

Horse's hoof handled short sword cane. The blade is released with the push of a
button. Stepped reed shaft, horn ferrule. Four sided blade: 12" l. Overall length:
34". *Courtesy of Ambassador Richard W. Carlson.* $625-690.

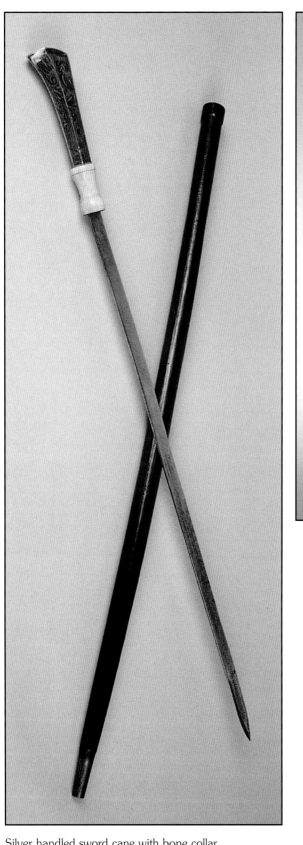

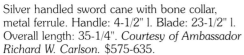

Silver handled sword cane with bone collar, metal ferrule. Handle: 4-1/2" l. Blade: 23-1/2" l. Overall length: 35-1/4". *Courtesy of Ambassador Richard W. Carlson.* $575-635.

Right:
Moroccan sword cane with filigreed metal elephant handle in brass and silver. Elaborate metal ferrule with wood tip. Rectangular blade: 24-3/4" l. Overall length: 38-3/4". *Courtesy of Ambassador Richard W. Carlson.* $725-800.

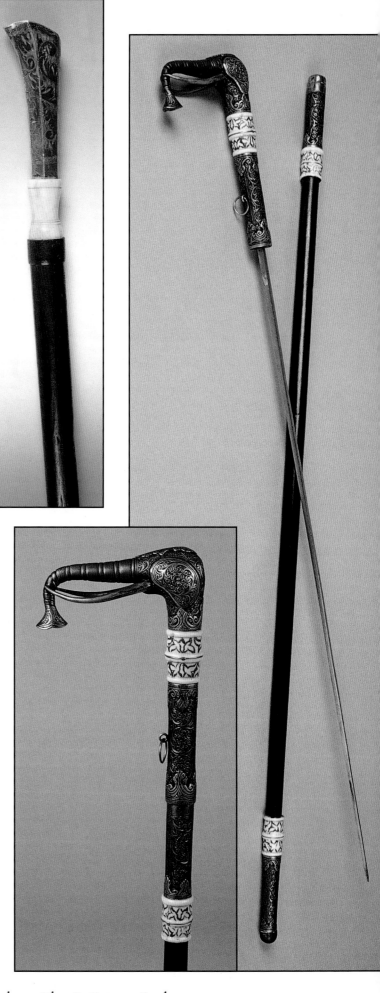

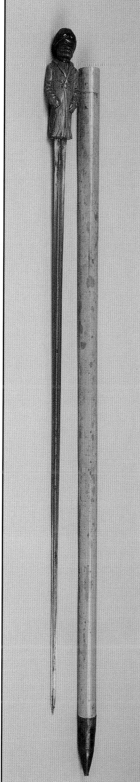

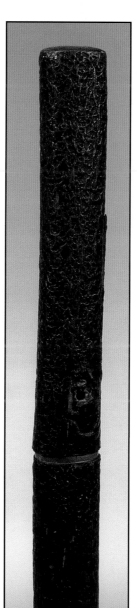

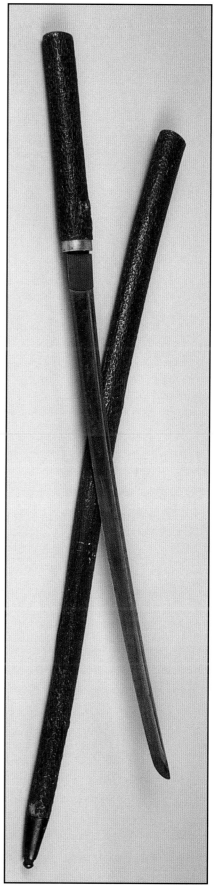

Below and right:
Japanese sword cane. The outer surface is covered in bark. The cane has an eyelet in the handle and the base of the shaft is protected with a metal ferrule. Blade: 25-1/4" l. Overall length: 35". *Courtesy of Ambassador Richard W. Carlson.* $475-525.

Above and right:
Figured handle sword cane with V-shaped sword blade and a pointed metal ferrule. Sword pulls free of shaft with a quick tug. Blade: 24" l. Overall length: 35-1/2". *Courtesy of Ambassador Richard W. Carlson.* $675-745.

Popular manufacturers of quality sword blades found within these canes included Solingen of Germany, St. Etienne of France, Wilkinson Company of England, and Toledo of Spain. Blued steel blades decorated with etchings from Solingen were quite popular. Wilkinson offered a sword stick with an antler handle and gold collar. Blades featuring elaborate decorative work and the Toledo name were also much sought for the strength of the blade. Many a sovereign and aristocrat has a sword or saber with a Toledo blade. Once introduced to Toledo steel by Spanish merchants, Japanese Samurai also sought Toledo blades for their *katana* weapons.

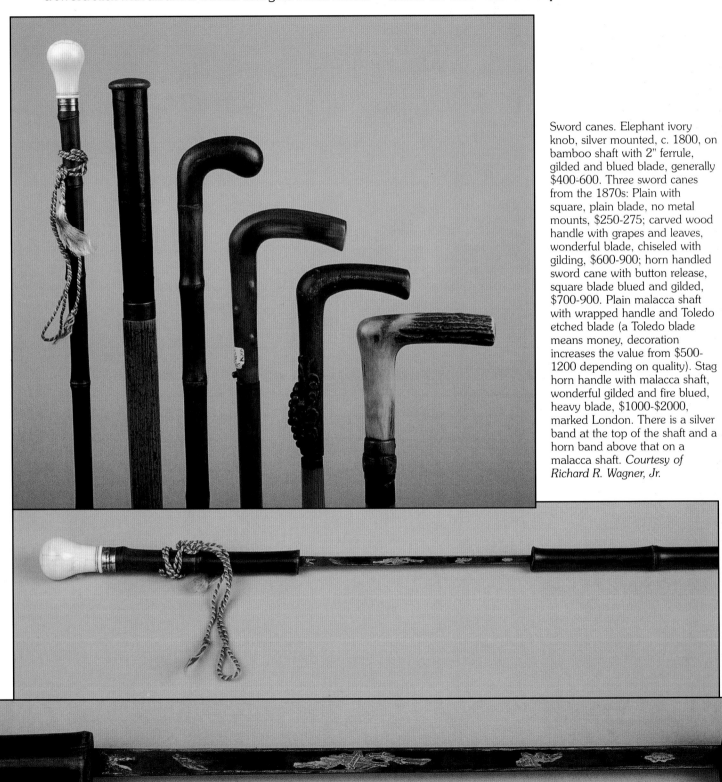

Sword canes. Elephant ivory knob, silver mounted, c. 1800, on bamboo shaft with 2" ferrule, gilded and blued blade, generally $400-600. Three sword canes from the 1870s: Plain with square, plain blade, no metal mounts, $250-275; carved wood handle with grapes and leaves, wonderful blade, chiseled with gilding, $600-900; horn handled sword cane with button release, square blade blued and gilded, $700-900. Plain malacca shaft with wrapped handle and Toledo etched blade (a Toledo blade means money, decoration increases the value from $500-1200 depending on quality). Stag horn handle with malacca shaft, wonderful gilded and fire blued, heavy blade, $1000-$2000, marked London. There is a silver band at the top of the shaft and a horn band above that on a malacca shaft. *Courtesy of Richard R. Wagner, Jr.*

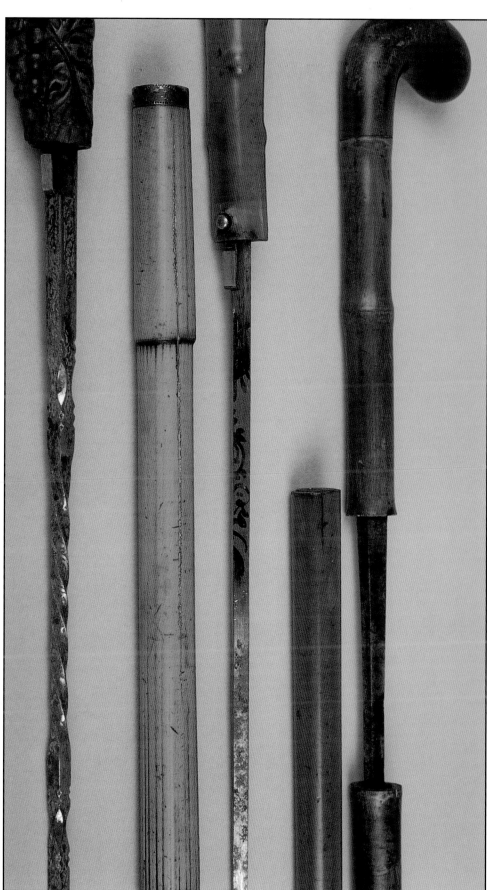

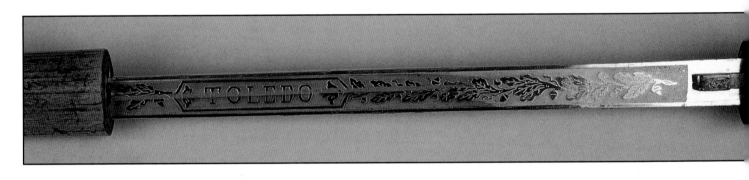

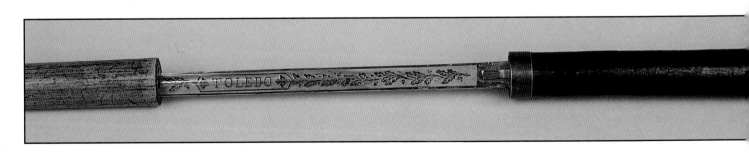

228 Sticks of Aggression, Sticks of Defense, Sticks at Play & System Sticks

During the colonial era in North America, colonists all carried daggers and swords. Blades served a variety of functions including self-defense, food procurement and preparation, and tool manufacture (including walking sticks). Large knives were quite popular among American frontiersmen for hunting, trapping, and settling disputes with fellow woodsmen or Native Americans.

During the nineteenth century, Americans preferred the large Bowie knife, especially on the frontier. Officers and gentlemen alike enjoyed carrying canes with daggers hidden in the shafts for self-defense, particularly on the expanding frontier or in areas embroiled in the growing debate over slavery prior to the Civil War.

Cane with interesting jackknife concealed in the handle and shaft; turning the collar frees the knife blade. It locks in place and is unlocked when you pull on the ring on the opposite side from the blade. Stepped reed shaft, "bullet type" ferrule. Blade: 5" l. Overall length: 32-3/4" with blade retracted.

Pocketknives have been popular for a very long time. Excavations at Roman archaeological sites have found them dating back to the first century A.D. Along the settled eastern seacoast of colonial North America, every man carried his pocket knife. Particularly popular and common among such knives has been the jackknife, ranging in size from four to seven inches when closed. The jackknife has a single large blade which folds into the handle. By the mid-eighteenth century, serious jackknives were being produced for fighting, lethal weapons that could measure up to two feet long with their blades extended. American soldiers during the Revolution carried jackknives with them at all times; in fact, the states of New York and New Hampshire required their soldiers to be so equipped. Officers and gentlemen of this period also enjoyed carrying walking sticks with slender daggers fixed to the handles and hidden in the shafts. With a quick pull of the handle, these daggers were always ready to parry the lunge of a jackknife-wielding thug. *Courtesy of Ambassador Richard W. Carlson.* $675-745.

Pistol cane with percussion cap mechanism. Turn and pull to free the pistol held in place by a pin in a slot within the long metal collar below the handle. Metal ferrule. Pistol: 11" l. Overall length: 34-1/2". *Courtesy of Ambassador Richard W. Carlson.* $625-690.

Gun canes were by far the most complex of the weapons canes. The earliest were wheel lock pistols installed in ducal sword canes. Wheel lock pistols in canes were in use from around 1510 to 1700. These were followed by flintlock pistols, which were housed in walking sticks from 1575 to 1825. Both wheel lock and flintlock pistols had their works attached to the handle and concealed within the cane shaft. To fire them, the user must first remove the pistols from the cane shaft.

The first gun canes using the entire length of the shaft as a barrel were produced in the early nineteenth century. These weapons used the ferrules to protect the end of the muzzle and had to be removed prior to firing. In muzzle loading weapons requiring wadding, ball, and gunpowder rammed into position in the barrel, the ramrod was attached to the ferrule. The firing mechanisms within these gun canes evolved over the years from percussion cap, to cartridge, and breech-loading mechanisms. In later models, the ferrules contain a small rod or pick acting as a cocking mechanism and cartridge remover.

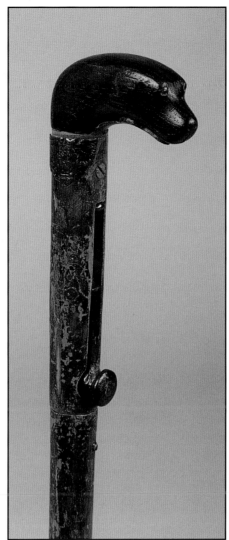

John Day patent design underhammer percussion cap gun cane produced from the early nineteenth century to c. 1860. The only wooden piece on the cane is the dog's head handle. The rest of the weapon is metal. This is a rifle instead of a pistol, using the length of the shaft as the barrel. It unscrews below the hammer to insert shot. Overall length: 34-1/2". *Courtesy of Ambassador Richard W. Carlson.* $1600-1760.

Left and below:
All steel Indian percussion cap gun cane. The hilt figure is a gold "koftari makaha" head (mythological water beast), the shaft is of steel, the silver and gold koftari contains the ramrod. *Courtesy of Richard R. Wagner, Jr.* $3000-4000.

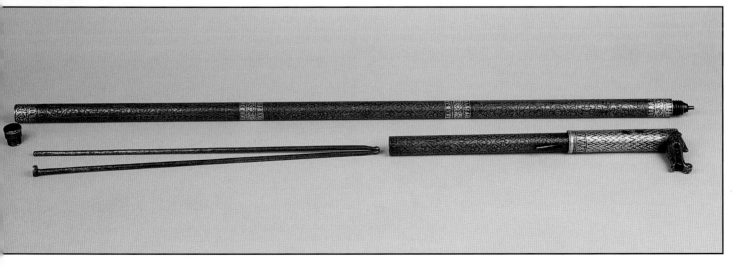

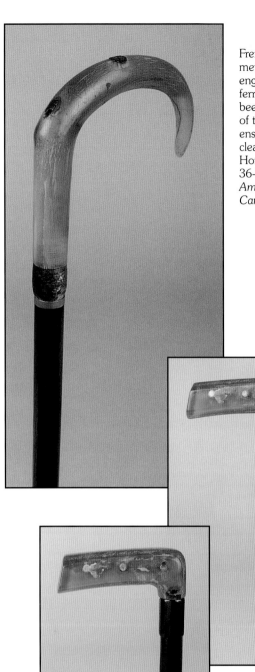

French cartridge gun cane, metal shaft, the hammer engaged and cocked with ferrule tines once ferrule has been removed from the end of the barrel. This system ensures that the barrel is clear when the gun is fired. Horn handle. Overall length: 36-1/2". *Courtesy of Ambassador Richard W. Carlson.* $1200-1320.

Cheroot cane for the cigar-smoking gentlemen who wanted to make a little noise. Cannon handle fires a single shot from its metal innards with the touch of a lit cigar to the touchhole. It was handy as a noisemaker when gunpowder alone was used. Handle: 3-1/2" l. x 2-1/4" h. Overall length: 34". *Courtesy of Ambassador Richard W. Carlson.* $825-900.

Two cheroot canes. Silver naval model with a binnacle on the handle, period engraving dated to the nineteenth century, rosewood shaft. Handle: 3-3/4" l. The other handle is nickel, measuring 2-3/4", on an oak shaft. *Courtesy of Richard R. Wagner, Jr.* Prices range from $1200-1500 depending on condition.

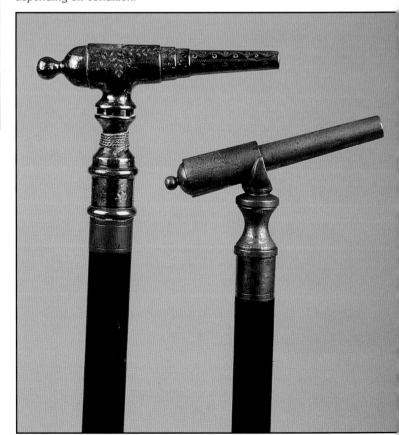

Modern gun cane from Darra, Pakistan, cartridge loading, turn the collar to release the trigger, plastic handle, metal shaft, plastic grip, the entire shaft is the barrel. Handle: 4-1/2" l. Overall length: 33-1/2".

Of Darra, Jack Anderson and Dale Van Atta reported in the *Washington Post,* May 6, 1987, "Darra is as much a page out of the American Wild West as any village in the world today. The main, muddy street is lined with dozens of shops sporting a startling array of weaponry—shotguns, rifles, pistols, machine guns, even an antitank and antiaircraft missile or two … The natives have been hand-tooling arms for more than a century in small factories behind the main thoroughfare … Townspeople even make pens that fire .25-cal. bullets." *Courtesy of Dale Van Atta.* $300-330.

Poaching in England

From 1671 to 1831, English law restricted the hunting of game animals to the aristocracy and the landed gentry. Until 1881, no tenant farmer could kill game stocked by the rural landowners for their hunting pleasure, even to prevent the loss of the tenant farmer's crops. In an increasingly industrialized island nation, with public grazing land and forests rapidly diminishing, hare, partridge, pheasant, and grouse were hard to come by and much sought after. A man of some means but without land of his own who could get his hands on a gun cane could provide himself and his family with some highly desirable main courses, provided he was both stealthy and a good shot. Stealth was required as landed aristocrats had their gamekeepers prowling the grounds at night and setting both spring guns with trip wires and mantraps to prevent game animal theft. Still, a poacher so equipped could quickly dispatch a game animal, hide it with brush for recovery later, and stroll away with his apparently innocuous cane in hand, the very picture of innocence in the eyes of the harried gamekeeper seeking the source of the gun's report. That was the theory at any rate.

Despite all deterrents, the poor supplemented their income trapping game for the London black market. Since it was difficult to procure, game animals were a delicacy and a considerate gift with which to impress loved ones and friends, and black market game was best; the animals in question were always in better condition as they had been trapped with wires or nets in secrecy rather than being perforated with shot.

Class tension in rural England was aggravated by these restrictive game laws and their reduction of access to coveted food sources. English aristocracy may well have felt the need to carry weapons canes, wondering if the surrounding tenant farmers would became overly incensed by the situation. There were simpler solutions available to land owners than bearing hidden arms at all times. Well aware of the tension, rural landowners with stocked game occasionally invited their less fortunate neighbors on hunts. Allowing locals without direct access to game animals to carry away part of the estates' ample supply helped ease the hard feelings. The surrounding farmers chafed a little less under the laws forbidding them from killing the landowner's animals when they strayed from the estate proper (creating a nuisance and causing considerable crop damage), when they were sure that they would be allowed to eat a few of those pesky creatures themselves from time to time.

During the latter half of the nineteenth century, hundreds of gun cane patents were filed. Among the best known and finest of the gun canes were the American made gun canes of the E. Remington & Sons firearms company. Eliphalet Remington, the company's founder, felt his firm needed a weapon for the civilian market and turned to John F. Thomas, a gunsmith employed by the company, who had designed a gun cane patented on February 9, 1858. The Thomas patent gun cane (U.S. Patent #19,328) was a percussion cap model. Production was believed to have begun in 1859, was interrupted by the Civil War, and continued in 1865. Early models were .31 caliber, firing either a lead ball or shot.

The Thomas Patent Remington gun canes came with a variety of handles, including two sizes of dog's head, ball & eagle's claw, knob, L-shaped, crooked, and modified crooked handles with a flat gripping area. These weapons also had rifled barrels and were covered in hard gutta-percha rubber or vulcanized rubber. Ivory handled models were offered in the 1870s. Models in varying colors were also offered by Remington, including coral, black, and brown.

By the late 1860s, Remington had redesigned their gun canes to handle .22 caliber rimfire ammunition with the Remington No. 1 Rifle Cane and .32 caliber rimfire ammunition for the Remington No. 2 Rifle Cane. At first these rimfire cartridge canes had an internal hammer but later models featured a firing pin.

As an interesting safety feature, the ferrules protecting the ends of the barrels were held in place with friction alone. Should the gun cane be accidentally fired with the ferrule in place, it would be harmlessly expelled with the shot. A ferrule held in place more tightly could cause the blocked barrel to explode during an accidental discharge or when fired by the absent-minded.

Serial numbers on the early percussion cap models ranged from 1 to over 270 while the rimfire models ranged from 1 to over 1740. Production ceased around 1886 when E. Remington & Sons was sold. The new owners changed the name to Remington Arms Company in 1888 and discontinued the line of gun canes. Total numbers of Remington gun canes are quite limited today and these items are highly sought.

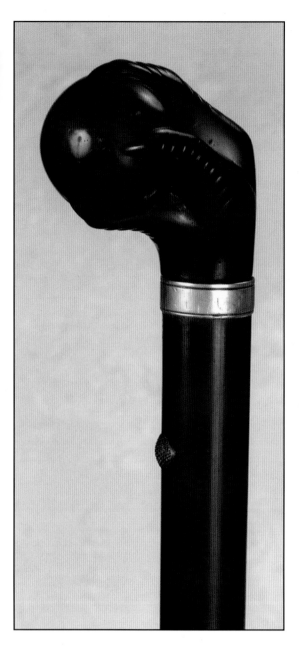

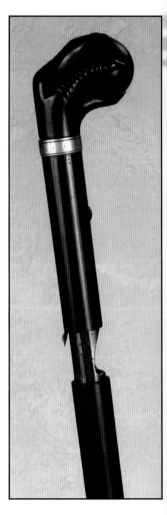

A rare Remington ball and eagle's claw handle percussion gun cane featuring a handle of molded gutta-percha and a shaft covered in a gutta-percha veneer. The collar is lined nickel-silver and measures 1/3". The shaft unscrews 3-1/2" down for the insertion of powder and a 44-caliber ball. It is cocked with a straight pull that reveals an open slot within which the percussion nib lies for loading with a percussion cap. A notched sight also rises when cocking the gun for aiming. A round trigger below the collar fires the gun. The removable 2" steel ferrule is marked, "J.F. Thomas, Patent, Feb'y 9 1858, Remington & Sons, Ilion N.Y. / 63." When the ferrule is removed the end of the brass barrel revealed is also marked "63." This gun cane is believed to date from c. 1859. Handle: 2" x 2-1/4". Overall length: 35". *Courtesy of Henry A. Taron, Tradewinds Antiques.* $12,000-18,000.

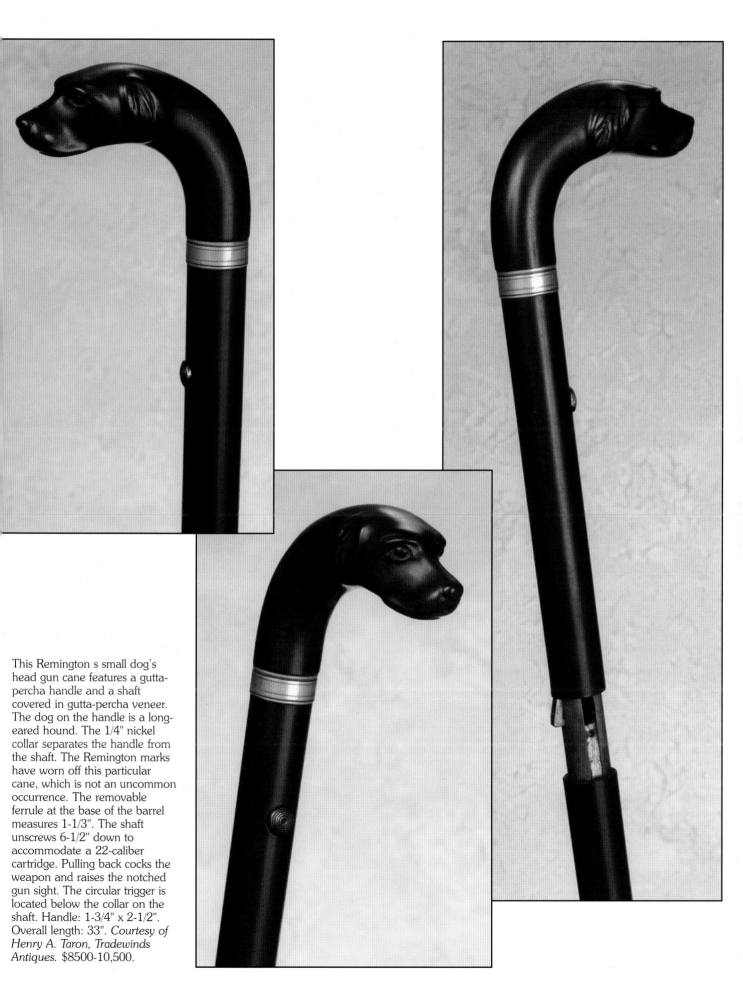

This Remington s small dog's head gun cane features a gutta-percha handle and a shaft covered in gutta-percha veneer. The dog on the handle is a long-eared hound. The 1/4" nickel collar separates the handle from the shaft. The Remington marks have worn off this particular cane, which is not an uncommon occurrence. The removable ferrule at the base of the barrel measures 1-1/3". The shaft unscrews 6-1/2" down to accommodate a 22-caliber cartridge. Pulling back cocks the weapon and raises the notched gun sight. The circular trigger is located below the collar on the shaft. Handle: 1-3/4" x 2-1/2". Overall length: 33". *Courtesy of Henry A. Taron, Tradewinds Antiques.* $8500-10,500.

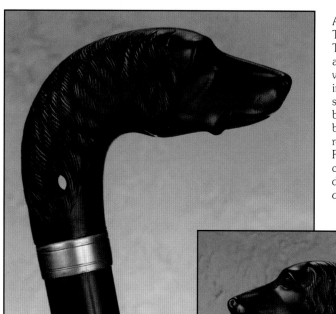

A much sought after and scarce large Remington dog's head gun cane. The L-shaped handle features the hound Remington is well known for. The professionally drilled hole for a wrist cord is a later addition, possibly at the time of purchase. The gutta-percha handle and shaft are joined with a 1/3" nickel collar. The gun unscrews 6" down the shaft to allow the insertion of a 32 caliber cartridge and the weapon is cocked with a straight pull that pops up a notched gun sight. The round trigger is found below the handle. The shaft is covered with gutta-percha veneer. The base of the shaft is protected with a 1-3/4" nickel ferrule marked "1736", revealing that this was the 1736th gun cane of this type manufactured by Remington. These canes have survived in small numbers and are considered among the very finest gun canes ever produced. This example dates from c. 1870. Handle: 3-1/4" x 2-1/2". Overall length: 35". *Courtesy of Henry A. Taron, Tradewinds Antiques.* $7500-10,000.

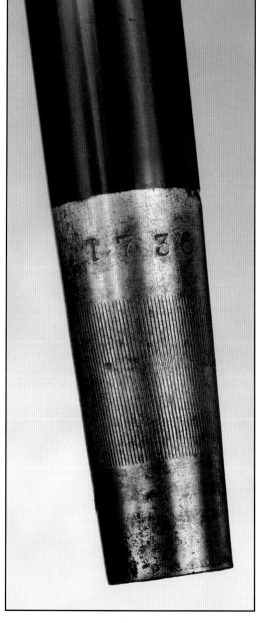

Sticks at Play

Walking Sticks in Dance, Juggling, & Step Shows

On a lighter note, walking sticks have often been used in playful ways throughout history. Walking sticks have appeared in movies such as *Top Hat* in the 1930s and *The Bandwagon* and *A Star Is Born* in the 1950s. Charlie Chaplin made good use of a very springy little crook handled cane in his films. Additionally, both magicians and clowns have found canes to be useful props.

During the medieval period, Egyptian men practiced an energetic folk dance known as the cane or stick dance, the *Tahtib*. Its origin is much earlier, as figures performing this dance may be found on the monuments and tombs of Luxor. A strong bamboo staff was used, the same staff an Egyptian peasant would carry with him for protection on a long journey. Men practiced the *Tahtib* to pass the time and as a form of self-defense. This dance was performed at festivals and celebrations.

Egyptian women also danced with canes, although in a more delicate manner. Women held canes while shimmying and swung the canes at near head level. Some suggest the women's cane dance is intended as a parody of the *Tahtib*. In time, the women's cane dance, the *Asaya*, was incorporated into belly dancing.

Members of the Kappa Alpha Psi fraternity have worn canes since the organization's establishment in 1911. Canes were carried by productive gentlemen of the community, and that was the image the Kappas wished to cultivate. In the 1950s, African-American Greek letter organizations developed "Step Shows" practiced by undergraduates. Kappas joined in, incorporating their canes into the intricate routines, including "Taps" where the canes were rapped on the ground in time to the music. By the 1960s, Kappa Alpha Psi members were decorating the canes they performed with in the fraternity's colors. During the 1970s, members began twirling their canes, adding a new dimension to their routines.

Juggling has been a favorite pastime since the earliest recorded history. Native Americans of the northern and southern hemispheres juggled, as did the peoples of China, Egypt, India, Iran, and Japan. When Europeans took up the art, juggling was coupled with sleight of hand until the late nineteenth century. During the latter years of the nineteenth century, salon jugglers took the stage. These talented individuals juggled objects commonly found in Victorian drawing rooms, including walking sticks, top hats, bouquets of flowers, and billiard balls.

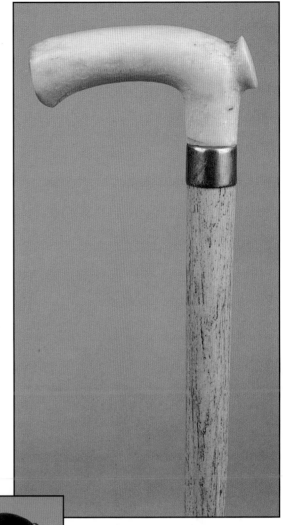

This walking stick has a unique history; it appeared as a prop in the 1941 movie *Dr. Jekyll and Mr. Hyde* with Spencer Tracy and Lana Turner. Nautical cane, walrus ivory handle, white metal collar, whalebone shaft. Handle: 2-1/4" h. x 4-1/4" l. Overall length: 34-1/2". *Courtesy of Richard R. Wagner, Jr.* $1500-1800.

Simple dog's head cane made from a single branch with applied eyes used as a prop by Fred Astaire when he danced with Ginger Rogers for one of their films. This particular cane was given to Ambassador Carlson by the actress Rosalind Russell, a friend of Fred Astaire. Overall length: 33-1/2". *Courtesy of Ambassador Richard W. Carlson.* $825-900.

Child's Play

During the nineteenth and twentieth centuries, children received small canes at carnivals and fairs. These simple sticks were brightly colored and cheaply decorated. Children have always enjoyed imitating adults and these small canes, as well as other more formal examples seen in the photographs displayed here, helped. Such sticks also allowed youth to practice proper cane etiquette in preparation for adulthood … or to lampoon their elders!

Two children's carnival canes with painted wood shafts and plain metal ferrules. Overall lengths: 34" each. *Courtesy of Dale Van Atta.* $40-60 each.

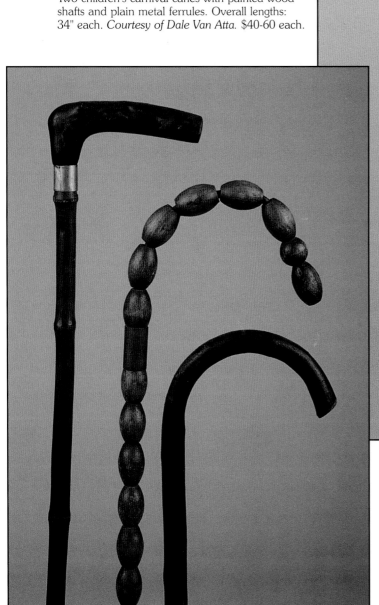

Three children's canes, heights: 20-22" h., in three styles: a horn handle on a bamboo shaft with a white metal collar; beads of wood on a metal crook rod and handle; a crook handle on a bark stick, and *Courtesy of Richard R. Wagner, Jr.* $30-60 each.

All together now, "Who's the leader of the club that's made for you and me? ..." Walt Disney's Mickey Mouse tops this 1930s cane. The sawdust and resin composition handle is painted with Mickey's smiling face. While age crazing has occurred, the paint job remains intact. Remnants of an original silk ribbon necktie remain around Mickey's neck. The hardwood shaft is painted bright red and is tipped with a metal ferrule. Handle: 3" x 2-1/2". Overall length: 36-1/2". *Courtesy of Henry A. Taron, Tradewinds Antiques.* $900-1300.

Sticks of Aggression, Sticks of Defense, Sticks at Play & System Sticks   239

Very thin, petite, child's ivory handled cane with a circular handle and a dog's head. Metal ferrule. Handle: 2-1/2" d. Overall length: 34-3/4". *Courtesy of Dale Van Atta.* NP (**N**o **P**rice).

Historical photographs portraying children with more formal sticks. *Courtesy of Richard R. Wagner, Jr.*

System Sticks

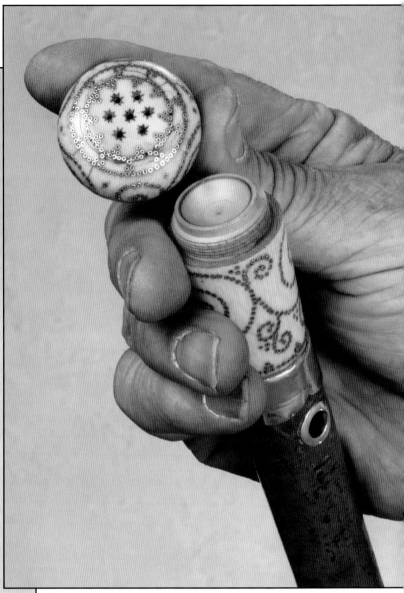

An eighteenth century English ivory pique pomander cane with an elephant ivory handle. The perforated top unscrews to gain access to the shallow compartment within. A small cloth soaked in a healthful, aromatic vinegar solution was placed within the hollow. Once the perforated lid was back in place, the user would sniff the rising vapors when the smells from the surrounding environment became too strong and/or conditions were considered unhealthful. Thus this stick served dual purposes; on the one hand it was an elegant accessory for the wearer, on the other it was intended to serve as protection against odor and disease. The handle is decorated with large "C" scrolls. The scalloped silver collar measures 2/3" and is inscribed "John Shaw, 1711." The shaft is full bark malacca, is pierced with round silver eyelets for the wrist cord, and the tip is protected by a 5-1/4" long brass and iron ferrule. Handle: 2-1/2" x 1-1/4". Overall length: 36-1/2". *Courtesy of Henry A. Taron, Tradewinds Antiques.* $6000-8000.

"Navigator's Cane" featuring a solid ivory sphere handle divided into twin hinged hemispheres detailed on the outside with a map of the world dating to the middle of the eighteenth century. The inner surfaces of the sphere are decorated in tortoiseshell on the upper half and inscribed with sundial notations on the lower half. A silver sundial completes the piece. This impressive knob handle is attached to a malacca shaft, has a gold collar, and bone ferrule. Handle: 2" diameter. Overall length: 31". *Courtesy of Kimball M. Sterling Auctioneers.* $2400-3200.

Also known as "gadget canes," these are walking sticks that have a second, hidden function within them. People who encounter them today find these intricate objects endlessly fascinating. Generally speaking, system sticks may be divided into four broad categories, although crossover items from one category to another will give you headaches if you spend too much time attempting to pigeonhole them into one category or another. That said, the four categories are: practical canes; professional canes; canes with integrated instruments; and canes with surprises. Practical canes include those with items such as candles and flashlights, dog whistles, items useful to travelers including shaving kits, makeup, or toothbrushes, items aiding those out hunting and hiking which include seats or compasses, even canes with dice and musical instruments. Professional canes hide the tools of trade within them and include measures for various professions, instruments for doctors, instruments for the musician, and tripods for photographers and surveyors. Canes with integrated instruments include sticks with microscopes, or instruments to measure time and distance. Finally, canes with surprises include automatons—those figural handles with rolling eyes, wagging jaws, and wiggling tongues—water squirting canes, and other equally interesting or ornery amusements for the lighter moments.

System sticks come of age in the nineteenth century. Over fifteen hundred patents were issued for these complex and imaginative objects from 1870 to 1915. The "tippler's stick" was used in the United States often during the Prohibition era. Contained within its hollow shaft and handle were a thin glass flask and tiny drinking glass with which to imbibe illegal alcoholic beverages carried discreetly with the cane wearer. Men with such tippler's canes frequented Chicago's Green Mill Cocktail Lounge, which featured jazz music and was a mob-owned speakeasy during the Prohibition years. Men wore tuxedoes and carried their hollowed canes while their ladies wore evening gowns and carried flasks in their purses. A trap door behind the bar led to a tunnel used to transport illegal booze up in a hydraulic elevator. Al Capone sat in the booth on the right, the one facing the door. Charlie Chaplin stopped by for a drink after a day's shooting at Essanay Studios. Benny Goodman played there and Billie Holiday sang.

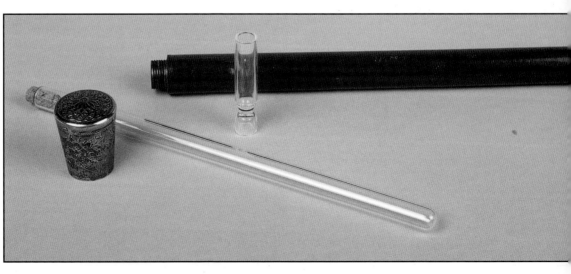

Russian silver handled whisky flask cane with cup. Metal ferrule. Overall length: 36". *Courtesy of Ambassador Richard W. Carlson.* $575-635.

Single shot tippler's cane. Handle fashioned to appear as horn. Overall length: 36-1/4". *Courtesy of Dale Van Atta.* $280-310.

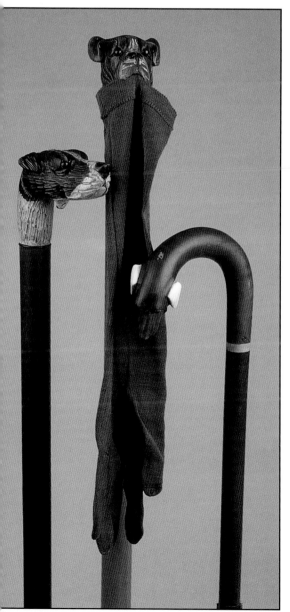

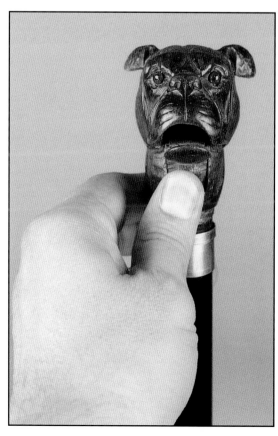

Left and Below:
Carved wood bulldog glove holding gadget cane with opening mouth and glass eyes. Silver collar, ebony shaft with 1-1/2" metal ferrule, late nineteenth century. Handle: 2-1/2" h. x 2-1/4" d. x 2" at widest. Overall length: 35". *Courtesy of The World of the Walking Stick.* $1250-1375.

Left:
Three dog's head glove holders. Dog with glass eyes, walnut shaft. Handle: 2-3/4" h. x 3-1/4" w. Overall length: 33-1/2". Bulldog (with glove) wood handle with glass eyes, silver collar, malacca shaft. Handle: 2-1/2" h. x 2" w. Overall length: 34-3/4". Wooden crook handle with elephant ivory ears, glass eyes, and a collar. Handle: 3-1/4" h. x 4" w. Overall length: 35". *Courtesy of Richard R. Wagner, Jr.* These each run in the $400-600 range.

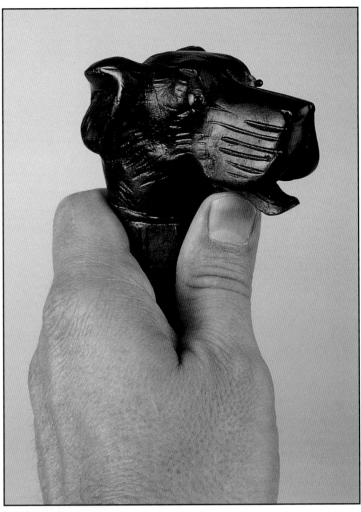

Dog's head glove holder gadget cane with moving mouth, bead eyes, wood handle, no collar, and a metal ferrule. Overall length: 37-1/2". *Courtesy of Dale Van Atta.* $600+.

German coin holder system stick, c. 1900-1910. The spring activated pewter handle features two coin inserts, also spring set. The handle is marked GERMANY. It has an ebonized shaft and black horn ferrule. Handle: 2-1/2" x 1-3/4". Overall length: 34-1/2". *Courtesy of Kimball M. Sterling Auctioneers.* $800-1200.

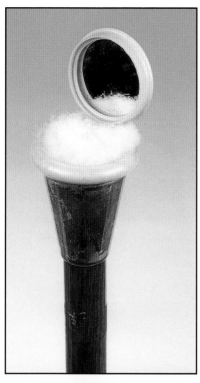

Left:
Ladies compact cane with Bakelite and silver handle, containing beneath the lid both a mirror and powder puff. Horn ferrule. Handle: 1-3/4" d. Overall length: 36". *Courtesy of Ambassador Richard W. Carlson.* $425-470.

Below and right:
Shaving kit gadget cane with brush and razor hidden within ivory handle and cane shaft, bone ferrule. Handle: 3" l. Overall length: 35-1/2". *Courtesy of Ambassador Richard W. Carlson.* $825-900.

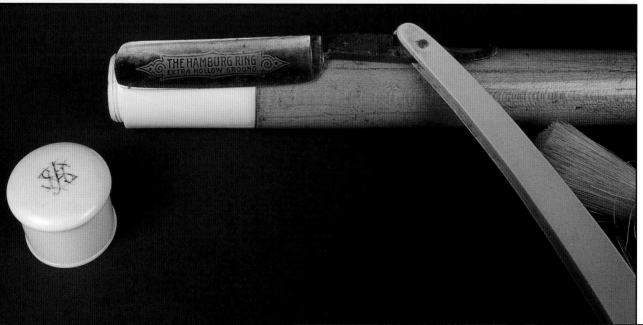

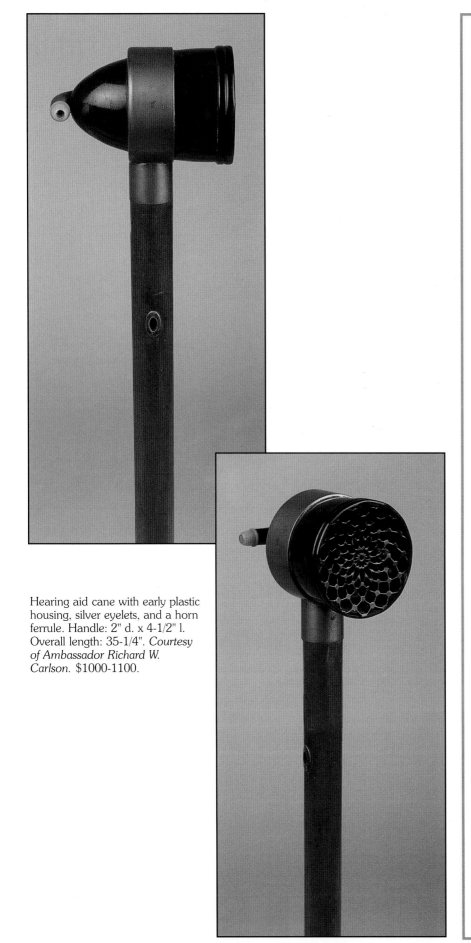

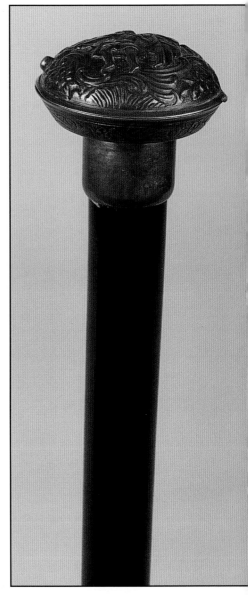

Watch cane, the watch under the metal handle includes a key under the mechanism in the base of the handle. Three figures decorate the embossed metal cover. Overall length: 36". *Courtesy of Dale Van Atta.* $2275-2500.

Hearing aid cane with early plastic housing, silver eyelets, and a horn ferrule. Handle: 2" d. x 4-1/2" l. Overall length: 35-1/4". *Courtesy of Ambassador Richard W. Carlson.* $1000-1100.

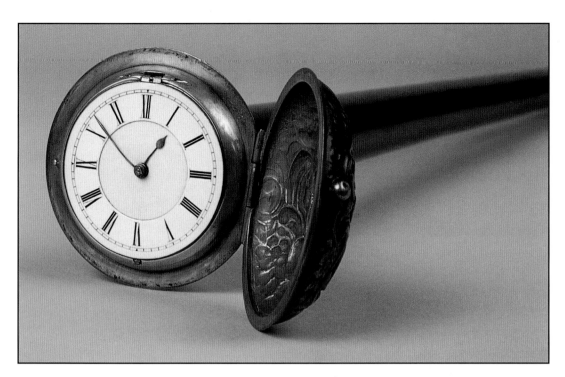

Brass handled watch cane with sweep second hand and rubber ferrule. Overall length: 35-1/2". *Courtesy of Ambassador Richard W. Carlson.* $425-470.

A music box is hidden beneath this mushroom knob handle. Press the small button on the side of the silver handle and the first two lines of the 1920s song "Smoke Gets in Your Eyes" is played. A built-in key is used to wind the music box once the top of the handle is opened. This intricate gadget cane is American and dates from c. 1925. The ebony shaft ends in a 3/4" horn ferrule. Handle: 1-1/2" x 2". Overall length: 33-1/2". *Courtesy of Henry A. Taron, Tradewinds Antiques.* $3500-5500.

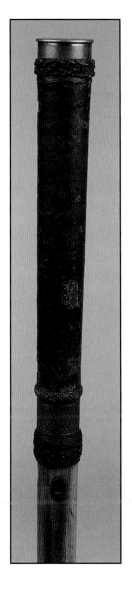

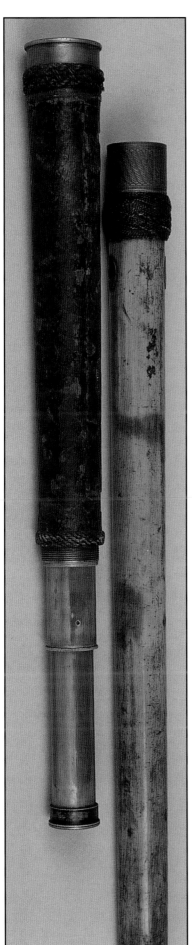

Left:
Telescope cane, mid-nineteenth century, brass mounts and eyelets (tip replacement) marked "R & J Beck 31 Hornhill, London." *Courtesy of Richard R. Wagner, Jr.* Period telescope canes of this type (this example has macramé) begin at $2000 and go up to $3500.

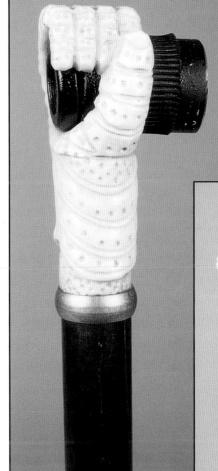

Above and right:
Telescope cane, small metal telescope (with excellent optics) held by a carved ivory gauntlet, replaced brass collar, snakewood shaft with replaced metal ferrule, probably Continental, late nineteenth century. Handle: 2-3/4" h. x 1-1/4" w. Overall length: 34-3/4". *Courtesy of The World of the Walking Stick.* $1950-2145.

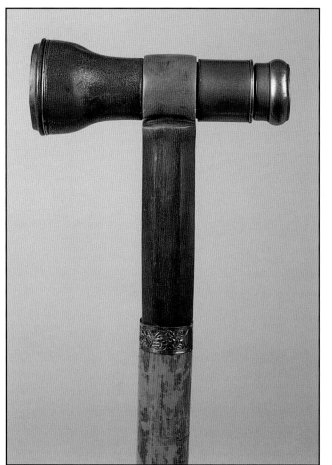

Telescope cane with a bone shaft and Bakelite ring with a silver telescope, brass thin collar, and malacca shaft. Overall length: 35". *Courtesy of Dale Van Atta.* $750-825.

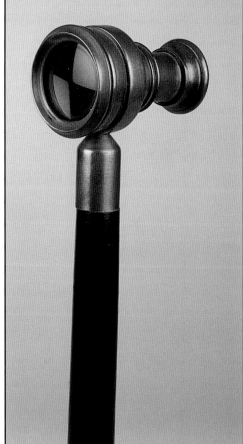

Left:
This small telescope in a brass handled gadget cane features an extending eyepiece for focusing. The base of the shaft is finished with a small metal ferrule. Overall length: 36-1/4". *Courtesy of Dale Van Atta.* $1100-1210.

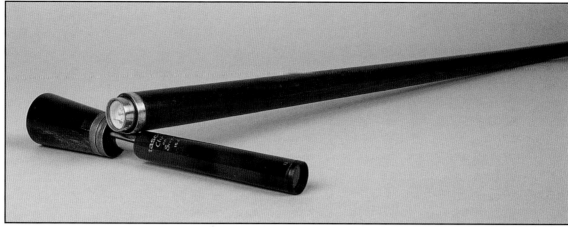

Composite handle and ferrule cane with a Tasco™ spyglass and compass inside (eyepiece in top of handle). Overall length: 36". *Courtesy of Ambassador Richard W. Carlson.* $325-360.

Crying baby handle with compass in top of head, thin metal collar, no ferrule. Handle: 2-1/4" l. Overall length: 33". *Courtesy of Ambassador Richard W. Carlson.* $575-635.

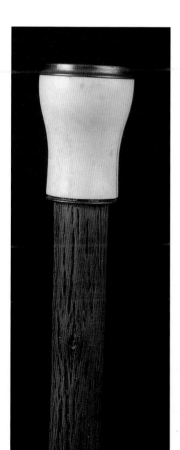

A brass compass insert is mounted in the bone handle of this cane. Overall length: 34-1/2". *Courtesy of Dale Van Atta.* $550-600.

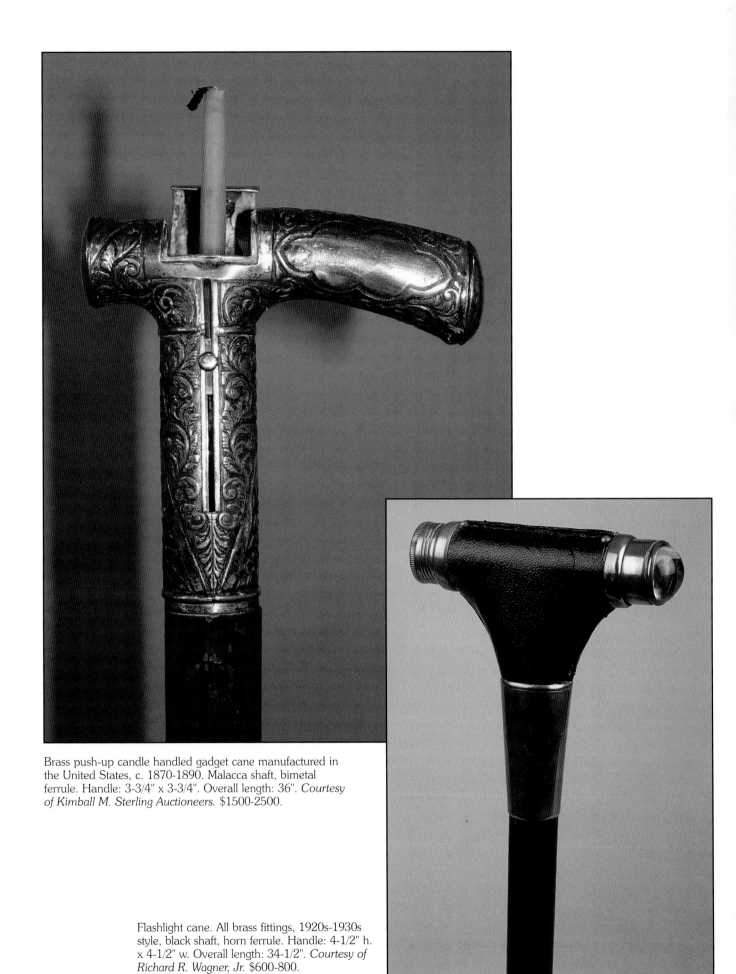

Brass push-up candle handled gadget cane manufactured in
the United States, c. 1870-1890. Malacca shaft, bimetal
ferrule. Handle: 3-3/4" x 3-3/4". Overall length: 36". *Courtesy
of Kimball M. Sterling Auctioneers.* $1500-2500.

Flashlight cane. All brass fittings, 1920s-1930s
style, black shaft, horn ferrule. Handle: 4-1/2" h.
x 4-1/2" w. Overall length: 34-1/2". *Courtesy of
Richard R. Wagner, Jr.* $600-800.

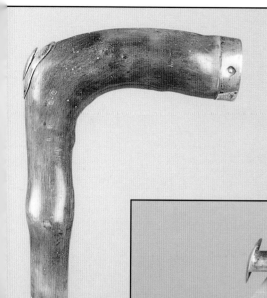

Left and below:
L-shaped pencil holder cane with sterling silver mounts, silver collar with English hallmarks and date mark for 1931. Stamped "Bencox", London. Knobby hardwood shaft with 1-1/8" metal ferrule. Overall length: 33". *Courtesy of The World of the Walking Stick.* $600-660.

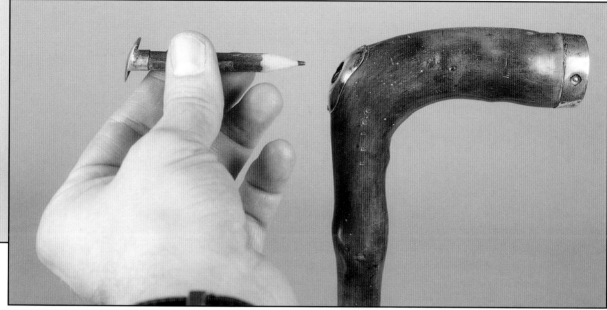

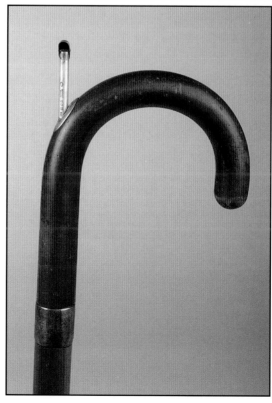

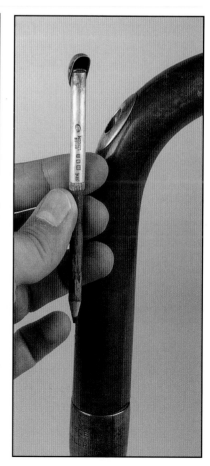

Pencil holder gadget cane with crook handle. The silver collar reads "F.H. Preece 57A Cromwell Road." The pencil's metal collar has British hallmarks and reads "Briggs London." Bone ferrule. *Courtesy of Dale Van Atta.* $1200-1320.

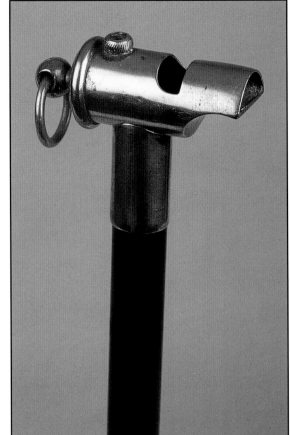

Nickel-plated whistle handled cane with a horn ferrule. Handle: 1-3/4" h. x 2-1/4" w. Overall length: 36-1/2". *Courtesy of Richard R. Wagner, Jr.* $400-600.

Two whistle canes: the metal example on the left is a dog leash whistle combination, the right hand example is made of horn handle, both with metal ferrules. Overall lengths: metal whistle, 34-1/2"; horn whistle, 36-1/2". *Courtesy of Ambassador Richard W. Carlson.* Metal handled dog leash whistle: $375-415; horn handled whistle: $295-325.

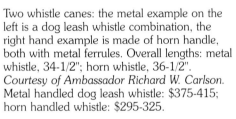

Left:
Whistle cane, whistle inset into early "plastic" ball, silver collar, branch shaft, metal ferrule. Handle: ball, 2" d. Overall length: 35-1/4". *Courtesy of Ambassador Richard W. Carlson.* $425-470.

Right:
Siren ball top metal cane with wood shaft and a silver metal ferrule. Blow into the top and two pierced disks rotate rapidly and produce the siren sound. Overall length: 37". *Courtesy of Dale Van Atta.* $425-470.

Ivory handled sewing kit system stick featuring an ivory thimble and a three-part ivory bobbin, plus a space hollowed out to hold a variety of needles. All these items fit within the ivory knob handle. The handle unscrews in the center. This is probably an English stick produced c. 1900. Malacca shaft. Handle: 1-5/8" x 1-7/8". Overall length: 36". *Courtesy of Kimball M. Sterling Auctioneers.* $750-1200.

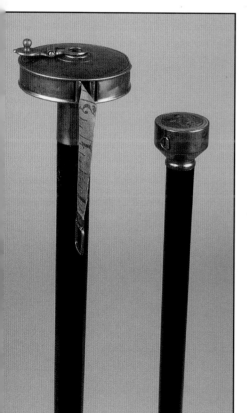

Two measuring tape sticks. The large reel on the left holds 33" of cloth tape. The top of the handle reads "Universal" Reg. U.S. Patent Off." The tape on right features a dog's head in relief in metal on the handle top. The cloth tape pulls from the side of the handle. Overall lengths: left: 34"; right: 36". *Courtesy of Ambassador Richard W. Carlson.* Together, they are valued from $1300-1430.

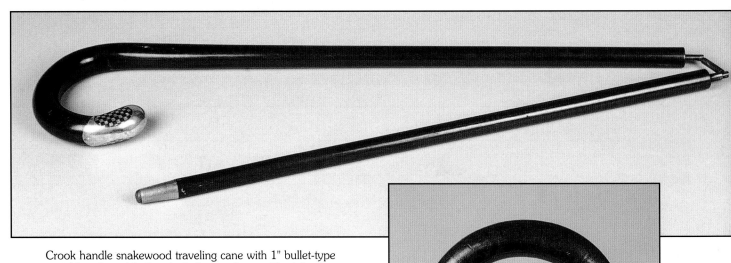

Crook handle snakewood traveling cane with 1" bullet-type
metal ferrule and hallmarked silver end cap with niello decoration. The cane unscrews 18-1/2" from the top of the crook
handle, c. 1890. Handle: 4-1/2" w. Overall length: 35-1/2".
Courtesy of The World of the Walking Stick. $1150-1265.

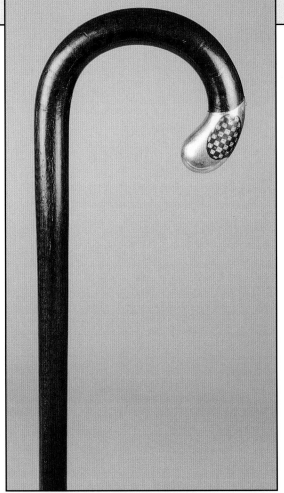

Crook handled stepped shaft traveler's cane, silver end
cap, metal ferrule with iron tip. Overall length: 35-1/4".
Courtesy of Dale Van Atta. $1000-1100.

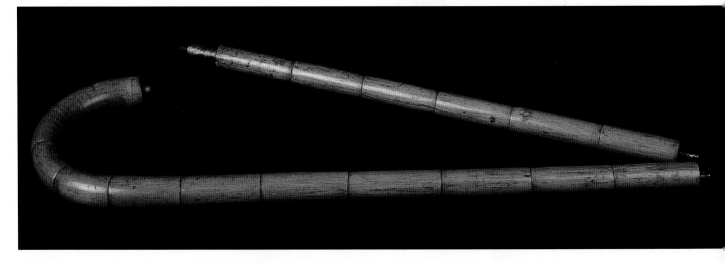

Below and right:
A 1939 World's Fair seat cane. Handle; seat; 6" d. Overall length: 35-1/2". *Courtesy of Dale Van Atta.* $250-275.

Right:
Spike handled cane (appears to be for mountaineering) with initials "TB" and "GB" in two separate ovals. Brass fittings hold the metal spike in place on a flat-sided shaft. Ferrule appears to be plastic. Handle: 4" l. Overall length: 38-3/4". *Courtesy of Ambassador Richard W. Carlson.* $325-360.

A rare and most unusual ladder gadget cane with an ebony flat mushroom knob handle, a very thick and heavy dark hardwood shaft, and a 1-2/3" brass ferrule. A 3/4" round pin protrudes from the ferrule to push into the ground to stabilize the ladder. A heavy 1" metal ring encircles the center of the shaft. Once removed, the shaft opens to reveal the ladder within, created with four metal crossbars. This is possibly a French design dating from c. 1910. Handle: 1" x 1-1/2" dia. Overall length: 37". Catherine Dike reports that one inventor suggested that several such canes could be fastened end to end and used by mountain troops when scaling vertical walls or crossing dangerous crevasses. (Dike 1983, 19) *Courtesy of Henry A. Taron, Tradewinds Antiques.* $6700+.

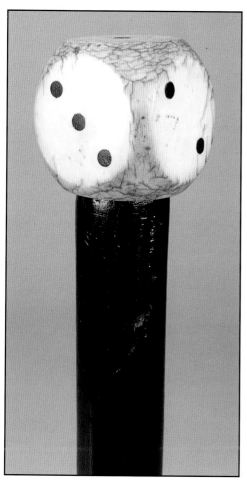

Gambler's stick with ivory die handle with ebony dots. The handle unscrews to reveal a space in the shaft that holds a small pair of ivory dice, ebony shaft, c. 1880. Handle: 1-7/8" x 1-7/8"x 1-7/8". Overall length: 34-1/4". *Courtesy of The World of the Walking Stick.* $950-1045.

Left and Below:
Ivory handle game cane with dominoes inside (bone dominoes), brass covered with leather beneath screw off handle, bone ferrule. Overall length: 35-1/4". *Courtesy of Ambassador Richard W. Carlson.* $825-900.

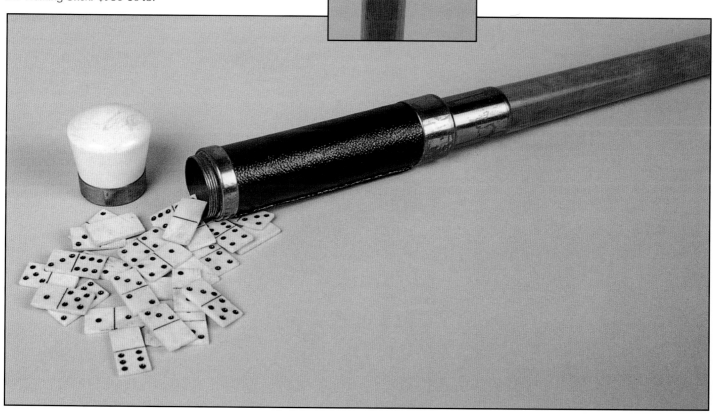

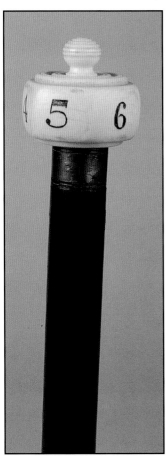

Gaming cane, handle removed to form a spinning top once the base spindle is screwed into the freed handle base. Overall length: 35-1/2". *Courtesy of Dale Van Atta.* $800+.

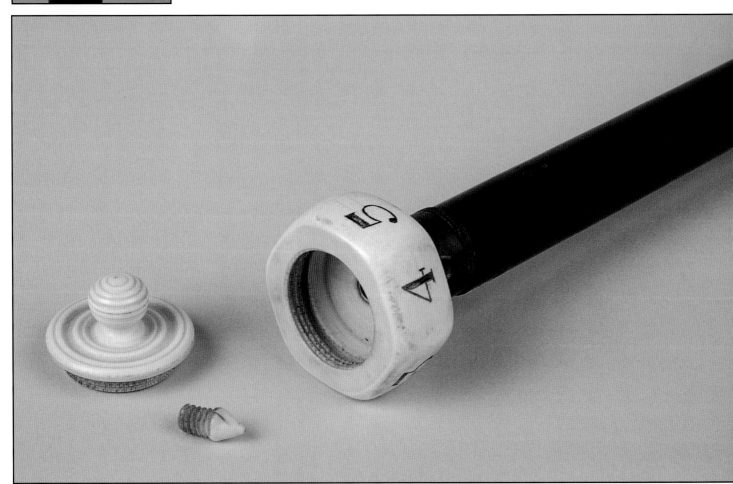

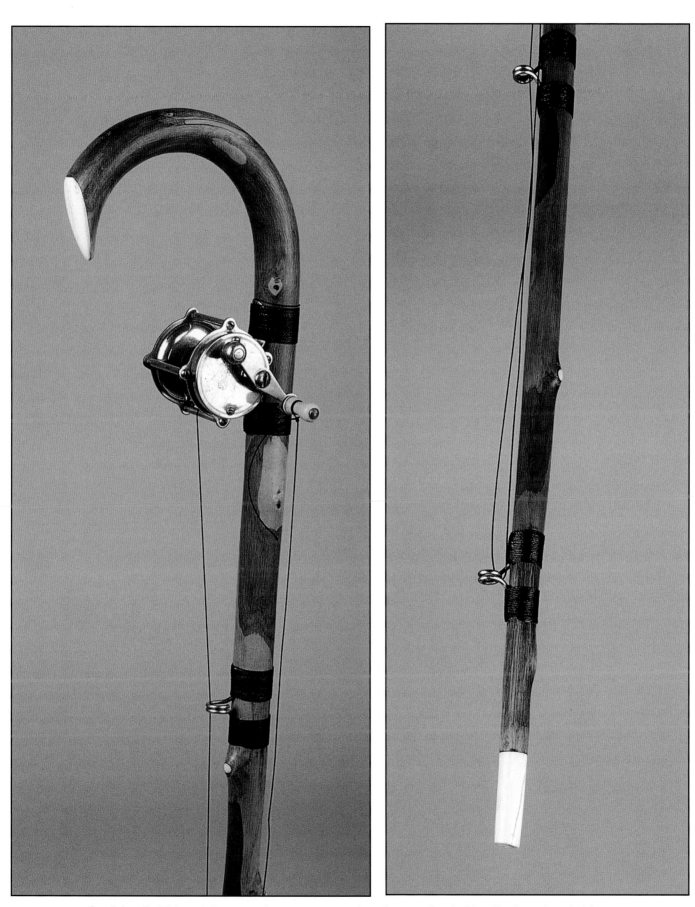

Crook handled fishing pole cane with ivory insets into branch tips and end of handle; the reel reads Atlas Portage. Ivory ferrule. An inventive Italian fisherman made this useful item in the 1930s in San Francisco, California. Overall length: 34-3/4". *Courtesy of Ambassador Richard W. Carlson.* $825-900.

Sticks of Aggression, Sticks of Defense, Sticks at Play & System Sticks   263

Above and right:
Scottish oryx horn and silver snuff box gadget cane made in the British Isles, c. 1890. The handle is a combination of sterling silver and lignum vitae. The wooden top is hinged, raising to reveal its deep snuff receptacle. The lid is decorated with a silver, stylized thistle, Scotland's emblem, and the initials "M.S." The hallmarks and inscription on the silver have been worn to illegibility from long use. The shaft is a straight length of oryx horn from the African gazelle. The shaft tip is protected by a 1-1/8" brass ferrule. Handle: 1-1/2" x 2". Overall length: 35-1/2". *Courtesy of Henry A. Taron, Tradewinds Antiques.* $950-1350.

Opposite page:
System stick pipe cane fashioned from one piece of hardwood with a 1/2" metal ferrule. The top portion of the cane unhinges to reveal a small wooden removable pipe that fits tightly into a receptacle in the shaft. Decorative silver beading surrounds the opening of the handle, late nineteenth century. Overall length: 35-1/2". *Courtesy of The World of the Walking Stick.* $650-715.

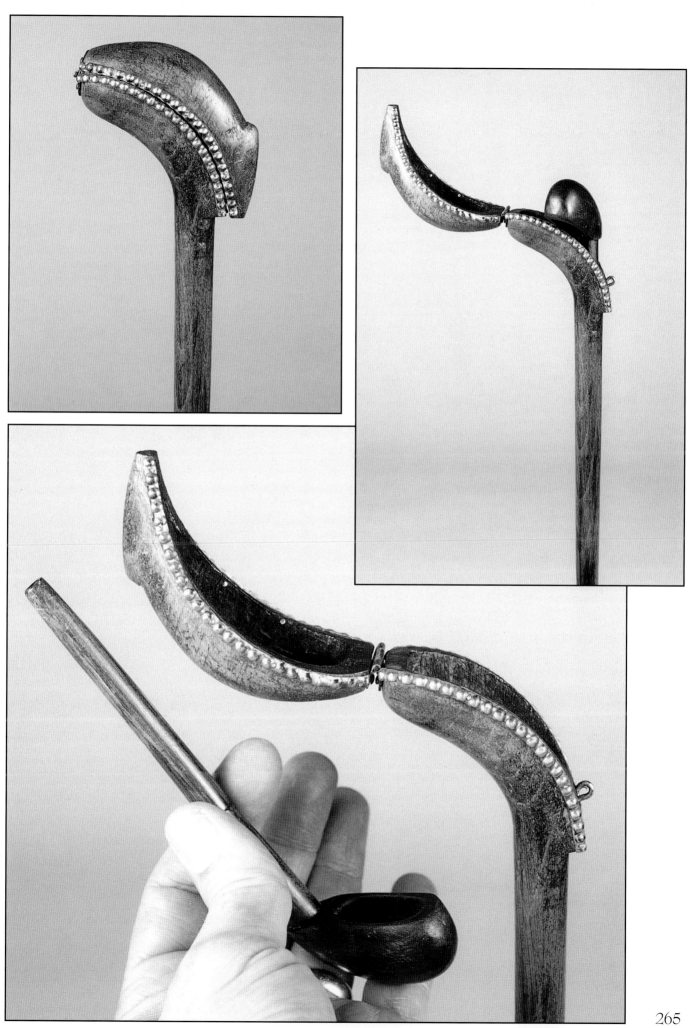

Two pipe smoker's gadget canes. The model on the left reads "Jerusalem" on the handle, which is also the pipe bowl. The base of the shaft has a horn ferrule. The example on the right has a metal ferrule. Overall lengths: 35-1/2" each. *Courtesy of Ambassador Richard W. Carlson.* Together, these canes are valued from $700-770.

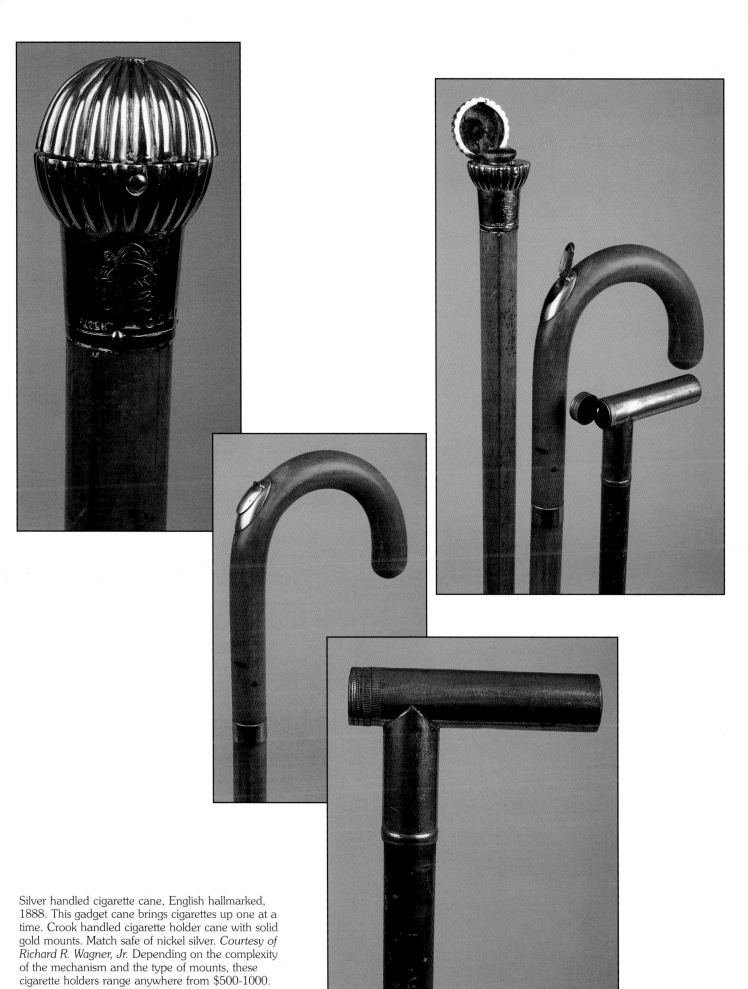

Silver handled cigarette cane, English hallmarked, 1888. This gadget cane brings cigarettes up one at a time. Crook handled cigarette holder cane with solid gold mounts. Match safe of nickel silver. *Courtesy of Richard R. Wagner, Jr.* Depending on the complexity of the mechanism and the type of mounts, these cigarette holders range anywhere from $500-1000. Match safes of this sort range from $400-700.

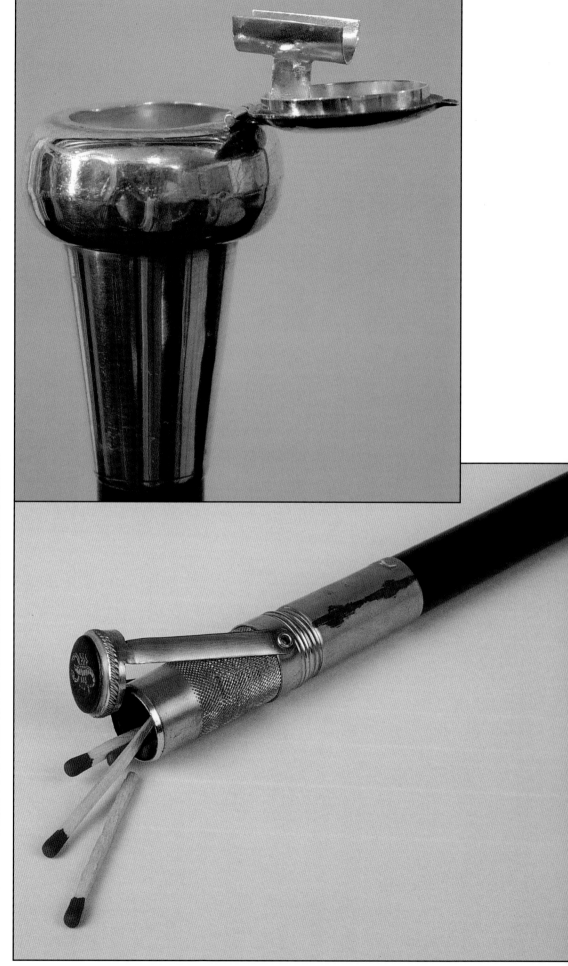

Silver-handled Continental smoker's cane, c. 1925, with a hinged lid in the mushroom shaped handle that opens to reveal a cigarette holder and ashtray. Ebonized shaft and black ferrule add to the air of elegance around this cane. Handle: 2-1/4" x 1-1/2". Overall length: 35-3/8". *Courtesy of Kimball M. Sterling Auctioneers.* $800-1200.

Gadget cane match holder decorated with a scorpion on the top. *Courtesy of Dale Van Atta.* $650-700.

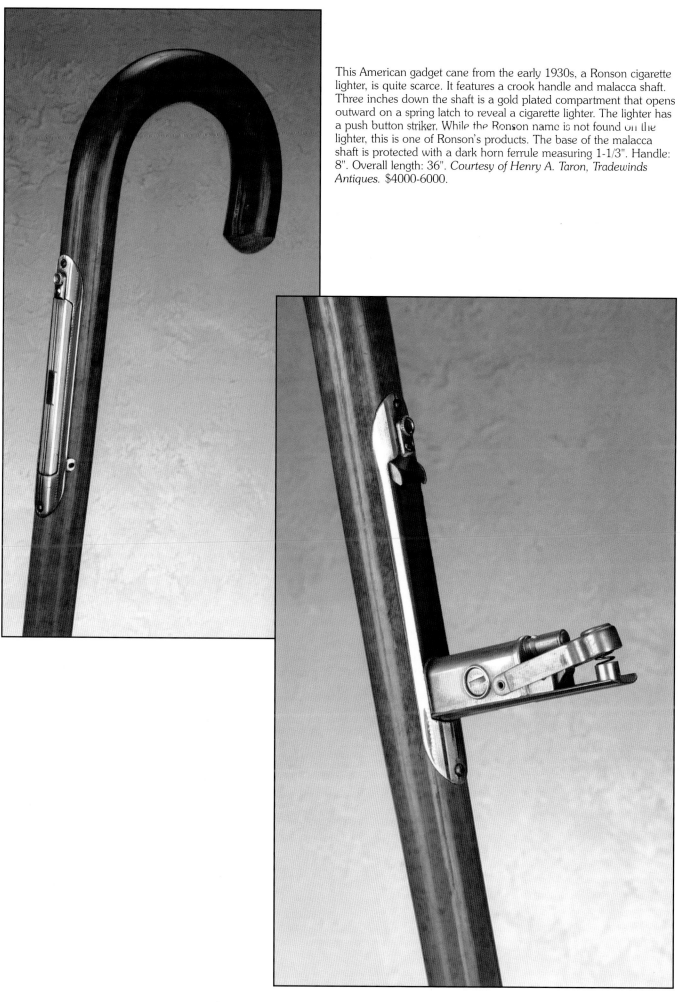

This American gadget cane from the early 1930s, a Ronson cigarette lighter, is quite scarce. It features a crook handle and malacca shaft. Three inches down the shaft is a gold plated compartment that opens outward on a spring latch to reveal a cigarette lighter. The lighter has a push button striker. While the Ronson name is not found on the lighter, this is one of Ronson's products. The base of the malacca shaft is protected with a dark horn ferrule measuring 1-1/3". Handle: 8". Overall length: 36". *Courtesy of Henry A. Taron, Tradewinds Antiques.* $4000-6000.

Here is a rare Continental, possibly French, ivory opium pipe cane featuring an elephant ivory handle carved and inked with a monogram of the owner and a crown. Around the handle is a carved scene of Napoleonic soldiers at a woodland camp. The figures are shown in high relief carving going about all the business required to make camp, including stacking long arms and removing saddles. Below the scene the ivory is turned in rings below the joint where the handle unscrews. A tiny threaded ivory fitting unscrews to be fastened to a separate vial of opium powder. To use the pipe, the long ivory ferrule (2-1/2") unscrews to expose a cork-covered mouthpiece. When the opium pipe was lit, the smoke was drawn down the length of the rosewood cane shaft. This piece dates from c. 1860. Handle: 3-1/2" x 1-1/3". Overall length: 33". *Courtesy of Henry A. Taron, Tradewinds Antiques.* $7000-9000.

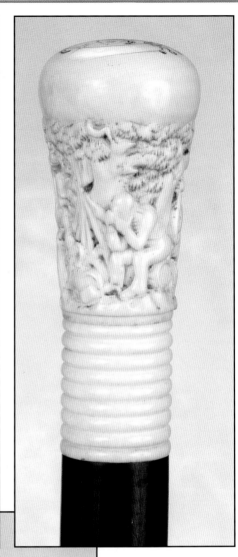

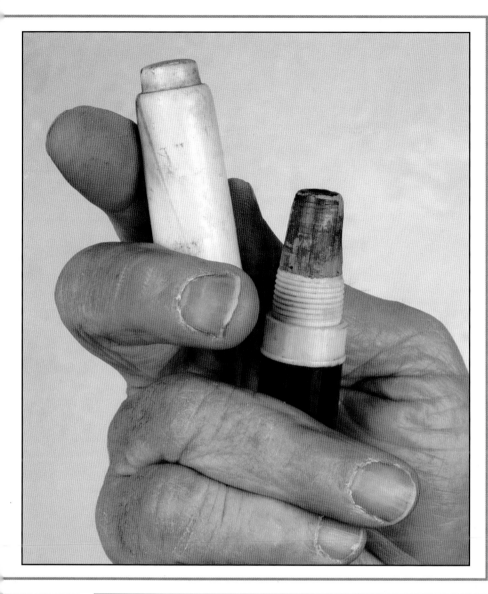

Below:
Gadget cane with "heroin spoon" in the handle, attached to the lid.
Courtesy of Dale Van Atta. $220-240.

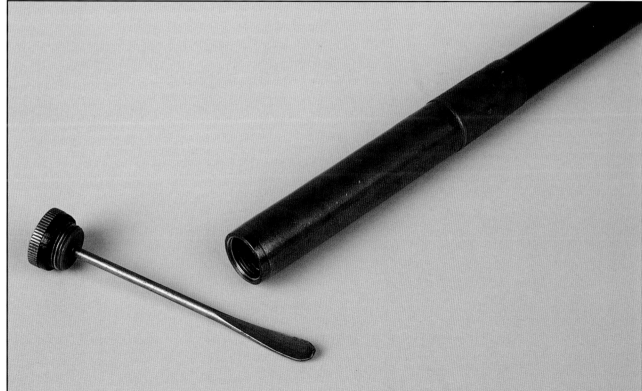

Boot / shoemaker's measuring cane, owned by a cobbler. Ivory disk handle, metal ferrule. Overall length: 36". *Courtesy of Ambassador Richard W. Carlson.* $725-800.

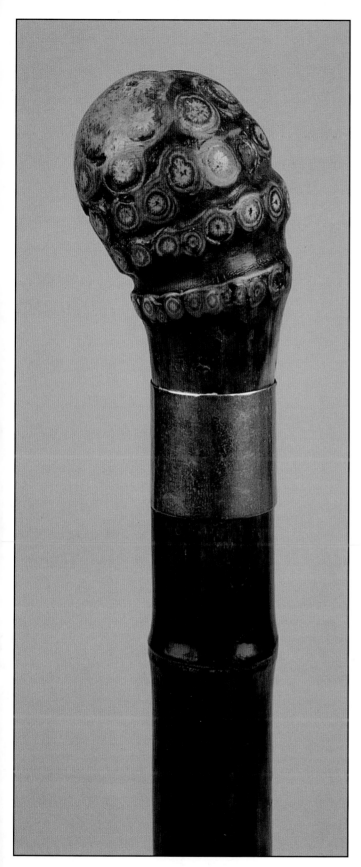

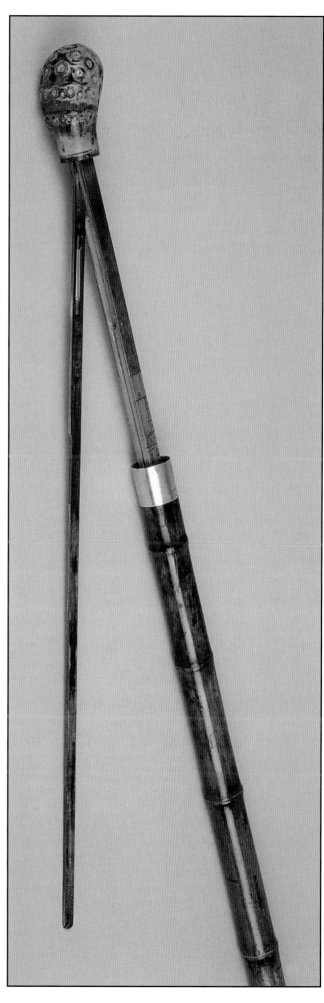

Horse measuring cane. (Such canes are reproduced today in aluminum, the earliest examples were also aluminum; later examples are made in brass). This example has a bamboo shaft, but they were made in all different woods and handle shapes. Make sure the level is in place and level's glass is unbroken. *Courtesy of Richard R. Wagner, Jr.* Antique horse measuring canes bring $450-650.

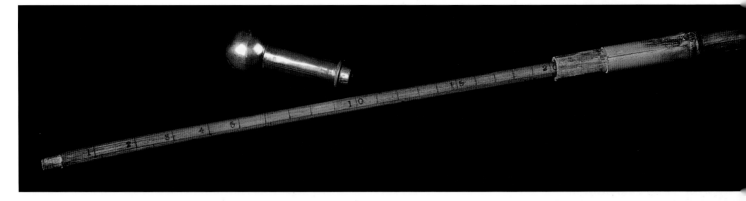

Beer measure held within the bamboo shaft and beneath a silver ball handle.
Metal ferrule. Overall length: 32-1/4". *Courtesy of Dale Van Atta.* $470-520.

Left and below:
French barometer gadget cane, small metal ferrule.
Handle: 2-1/4" d. Overall length: 36-1/2". *Courtesy of Ambassador Richard W. Carlson.* $775-855.

American logging crew chief's marker cane, c. 1880. This cane was used by the head of a timber logging crew to mark trees to be felled. It features an iron handle, burned stepped malacca shaft, and bimetal ferrule. Handle: 3" x 3-1/2". Overall length: 33-3/4". *Courtesy of Kimball M. Sterling Auctioneers.* $500-800.

American railroad construction crew chief's testing stick, c. 1890. This stick served two purposes. The combined length of the decoratively carved and burnt cane shaft and iron handle measured the correct distance between the rails to ensure uniformity of width, while the iron hammer handle was used by the crew chief to tap the rails and determine whether the rails were properly fitted together by the tone his tap produced. Handle: 4" x 2-3/4". Overall length: 36". *Courtesy of Kimball M. Sterling Auctioneers.* $500-800.

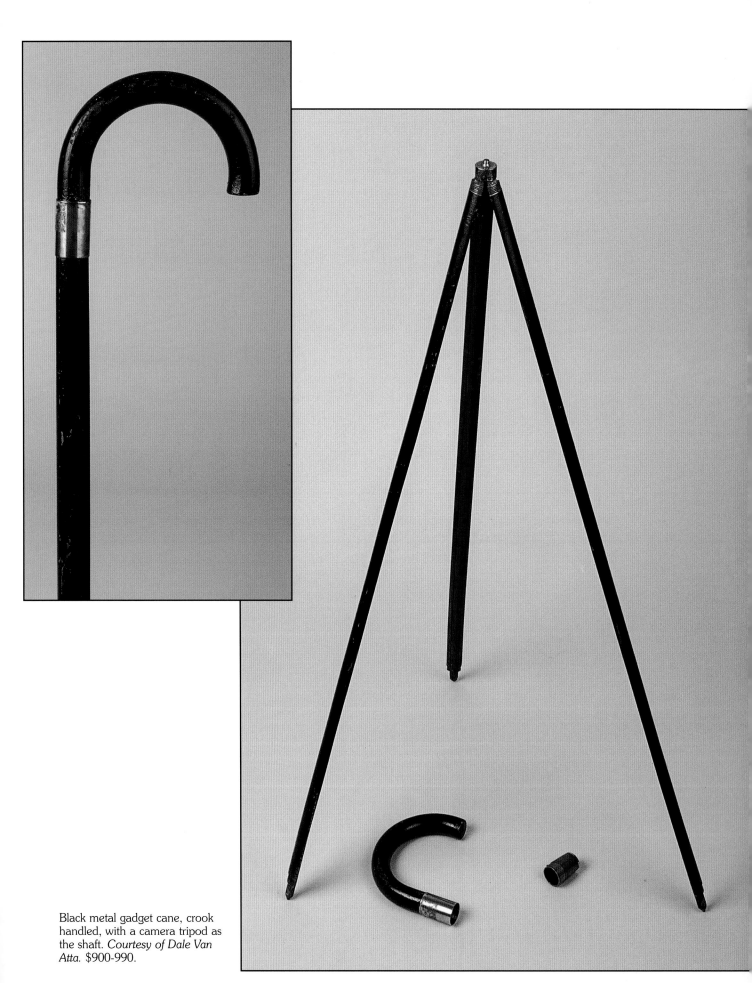

Black metal gadget cane, crook handled, with a camera tripod as the shaft. *Courtesy of Dale Van Atta.* $900-990.

Photographer's light meter stick with the meter in the handle, metal ferrule. Handle: 2" d. Overall length: 36". *Courtesy of Ambassador Richard W. Carlson.* $725-800.

Below and right:
A cappella tuning cane (for choirs), purchased by the current owner in Vienna, Austria. Malacca shaft, metal head with tuner, metal collar, foliate decoration. On the collar is written "Patent J. Neschuta." Overall length: 35-1/2". *Courtesy of Dale Van Atta.* $1580+.

Brass handle (leather covered) field microscope cane with bone ferrule. Overall length: 36". *Courtesy of Ambassador Richard W. Carlson.* $1200-1320.

Right:
Miniature floating turtle figure with moving head, legs, and tail under a fixed, plated shell. This little turtle is housed beneath a flat glass top. The knob handle is burned and darkly stained and the joint between handle and shaft is hidden beneath a decorated metal collar. The shaft ends with a bimetal ferrule. Handle: 2" x 1-3/8". Overall length: 34". *Courtesy of Kimball M. Sterling Auctioneers.* $400-800.

Below and below right:
Spitting Chinaman gadget cane on a bamboo shaft, small metal ferrule. Could squirt water or something more caustic. The braid in the back was the trigger. Handle: 2-1/4" long, including braid. Overall length: 37-1/2". *Courtesy of Ambassador Richard W. Carlson.* $675-745.

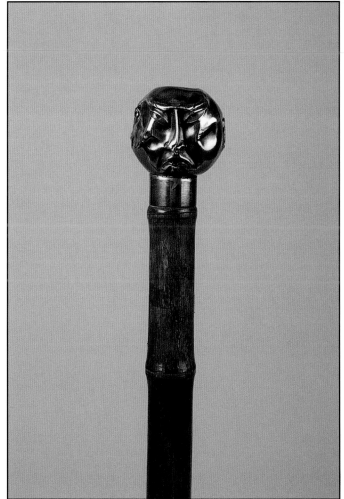

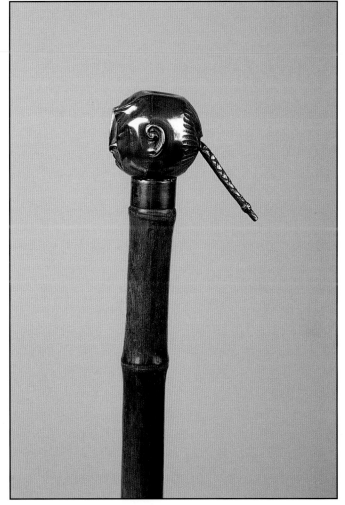

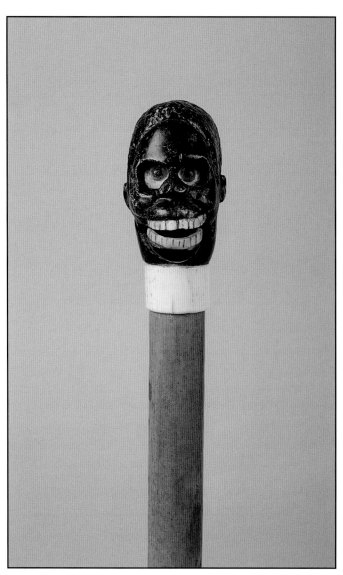

Automata gadget cane, move the lever at the back of the head and the eyes roll and mouth gapes. Bone collar, horn ferrule. Overall length: 35-3/4". *Courtesy of Ambassador Richard W. Carlson.* $675-745.

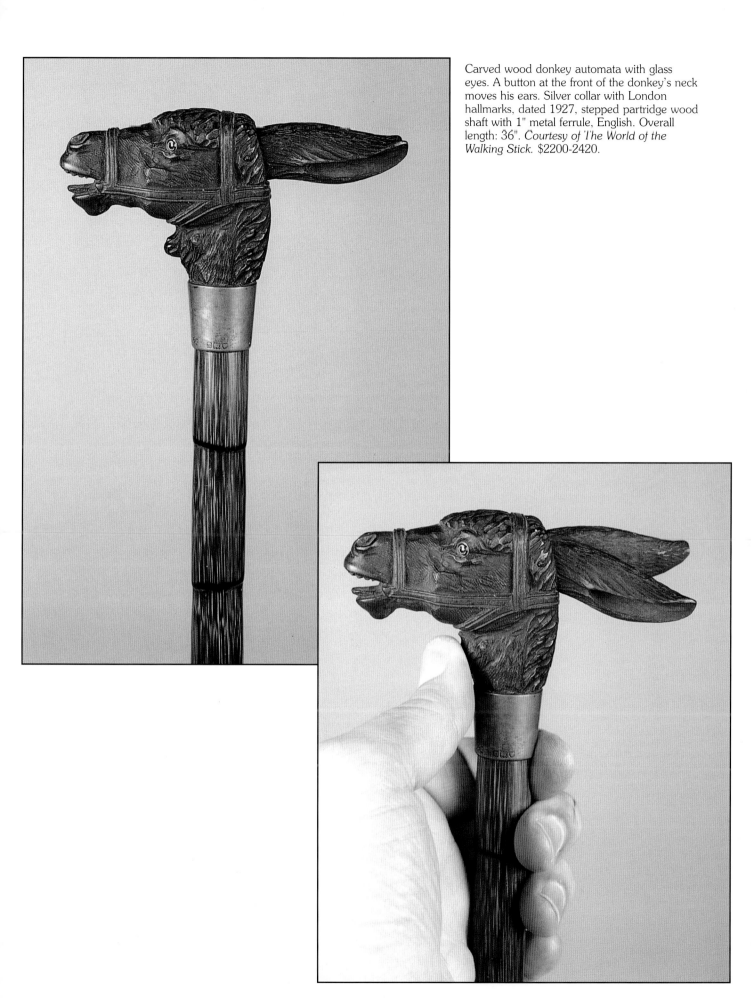

Carved wood donkey automata with glass
eyes. A button at the front of the donkey's neck
moves his ears. Silver collar with London
hallmarks, dated 1927, stepped partridge wood
shaft with 1" metal ferrule, English. Overall
length: 36". *Courtesy of The World of the
Walking Stick.* $2200-2420.

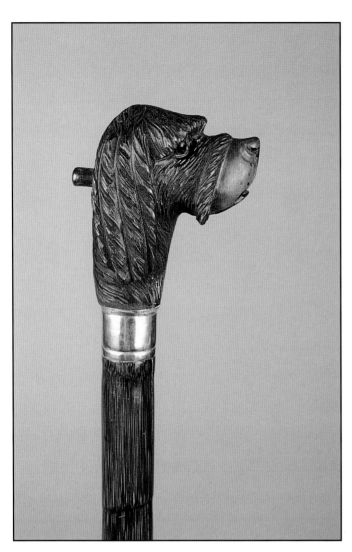

Carved wood dog automata walking stick with large floppy ears and glass eyes. Press the button at the back of the dog's head and the tongue sticks out. Silver collar, stepped partridge wood shaft with 1-1/2" white metal ferrule, probably Continental, c. 1900. Overall length: 34-1/4". *Courtesy of The World of the Walking Stick.* $950-1045.

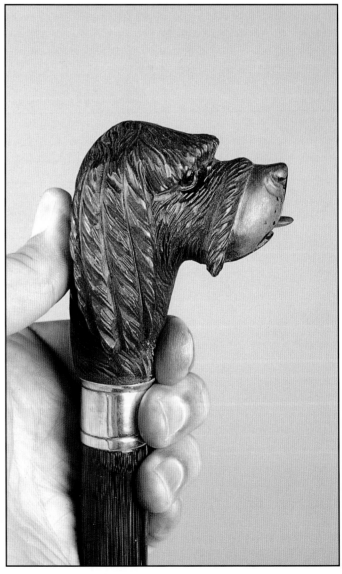

If you are imagining that system sticks are all a thing of the distant past, that is not quite true. Here is a partial listing of system sticks patented between 1970 and 1994:

Date	Patent #	Stick
1970	3,546,465	Typhlocane [long cane] with range extending obstacle-sensing devices
1985	4,556,075	Two-in-one quick release cane
1988	4,787,405	Multi-purpose stick
1989	4,796,648	Ergonomic cane having oval, tapered short handle and triangular shank
1990	4,962,781	Collapsing rolling cane
1993	5,188,138	Walking stick with wheels
1994	5,331,988	Walking stick with alternative decorative cover
1994	5,351,704	Walking cane for illuminating the footpath of user
1994	5,392,801	Self-righting walking cane

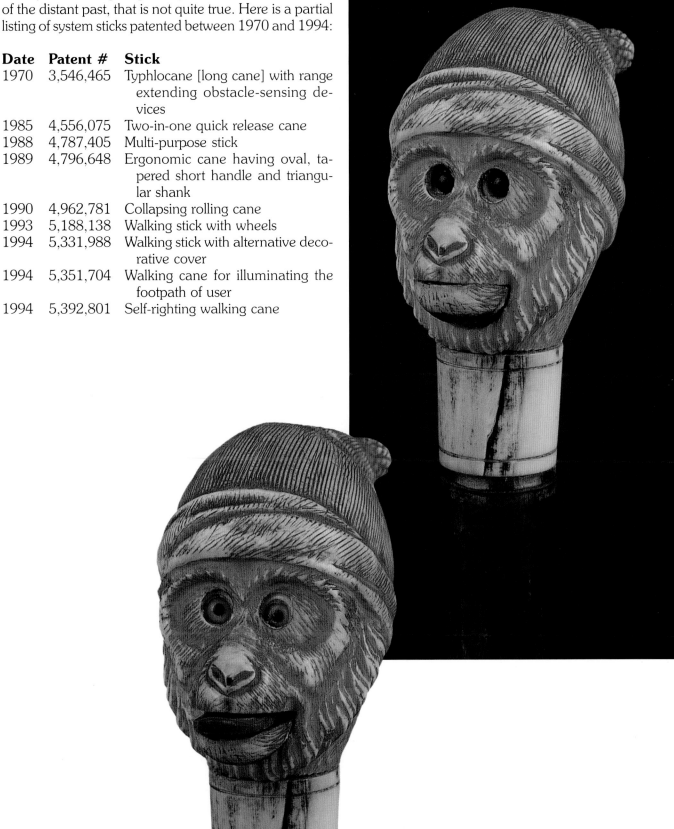

Monkey automata cane carved in an ivory handle and fitted to a bamboo shaft. When the lever in the back is pushed down, the eyes roll to change color and the tongue sticks out. *Courtesy of Richard R. Wagner, Jr.* $3500-5000.

Bibliography

Anderson, Jack and Dale Van Atta. "Dodge City, Pakistan." *The Washington Post,* May 6, 1987.

Arthur, Pat & Ann. "Memento Mori." *The Cane Collector's Chronicle* 14(1), July 2003.

Bancroft, Hubert Howe. *The Book of the Fair.* Chicago, San Francisco: The Bancroft Company, 1893.

Beeman, Linda L. "Fabergé." *The Cane Collector's Chronicle* 7(4), October 1996, pp. 1-5.

_____. "The Sultan's Birthday Stick." *The Cane Collector's Chronicle* 8(1), January 1997, p. 4.

_____. "Talking Canes. Historic Reliquaries." *The Cane Collector's Chronicle* 8(1), January 1997, pp. 1-3.

Bernal, Roy. "Tribal Sovereignty." *Eight Northern Indian Pueblo 1999 Visitor's Guide.* New Mexico: The Eight Northern Indian Pueblo Council, 1999.

Blegen, Theodore C. *Norwegian Migration to America 1825-1860.* Northfield, Minnesota: The Norwegian-American Historical Association, 1931.

Brooklyn City Business Directory. Brooklyn, New York, 1873.

Callahan, Charles H. *Washington: The Man and the Mason,* Washington, D.C.: Memorial Temple Committee of the George Washington Masonic National Memorial Association, 1913, 355-357.

Carter, Howard and A. C. Mace. *The Discovery of the Tomb of Tutankhamen.* New York: Dover Publications, Inc, 1977.

Cashman, Irene. "Collectible Canes & Walking Sticks." *Antiques and Collecting Magazine,* n.d.

Curtis, Deborah. "The walking stick has place in history." *Vigo County Historical Society,* May 4. 1986.

Daily Mail Reporter. "Booklets, straps, and canes seized. Detectives search leader's home." *Daily Mail,* 10 January 1953.

_____. "Police Seize Canes in Swoop on Offices." *Daily Mirror,* London, 10 January 1953.

Davis, Richard Beale, ed., *Chivers' Life of Poe.* New York: E.P. Dutton & Co., 1952 (Chivers's recollections are not considered an entirely impartial source, however what he has to say about cane walking is interesting).

Deetz, James. *Invitation to Archaeology.* Garden City, New York: The Natural History Press, 1967.

Dike, Catherine. *Cane Curiosa: From Gun to Gadget.* Paris: Les Editions de l'Amateur, 1983.

Dishneau, David. "Carver lived in shadows, but his folk art gains acclaim." *South Coast Today, The Standard Times,* 1998.

Dogood, Silence. "To the author of the New England Courant." *The New-England Courant,* September 24, 1722.

Drayman-Weisser, Terry. "Caring for Antique Ivory." *The Cane Collector's Chronicle* 4(1), January 1993, p. 3.

Espinós, Rafael. "The 1500 Possibilities of the Elegant Cane." *La Vanguardia,* October 27, 1991, "Casa y Ambiente" section, p.8.

Fife, Sharon A. "Baptist Indian Church: Thlewarle Mekko Sapkv Coko." *Chronicles of Oklahoma,* Winter 1970-1971, volume XLVIII, number 4, pp. 450-466.

Frank, Stuart M. "Scrimshaw: 'Ingenious contrivance…in the hours of ocean leisure'." New Bedford Whaling Museum, Expanded Information on Scrimshaw. <http://www.whalingmuseum.org/kendall/amwhale/am_scrim_extend.html> 4/25/2003.

Fulton County, Indiana, Newspaper Excerpts, 1858-62.

Fyson, Donald. "Blows and Scratches, Swords and Guns: Violence Between Men as Material Reality and Lived Experience in Early Nineteenth-Century Lower Canada." A paper for the 78th annual meeting of the Canadian Historical Association, Sherbrooke, Canada, June 1999.

Gavazzoni, Chris. "Green Mill full of Jazz, History, and Mystery." *Columbia Chronicle Online,* 33(24), 2001, pp.1-3. <http://www.cchronicle.com/back/00may01/ae4.html>

Gentleman, A. *The Laws of Etiquette; or, Short Rules and Reflections for Conduct in Society.* Philadelphia: Carey, Lea, and Blanchard, 1836.

Gilbert, Anne. "Walking cane can be the talk of the town." *The Charlotte Observer,* Saturday, February 1, 2003.

Gladstone, Valerie. "A Leg Up On Canes." *The Wall Street Journal,* August 7, 1998.

Gramercy Books. *Sears, Roebuck and Co. Catalog No. 111.* Avenel, New Jersey: Random House Value Publishing, Inc., 1993.

Graybeal, Jay A. "John H. Mitten, Oldest U.S. Newspaper Man." *Carroll County Times*, (Maryland) 22 November 1998.

Grescoe, Taras. "Quebec's Carnival." *National Geographic Traveler*, 2001.

Hoover, Alan. "Staffs, Canes and Walking Sticks," *Discovery Magazine*, 1997.

Hopkins, Alfred F. "Sticks and Swords." *The Regional Review* II (4), April 1939.

Industries and Wealth of the Principal Points in Rhode Island, being the city of Providence, Pawtucket, Central Falls, Woonsocket, Newport, Narragansett, Bristol & Westerly. New York: A. F. Parsons Publishing Co., 1892.

"Isle of Wight Shipwrecks: Royal George." BBC – h2g2.

Jeannin, Judy. "New Jersey woman found her passion into a business." *Bergen Record*, August 3, 1998.

Johnson, Don. "C. Wesley Cowan, Montgomery, Ohio. A Cornucopia of Canes." *Maine Antiques Digest*, February 2001.

Joseph, J.W. "Unwritten History of the Free African-American Village of Springfield, Georgia." *Common Ground. Archaeology and Ethnography in the Public Interest* 2(1), Spring 1997.

Kadri, Youssef. "A Few Thoughts on Caring for Old Canes." *The Cane Collector's Chronicle* 4(1), January 1993, p. 4.

Klever, Ulrich. *Walkingsticks*. Atglen, Pennsylvania: Schiffer Publishing, 1996.

Kyle, Robert. "Richard Opfer's Cane Collection at Auction." *Maine Antique Digest*, 1995.

Larkin, Jack. *The Reshaping of Everyday Life. 1790-1840*. New York: Harper & Row, Publishers, 1988.

Latif, Angie. "The steps of belly dance." *Arabia.com*, January 20, 2001.

Leitch, Alexander. *A Princeton Companion*. Princeton, New Jersey: Princeton University Press, 1978.

Lester, Katherine Morris and Bess Viola Oerke. *Accessories of Dress*. Peoria, Illinois: Charles A. Bennett Publications, 1940.

Libby, Jean. "Technological and Cultural Transfer of African Ironmaking into the Americas and the Relationship to Slave Resistance." Included in *Rediscovering America: National, Cultural, and Disciplinary Boundaries Re-examined*. Baton Rouge, Louisiana: Louisiana State University, 1993. <http://www.afrigeneas.com/slavedata/Paper-LSU-1492-1992.html>

Lindbeck, Jennifer A. & Jeffrey B. Snyder. *Elegant Seneca*. Atglen, Pennsylvania: Schiffer Publishing, 2000.

MacDougall, Robert. "Strange enthusiasms: a brief history of American pseudoscience." *21stC* 3(4), Special Section/Strange Science. <http://www.Columbia.edu/cu/21stC/issue-3.4/macdougall.html>

McWilliams, John and Courtney Scott. "Wah-Hoo-Wah: The Dartmouth Indian. The Indian's Long History." *The Dartmouth Review*, October 23, 1996.

Massey, Richard. "Folk art exhibit at University Museums captures South." *The Daily Mississippian*, 26 February 1998.

Meyer, George H. with Kay White Meyer. *American Folk Art Canes: Personal Sculpture*. Bloomfield Hills, Michigan: Sandringham Press, 1992.

Middleton, Dr. Sue. "Canes, Berets, and Gangsta Rap: Disciplining Sexuality in School, 1920-1995." Paper presented in a symposium, Rethinking the Lives of Women Educators: Poststructuralist and Materialist Feminist Approaches, at the Annual meeting of the American Educational Research Association, New York, April 8-12, 1996.

Monek, Francis H. *Canes Through the Ages*. Atglen, Pennsylvania: Schiffer Publishing, 1995.

Neumann, George C. *Swords and Blades in the American Revolution*. Texarkana, Texas: Scurlock Publishers, 1991, pp. 239-247.

Nirschl, Fr. Nicholas, O. Praem. "Pueblo Governors' Canes." *Norbertine Community News*, (New Mexico), n.d., p. 2.

Norris, Robert. *Memoirs of the Reign of Bossa Ahádee, King of Dahomy, an Inland Country in Guiney. The Which Are Added, the Author's Journey to Abomey, the Capital; and a Short Account of the African Slave Trade*. London: W. Lowndes, M.DCC.LXXXIX. Electronic Edition. Chapel Hill, NC: University of North Carolina, First edition, 2001. © This work is the property of the University of North Carolina at Chapel Hill. It may be used freely by individuals for research, teaching, and personal use as long as this statement of availability is included in the text.

Northrop, Henry Davenport. *Wonders of the Tropics or Explorations and Adventures of Henry M. Stanley and Other World-Renowned Travelers*. Philadelphia, Pennsylvania: National Publishing Co., 1891.

"Overview of Scrimshaw – The Whalers' Art." New Bedford Whaling Museum/Research. <http://www.whalingmuseum.org/kendall/amwhale/am_scrim_extend.html> 4/25/2003.

Page, Dave. "Carter Glass. A brief biography." Minneapolis, Minnesota: Federal Reserve Bank of Minneapolis, December 1997.

Park, Edwards. "The Object at Hand." *Smithsonian Magazine*, October 1995.

Peck, Deborah. "Multicultural Education: A Calendar of Ethnic Festivals and Celebrations." *Yale-New Haven Teachers Institute*, May 1982.

Pool, Daniel. *What Jane Austen Ate and Charles Dickens Knew. From Fox Hunting to Whist—the Facts of Daily Life in 19th-Century England*. New York: Simon & Schuster, 1993.

Potier, Beth. "Finding hidden veins of cultural treasure." *Harvard Gazette*, October 4, 2001.

Rilly, Claude. "Witchcraft at the Louvre: HEKA, Magic, and Bewitchment in Ancient Egypt." Culturekiosque.com, 11 March 2001.

Roach, Susan. "The Journey of David Allen: Transformations through Public Folklore," In *Public Folklore*, ed. Robert Baron and Nicholas Spitzer. Washington and London: Smithsonian Institution, 1992.

Roberts, Larry. "Florida Souvenirs 1890 to 1930." *Antiques & Art Around Florida,* Summer/Fall 2001.

Roche, Jim. "Jim Roche on the Artists and Unsigned, Unsung, Whereabouts Unknown … Made-Do Art of the American Outlands." [Commentary compiled from video interviews with the curator. Jim Roche, Professor, Department of Fine Arts, Florida State University, Tallahassee, Florida, 1993.]

Rosenzweig, Roy. "Interview with Orville Vernon Burton." *The History Teacher* 35(2), February 2002. <http://www.historycooperative.org/journals/ht/35.2/rosenzweig.html>

"A Rush to the Gold Washings." *California Star*, June 10, 1848. Article reprinted in the files of the Museum of the City of San Francisco. <http://www.sfmuseum.org/hist6/star.html>

St. Germain, Priscilla Weldon. "Record Louisiana Portrait Sold." *Maine Antique Digest*, January 2000.

Smith, Charles Manby. *Curiosities of London Life, or Phases, Physiological and Social or the Great Metropolis.* 1853.

Snyder, Jeffrey B. *Canes: From the Seventeenth to the Twentieth Century.* Atglen, Pennsylvania: Schiffer Publishing, 1993.

_____. *Historical Staffordshire: American Patriots & Views.* Atglen, Pennsylvania: Schiffer Publishing, 1995.

_____. *Stetson Hats and the John B. Stetson Company 1865-1970.* Atglen, Pennsylvania: Schiffer Publishing, 1997.

Sterling, Kimball M. *Absolute Cane Auction* catalog, September 7, 2003.

Stewardson, Jack. "Centenarian receives Boston Post cane." *Standard Times*, November 27, 2002, page A9.

Strong, Philip. "History of White Cane Safety Day." American Council of the Blind, n.d.

Switzer, Maurice. "Passing of a great educator," *The First Perspective Six Nations Reserve*, n.d.

Taron, Henry A. *Tradewinds Antiques Antique Cane Auction* catalogs, 2001-2003.

Taylor, Jim. "Horns, Bones, Tusks, Antlers and Hooves." Oregon Knife Collectors Association, 1999.

"TED Case Studies: Mammoths and Ivory Trade." <http://www.American.edu/TED/mammoth.html>

Tennesseans in the Civil War, Volumes 1-2. Nashville, Tennessee: Nashville Civil War Centennial Commission, 1964.

Tomes, Robert. *The Bazar Book of Decorum. The care of the person, manners, etiquette, and ceremonials* … New York: Harper & Brothers, 1873.

Truzzi, Marcello. "On Keeping Things Up in the Air." *Natural History* 88 (10), December 1979.

Twain, Mark. "Presidential Presents." *Alta California,* February 5, 1868.

University of Wisconsin Sea Grant. *1700s-1800s Underwater Exploration Timeline.* Madison, Wisconsin: University of Wisconsin Sea Grant Institute, 2001. <http://www.seagrant.wisc.edumadison jason11/timeline/index_1700.html>

Van Wyhe, John, Ph.D. "The History of Phrenology on the Web." <http://pages.britishlibrary.net/phrenology/overview.html>

"Vaudeville, A History." <http://xroads.Virginia.edu/~ma02/Easton/ vaudeville/vaudevillemain.html>

Vigny, Pierre. "The Walking-Stick as a Means of Self-Defense." *Health and Strength*, July 1903, pp. 253-254.

Wainwright, Katie. "Strolling & Swaggering." *Inside Northside Magazine*, August/September 2002.

Watson, John F. *A Collection of Memoirs, Anecdotes, and Incidents of the City and Its' Inhabitants of the Earliest Settlements of the Inland Part of Pennsylvania from the Days of the Founders. Intended to Preserve the Recollections of Olden Times, and to Exhibit Society in its Changes of Manners and Customs, and the City and Country in their Local Changes. (Watson's Annals of Philadelphia and Pennsylvania)*, Vol. I: River-Front Bank, 1857.

"When Walking Sticks Were a Fashion Statement." Official news releases from the Church of Jesus Christ of Latter-day Saints, 28 June 2001.

"Why Do Kappas Carry Canes?" The University of West Alabama's Iota Theta Chapter of Kappa Alpha Psi Fraternity Inc. <http://www.angelfire.com/al/nastynupe/ KaneHistory.html 11/15/2002>

Wilson, Susan. "An Elephant's Tale. An Unadulterated and Relatively True Story Chronicling the Life, Death, and Afterlife of Jumbo, Tufts' Illustrious Mascot." *Tufts online Magazine.* Spring 2002.

Wintz, Jack, O.F.M. "The Old Missions of New Mexico—Still Alive After Four Centuries." *St. Anthony Messenger*, October 1998.

WITHERELLS.COM Catalog Pages.

Yates, Riley. "Daniel Webster's desk switches hands." The Boston University Washington Journalism Center, 12 October 2002.

Yucel, Erdem. "Devrek canes – among the world's finest." *Turkish Daily News*, Features Section, January 24, 1999.

Index

US $69.95
9 780764 320415
ISBN: 0-7643-2041-6
56995